D0883090

A12901513101

WITHDRAWN

You're Only Young Twice

You're Only Young Twice

Children's Literature and Film

Tim Morris

I.C.C. LIBRARY

University of Illinois Press

Urbana and Chicago

PR
990
.M67
2000

© 2000 by the Board of Trustees of the University of Illinois
All rights reserved
Manufactured in the United States of America
♾ This book is printed on acid-free paper.

Library of Congress Cataloging-in-Publication Data
Morris, Timothy, 1959–
You're only young twice : children's literature and film /
Tim Morris.
   p.   cm.
Includes bibliographical references (p.   ) and index.
ISBN 0-252-02532-6 (alk. paper)
1. Children's literature, English—History and criticism.
2. Children's literature, American—History and criticism.
3. Children's literature—Film and video adaptations.
4. Motion pictures and literature.
5. Children—Books and reading.
I. Title.
PR990.M67   2000
820.9'8982—dc21   99-6617
CIP

C 5 4 3 2 1

For Margaret Louise,
for Thomas,
and for Fran

They force the baby to be Hook.
The baby! That is where the canker gnaws.
—Captain Hook

CONTENTS

ACKNOWLEDGMENTS

I want to thank the students in ENGL 4365, Children's Literature, at the University of Texas at Arlington very much for listening. I am grateful to Ann Lowry for her unwavering encouragement of this project, which began when she suggested I write this book instead of another and continued at every stage. I also want especially to thank Betsy Hearne, Stacy Alaimo, and Melanie Eckford-Prossor for reading the manuscript and offering many challenging suggestions. I also want to acknowledge the help of the Interlibrary loan staff at the University of Texas at Arlington.

Many people shared their excitement about children's culture with me as I worked, including D. Lynn Atkinson, Nannette Brenner, Phil Cohen, Martha Cutter, Denise DeArmond, Maggie Dwyer, Anne Fadiman, Janice Finney, A. C. Goodson, Cynthia Haynes, Jan Rune Holmevik, Heidi Jacobs, Don Johnson, Joanna Webb Johnson, Hans Kellner, Dallas Lacy, Jo Lacy, Lori Lebow, Elaina Macmillan, Gyde Martin, Samantha Masterton, Cedrick May, John McGowan, Susan Bridget McHugh, Joy Mosher, J. Mark Noe, Michael Oriard, Simon Ortiz, Debi Reese, Ken Roemer, Micki Roemer, Don Root, Patricia Sierra, Harry Stoneback, Rajani Sudan, Deeanne Westbrook, Jim Wood, Nancy Wood, and the parents, teachers, and students of Duff Elementary in Arlington, Texas. Thanks, everyone.

I love Margaret Morris, not least for helping me complete this book. Fran Morris insisted that I watch *Hook* so that I could get the rest of the story of *Peter Pan,* and I did. This book is dedicated to him and to two of his cousins, the three people I read to most when they were children.

1

YOU'RE ONLY YOUNG TWICE:
ADULTS, CHILDREN, POWER, CULTURE

I teach in a university English department in which adults, children, power, and culture are strongly linked. The nature of the connections, however, is frequently ignored. We require our majors to take a course in children's literature if they are seeking teacher certification. Our children's literature courses are always full, but always taught by adjunct faculty. Children's literature is neglected in hiring plans and curriculum discussions, even though its study accounts for a large percentage of our undergraduate enrollment. We offer no graduate courses in children's literature, have no lecture series or other activities devoted to it. Our library holdings in children's books consist of a few hundred ragged volumes of school texts closeted off in an airless room. These signs of neglect are no accident; they are part of a larger power relation.

When I go to my son's public elementary school, by contrast, children's literature is front and center—in a library that occupies a large corner of the building, in book fairs, reading programs, and posters. Library science has made a large commitment to books for kids, and kids' educators have made literature a priority.

This reversal of priorities as one goes from university to elementary school is not simply a function of the different audiences served by the two institutions. The university serves children too, indirectly. Many of our graduates become elementary teachers. Yet it seems that part of what we teach them is the unimportance of their own calling. The books that young children like are less culturally important in the university than are the books that adults admire.

I began to think about this dynamic more and more in recent years because I was a university teacher with a grade-school-age child. I wondered why his culture was so much less important than mine was. I wondered why public school teachers, when they enter our graduate program to work on master's degrees, invariably claim they enrolled because they want to teach literature to adults.

In my work I was complicit in a cycle of prestige and shame. I gained prestige from teaching adult undergraduates who became teachers of young children. Part of what I taught these undergraduates by omission, as I stayed silent on children's issues, was the worthlessness of serving the children that they would teach. Later in the cycle, these same people would reenter the university as graduate students, dissatisfied with the lack of prestige accorded to teachers of children. They would then redouble my own prestige, because graduate instruction is more prestigious than is undergraduate. If it's good to teach adults, it's even better to teach older adults. By a weird logic, the most powerful teaching situation of all was the one I experienced in my first semesters of graduate teaching: nearly all of my graduate students were older than I was. That was as powerful as I will ever get in this business.

My experiences as a parent and a college English teacher made me want to work against the system that kept this power flowing in my direction. I don't want to paint this as a grand rebellion or to exaggerate the power I wield, however. I garnered a kind of local and immediate power that may reflect larger circulations in mass culture. I imagined that if I started an eddy in my backwater going in the opposite direction, it might have an effect further down the stream.

In particular, reading to my son got me thinking. My wife and I read to him, starting with *Hop on Pop* when he was a year old, moving on to Arnold Lobel and then to Junior Illustrated Classics, and continuing through Goosebumps when he was six and seven. At the time of this writing he is nine and reads great long Animorphs and Harry Potter books to himself. He's on his own. But during those first six years or so of intensive parental reading, I realized that I liked the books I was reading to Fran a lot better than the scholarly books on American poetry that I was reading (and writing) in order to earn tenure and keep my prestigious job. In fact, I liked *Hop on Pop* considerably better than some of the Modern Library's hundred greatest English novels of the twentieth century. It is a much more interesting text than, for instance, Theodore Dreiser's *American Tragedy.* But I could not find a language in which to articulate that value judgment.

This language did not exist in the circles of traditional American literary scholarship. It did not exist even in the circles in which the canon was being rethought and redrawn in the 1980s and 1990s. Restructuring the canon to include texts by women and nonwhite writers did not extend to an inclusion of texts for children. In fact, newly included texts and writers needed to be made sufficiently "serious" to legitimate scholarly interest, so books for children were often excluded. As Joanna Johnson points out to me, there has been a tendency ever since the first American best-selling women writers—Susan Warner, Harriet Beecher Stowe, Louisa May Alcott—to juvenilize the work of women authors. In a culture that devalues children, recuperation of these writers almost necessitated the reprinting and reexamination of their works for adults or, in some cases, the rethinking of texts like *The Wide, Wide World* and *Little Women* in terms of their potential address to adults.

Also, as Fran grew, I began to watch a lot of children's movies, something I had stopped doing during those couple of decades between my own childhood and my young parenthood. I realized that here was a cultural dynamic almost completely ignored by scholarship—whether by the cultural studies approaches to serious (or not-so-serious) adult film that are increasingly important in English departments or by the approaches to children's literature that flourish among children's librarians and children's literature specialists. Unlike books, through which a child can perhaps establish a semiprivate identification with Sam-I-Am or Arthur the aardvark, these movies deliberately address the whole American family conceived as a tableau—whether across an aisle of seats in a theater or, increasingly, as VCRs conquer the world, on the family sofa. These films tell American families how to behave as families, among other things. Power circulates there too—but how? And how is one to see it, except by surrendering to its images?

This book is a series of observations of power relations as they are expressed through children's culture. I make no claims to a general theory of the operation of children's culture, even in the nineties. The field is vast. If my observations cohere, it is a coherence around one kind of typical suburban experience shared by parents who had a child born in the late eighties. In a sense I did no "research" for this book, though I did a lot of reading and viewing. The culture instead came to me and impressed itself upon me.

My specific observations include those about classics like *Black Beauty, The Secret Garden,* and *Peter Pan,* which are still just as much a part of children's culture today as they had been in their own time (if not more so). They also include thoughts on ephemera like contemporary children's series novels and children's films—though ephemera are always replaced by other ephemera when they vanish and therefore paradoxically constitute one of the most stable elements of culture.

I offer here suggested resonances that do not pass any test of rigorous scholarly connection but serve to show how interwound children's culture can be and how that culture is connected to adult power dynamics. We take so for granted the inequities of power in the relations between adults and children that we often miss seeing that all interactions between adults and children involve negotiations of cultural power. We have power over others because we are more adult than they are. Or we are more adult than others are because we have power over them. (That is why my graduate students, of course, want to teach adults.) The ultimate insult is to call someone else immature. That's why we laugh at the T-shirt slogan You're only young once, but you can be immature your whole life.

Insults based on gender and race, intelligence and ability, sexuality and class are socially inappropriate. Most of us have internal censors that forbid them. Insults based on childishness are the last frontier; they are always OK. Who thinks twice about insulting someone by saying that he or she has the attention span of a three year old? Except to add Groucho Marx's fillip: "You've got the brain of a three-year-old child, and I bet he was glad to get rid of it." Is *childist* a word? *Ageist* is, but it refers to prejudice against the old. Prejudice against the young, it seems, is a condition of life. Even finding one's inner child, in popular psychology, is done in the service of growing up more completely.

Of course, childishness can be funny, but it is funny and insulting in much the same way that death is funny and insulting. We are all going to die, so we can talk about dying in general terms as an all-purpose metaphor or as a joke without personal offense, unless we're close to it. (Death is funny, but a friend dying of AIDS is not.) We were all (or are still) children, so childishness is funny in much the same way. It is precisely when someone is close to childishness that the humor and the insult of calling someone a child becomes most intense and most apparent. No one is more anxious about being a child than an adolescent.

Power is the primary source of this anxiety. The appropriation of power over another person by placing one's self in the relation of adult to that person, who becomes implicitly a child, can be called juvenilizing. Juvenilizing is by no means a trivial or benign power relation, because the relation of adult to child is seldom trivial or benign. We can observe the power relation of juvenilizing in literary theory, in which sophisticated reading can be conceived as adult and naïve reading as necessarily childish. Karlheinz Stierle sees a rupture between incompetent childish reading, which involves identification with the text, and competent adult reading, which is critically self-conscious. Stierle characterizes the reading experience of "the child":

> Depending on the vividness of the illusion, the reader may be compelled to identify with fictional roles. . . . The child's experience of the imaginary . . . is the purest and least restricted form of this type of reception. For him the imaginary world of the fairy tale is real presence, its verbal mediation is still unperceived. . . . The illusory character of fictional communication—not yet recognized by the child—would remain meaningless, however, if it were not sustained by a certain conceptual coherence created within the specific articulation of the fictional text itself. Though the child can still ignore this relationship between illusion and conceptual coherence, its recognition is a prerequisite to aesthetic experience once the referential illusion has seriously been questioned. (84–85)

Stierle's concept of a hierarchy of reading competences, with the child's competence at the bottom (and identified with that of the most naïve adult reader) supplies some of the basic assumptions that the theory of "adult" literature makes about the study of children's literature.

In Stierle's theorizing, one senses that the child must always be derided and trivialized. For Stierle, and for many literary theorists, children's concerns are never as weighty as those of adults. High literature is at one pole of a continuum and the other pole is occupied not so much by *bad* literature as by *children's* literature. (Yet, as we shall see, there is a place even in the hierarchies of theory where the high pole reaches down to meet the low: the place where nonsense introduces Margaret Wise Brown to Gertrude Stein, in spite of all the surveillance that goes on in the middle of the continuum.)

The juvenilizing tendency in literary theory preserves the realm of adult texts as one of high and serious culture. As Peter Hollindale argues, "[The] practice of devaluing childhood and children's literature when we are really protecting our concept of adulthood (and exposing our unease about it) is extremely common in derogatory estimates of children's books" (36). When students in my poetry classes feel uneasy and make derogatory comments about a modernist author, they compare him or her to Dr. Seuss. Exactly, I sometimes say. Seuss is another great literary modernist. If they knew how serious I was, they'd be even more uneasy.

Juvenilizing children's books and genre fiction alike serves to repress concerns of great importance, relegating them to a land of children's literature where nothing is really taken seriously—and therefore where almost anything can be said, the privilege of both child and courtly fool. Chief among these concerns is violence, a violence linked by theorists such as Alice Miller and Philip Greven with how punished children become violent, punishing adults. In European-American history, Miller and Greven argue, nurturing has been inseparable from punishment. The roots of adult violence lie in the violence done to children.

Philip Greven, in *Spare the Child: The Religious Roots of Punishment and the Psychological Impact of Physical Abuse*, examines the tradition of corporal punishment in Anglo-American Protestant culture, from the time of the Puritans to the present-day fundamentalist insistence on physical punishment. For Greven, children never outgrow the experience of physical beatings: "Punishment . . . shapes our attitudes toward

6

authorities of all kinds, and imprints upon our psyches enduring responses, both positive and negative, toward all forms of authority—parental, educational, penal, ecclesiastical, and political. The coerciveness of physical punishment plays an extraordinarily important role in the designs that we construct about the world and our roles in it. . . . Authoritarianism . . . constitutes one of the most enduring outcomes of physical punishment of children" (8). The violence employed in the power struggle between parents and children—a terribly one-sided violence, at least while the children are powerless to fight back—is never, for Greven, simply confined to the home: "The impact of physical punishment . . . [travels] through time inside our bodies, minds and spirits and [lives] on long after our individual deaths through the legacies we bequeath to our children and grandchildren" (5).

Greven, a historian, is indebted to the German psychoanalytic theorist Alice Miller for much of his analysis of the psychology of punishment. Both Greven and Miller believe that the relation of parent to child is too often seen as a competition that the parent must win—and that the defeated child renews with his or her own children. "In beating their children," writes Miller, "they are struggling to regain the power they once lost to their own parents. For the first time, they see the vulnerability of their own earliest years, which they are unable to recall, reflected in their children. . . . Only now, when someone weaker than they is involved, do they finally fight back, often quite fiercely" (16).

Not every parent-child relationship is a scene of struggle. Nevertheless, Miller and Greven both argue that real struggles between parents and children that end in a forcible imposition of the parents' will are embedded in a cultural context that encourages adults to see the training of children as a battle to be won by any means. Greven points to the brisk trade in corporal-punishment manuals, especially in Christian bookstores (60–81). Miller sees encoded in the word *pedagogy* a sense of "self-defense on the part of adults, as manipulation deriving from their own lack of freedom and their insecurity" (100). Miller's use of the term *pedagogy* is somewhat different from the more common meaning in American education of a methodology for education. She uses *pedagogy* to refer to a whole system of child rearing.

Both Miller and Greven see child rearing in the West as a zero-sum competition in which adults must win what children lose. Greven notes that advocates of corporal punishment see the family not as a cooperative group but as an arena for decisive competition. "Win or lose: these are seemingly the only alternatives available to such parents. No choice is offered children except to surrender their wills to the wills and superior force of their parents. In the warfare between parents and children, the parents expect to win. If not, the war continues until such time as the children submit and obey" (69). The pervasiveness of a violent power relation between adults and children, in European and American cultures, leads to a concern with violence in texts that most closely represent children. The war between parents and children is in deadly earnest. Its ideological underpinnings are textual and cinematic.

Nowhere are lessons of violence more thoroughly underscored for children than in the Bible. Scriptural justification underpins Christian advocacy of punishment. As Greven shows (50–54), neither Jesus nor Paul comes close to advocating the punishment of children, a practice promoted in the New Testament only by the anonymous Epistle to the Hebrews. Instead, Christians justify corporal punishment most often by citing the Old Testament, both in terms of its specific proverbial encouragements of beatings ("He that spareth the rod hateth his son: but he that loveth him chasteneth him betimes," Proverbs 13:24) and by the many Old Testament stories involving the theme of God's punishment.

Given the insistence of so many fundamentalist Christians on the moral sanctity of punishment, it is intriguing to note which Bible stories recur in children's Bibles and Bible storybooks. Cain and Abel, Abraham and Isaac, David and Goliath, the persecution of David by Saul, Daniel and the lions, Jonah and the whale. Most enduringly popular, as book, play, story, and toy, is the tale of Noah and the ark. These are stories of punishment or of the miraculous deferral or suspension of punishment. They center on violence or the potential for violence. In the latter three cases, they are *animal* stories as well. We might well ask why, out of all the stories in Hebrew scripture (none of which is originally directed to children), some have been so naturally appropriated by Christian culture for children. Why do these stories concern the promise or the forbearance of punishment? Perhaps they share motifs of violence with folktales. The stories collected by the Grimm brothers are also full of animals and violence. But the specifically religious invocation of violent punishment has unsettling consequences for an American culture strongly influenced by Protestant ideology. A key element of that culture is the children's story.

These Bible stories offer deeply ambivalent portrayals of punishment and vengeance. Some of the more troubling Bible stories about punishment and violence, however, are almost never retold in children's versions: the rape of Dinah (Genesis 34), the Levite and the concubine (Judges 19), David and Uriah (2 Samuel 11–12). Each story features sex as well as a brutal execution of punishment or revenge, pointing to yet another dynamic that can surround children's stories: the elision of language that represents sex.

In a video store in Arlington, Texas—the buckle of the Bible Belt—I once heard a woman ask the clerk, a man in his twenties, whether the film *Braveheart* would be suitable for her pre-teen daughter. The clerk, visibly remembering the film, began to turn a little green and allowed as how the picture was "a little rough." "But it's just violence," the woman prompted him. "There's no bad language, is there?" The clerk made a quick mental scan of the movie and assured her that violence would be her primary worry. "That's all right, then," she said, picking up the tape. "As long as there's no language. Language is what I worry about." Language, indeed, is what we all worry about.

Philip Greven connects memories of his punishments from early childhood with the children's books that sustained him through them. He mentions in particular Munro Leaf's *The Story of Ferdinand* and Watty Piper's *The Little Engine That Could:* "Stories such as these helped me make sense of my life and myself as a boy. They helped me cope with the anxieties and the fears generated by punishments as well as rationalize my own boyhood proclivity toward nonviolence and the life of the mind" (xi). This testimony to the antiviolent stance of some children's texts underscores the nature of the ideological struggle within children's literature. Written and selected by adults, children's books nevertheless do not predictably take the adult "side" in the pernicious competition described by Miller and Greven. As often as not the children's text will act as an advocate for the child in the face of oppression.

Childhood is a form of Otherness, possibly its archetypal form. Children are always insufficient, always wrong, always in need of guidance and correction. In this they parallel many who are Other to the central default-value individual of Western culture: the heterosexual, cultured, white adult male human. Like the animal, the "savage," the woman, the person of color, and the queer person, "the child" helps define the default value by offering its negative. You are a man because you are not a boy. Yet the male child is also the only manifestation of the Other that the default-value person once was, though he cannot grow young again (except in the movies).

In the case of "the child," the Other is Us. Each adult was once an individual child. When we conceive of children's literature as a minority literature, that continuity is crucial. Adults have deep-seated responses to children's books because these adults were once children. Their identity is continuous with that of the children they were. Alice Miller's insights enable us to recognize the traumatized child fighting back in the form of the adult child-beater. These same insights can help us to recognize that adults read (and write) children's books not just as expressions of conscious adult ideologies but also as their own response to their lived experience as children.

Roald Dahl's *Boy* (1984) brings together issues of punishment and violence, children's power relations to adults, the persistence of memory and identity between adult and child, and the uncertainties of definition that surround children's culture. *Boy* begins by contesting its own generic identity:

> An autobiography is a book a person writes about his own life and it is usually full of all sorts of boring details.
>
> This is not an autobiography. I would never write a history of myself. On the other hand, throughout my young days at school and just afterwards a number of things happened to me that I have never forgotten. (9)

Instead of being called a memoir, *Boy* is subtitled *Tales of Childhood*, to mark it as a set of disparate episodes with no connecting thread. "None of these things is important," Dahl goes on to say; they are simply episodes, with no narrative continuity, no significance beyond a happening that has become engraved in his memory.

Salient in these opening sentences is a problem of address common to many texts that fit uneasily between adult and child audiences. *Boy* is clearly intended as a children's book. The cover illustration is by Quentin Blake, who collaborated as illustrator on Dahl's later children's books, including *The BFG* and *The Witches*. The sentences are short and use a basic vocabulary and thus are clearly geared toward a child's reading level. But Dahl also gives the impression, difficult to quantify, that he is attempting to engage an adult reader at the same time. Dahl's swipe at the boring nature of autobiography is at once pseudo-instructional (the distinguishing characteristic of an entire genre cannot actually be that it is boring), presumptive of some familiarity with boring autobiographies (so that the adult reader appreciates the humor of twitting them for their tedium), and an outright misleading statement that may persuade an inexperienced reader but will strike a savvier one as protesting too much. *Boy* is, in fact, an autobiography. Its claim to exemption from the genre because it lacks a narrative line is no more than a statement about how all autobiography is constructed out of the disparate images of memory.

The "tales of childhood" in Dahl's *Boy* are indeed not connected with a narrative line. Years of the narrator's childhood pass without comment and whole areas of his family history are left unexamined. The episodes that get told, however, return insistently to motifs both of punishment and of unlooked-for delight. The stories, humorous or horrifying (or both at once, a Dahl trademark), are told with constant explanation, as if to an audience of children. Long-ago events are made intelligible to children of a later generation to whom they are temporally (and perhaps geographically) foreign.

Punishment recurs throughout the stories. Dahl recounts three separate memories of canings inflicted on him, and on other students, at three different schools: Llandaff Cathedral School, St. Peter's School, and Repton. The caning episodes fall into a pattern, like a recurrent nightmare. First is the anticipation of a call to the headmaster's office, then the cane itself—which recurs as an illustration, a simple but terrifying line drawing (45, 109, 130), then the pain and humiliation of the beating, and then a reflective commentary. *Boy* is not just an anti–corporal punishment manifesto. It is quite possible that these memories of corporal punishment came to be here just as Dahl insists in his opening disclaimer: as episodes imprinted on his memory. The effect of the text as final product, however, makes an argument against the barbarity of caning. Dahl as a boy is unable to understand, however, why the adults around him, no matter where he finds himself, resort over and over again to this same worn-out motif.

The caning episodes are narrated with characteristic double-address. The primary implied reader is always a child. The exposition is slow, as if to a child unfamiliar with the customs. In the first caning scene, even the weapon is assumed to be unfamiliar, and it is illustrated and described: "a long yellow cane which curved round the top like a walking stick" (45). Several other boys are beaten before it is Dahl's turn. "The watching and waiting were probably even greater torture than the event itself" (47). Then, the caning is described: the crack of the stick, the oddly delayed pain, the marksmanship of the headmaster as he lands one blow after another on the same wound. "Even today," writes Dahl, "whenever I have to sit for any length of time on a hard bench or chair, I begin to feel my heart beating along the old lines that the cane made on my bottom some fifty-five years ago" (131).

In these descriptions, the victims (Dahl and his friends) are individuals. The masters who wound them are implacable, impersonal forces. To be sure, the headmasters are identified. In an irony dwelt on at some length, the master of Repton who beats Dahl's friend Michael later becomes Archbishop of Canterbury and crowns the Queen of England. But the circumstances of the beatings, during which the boy has his back turned to his assailant and is denied any sympathy, emphasize a circumstance of violence that turns the individual into an impersonal role. Such depersonalization causes Dahl, as the narrator of *Boy,* to wonder about the coherence of personality. He says of the future archbishop: "Do you wonder then that this man's behaviour used to puzzle me tremendously? He was an ordinary clergyman at that time as well as being Headmaster, and I would sit in the dim light of the school chapel and listen to him preaching about the Lamb of God and about Mercy and Forgiveness and all the rest of it and my young mind would become totally confused" (132). The perspective of adult memory brings no answers. Dahl can say only that "there must be something very wrong about the whole business" (132). Narrating to an implied child prevents any analysis beyond the bare assessment that something is "very wrong."

Directions toward the adult reader, whether over the shoulder of a child or alone, litter the pages of *Boy* in an apparently desultory way. One is that the violence of British headmasters may have cultural roots. After his first beating, Dahl's Norwegian mother fumes, "They don't beat small children like that where I come from" (50). That this endemic British violence may be the result of a cycle of violence, the masters addicted to caning because they were themselves caned when students, is a theme made stronger, perhaps, by Dahl's unwillingness to voice it. The beginnings of adult violence are in the school system itself, with the upperclassmen "Boazers" at Repton lording it over the "fags" from the younger classes, who are their unofficial servants. Dahl, like Leaf's Ferdinand, breaks the cycle of violence. Though he becomes a star at sports, he is never made a Boazer. He avoids transmitting the violence in his own experience to another generation.

An undertone to the theme of caning is the theme of ineffectual adult intervention. Dahl's mother is outraged by the first beating he receives, but she remonstrates with the headmaster to no avail. After his second beating, one of Dahl's classmates tells him that he'll write to his own father (Dahl's father is dead) and get the matter set to rights. "Little Highton sat down and wrote to the father he admired so much, but of course nothing came of it. It was nevertheless a touching and generous gesture from one small boy to another and I have never forgotten it" (111).

The most startling episode in *Boy* is not a school scene but a medical scene, only three pages long. Soon after Dahl's beating in Wales that has made her so furious, his mother takes him to a doctor in Oslo, saying, "I think you've got adenoids." He does, but not for long. The doctor suddenly cuts out Dahl's adenoids, using no anesthetic. "He spoke gently, and I was seduced by his voice. Like an ass, I opened my mouth" (65), remembers Dahl, as if any refusal on his part could have done more than prolong the pain. The phrasing reflects how the narrator internalizes a sense of guilt for the assault inflicted on him by others.

"I grabbed my mother's hand and held on to it tight. I couldn't believe that anyone would do this to me" (66). The ostensible villain here is the doctor. But the real focus of the narrator's anger is his mother. Unable to voice his anger toward the adult who will not protect him from school beatings and who has followed up this failure by delivering him into the hands of the sadistic doctor, the narrator is reduced to silence. His mother makes him walk home. She then treats him with indifference until his grandmother insists on a little solicitude, saying, "After all, he's had an operation" (66). Throughout this brief passage, Dahl never openly identifies his mother as the person who oppresses him. He marvels in a detached way at the cruelty of the doctor and the nonsense of such a medical custom. He concludes with a comment that is distanced and a bit droll: "That was in 1924, and taking out a child's adenoids, and often the tonsils as well, without any anaesthetic was common practice in those days. I wonder, though, what you would think if some doctor did that to you today" (66). Dahl's private trauma does not become political here, but it does become textual. Presented as an "unimportant" event, it can resonate back through Dahl's books for children, through the menacing or detached adults of *James and the Giant Peach* and *The Witches*, the dream of a protector who appears to threaten and then relents in *Charlie and the Chocolate Factory*.

The struggle for power between Dahl and his mother in the adenoid scene is hardly a struggle. Dahl must submit to mutilation. The struggle is turned inward to become part of the individual who survives the mutilation. It becomes outward only in texts that revolve around helplessness and reprieve. In this way the politics of children's pain becomes more basic than any possible articulate or activist politics. Children's books are not tracts about punishment. But the role of literature in representing the imposition of adults' wills on children makes these texts a proving ground for seeing how all culture, at some level, reflects our first education in the realities of power.

2

BEAUTIES:
COMING TO *BLACK BEAUTY*

Can a mistaken assumption be the start of understanding? One might say that this happens whenever one reads—that one proceeds from a mistaken assumption and refines one's sense of things toward newer, slightly less mistaken assumptions. This is the basic insight in Hans-Georg Gadamer's notion of hermeneutic prejudice: "A person who is trying to understand a text is always projecting. He projects a meaning for the text as a whole as soon as some initial meaning emerges in the text. Again, the initial meaning emerges only because he is reading the text with particular expectations in regard to a certain meaning. Working out this fore-projection, which is constantly revised in terms of what emerges as he penetrates into the meaning, is understanding what is there" (267). Gadamer sets ideal conditions for fore-projection. He assumes that a reader comes to the text exerting intellectual powers in good faith toward the pursuit of knowledge. This reader is open-minded and recognizes preconceptions and prejudices (in the positive sense) as necessary components of active reading. Such a reader was not me when I first came to *Black Beauty*.

When I first read *Black Beauty* I was not looking for knowledge or understanding, and my fore-projections were not those of the engaged hermeneut. I was looking for something to help my son get to sleep. It had to be something with pictures so that he could follow the story (he was six). I was looking for a text that would allow my mind to wander, something that I could read aloud while I thought about other things, in the way familiar to those who read aloud to young children. I figured *Black Beauty* to be easy, and I was wrong.

Figuring the book to be easy was not the greatest of my prejudicial errors. When I leaned back in bed at the age of thirty-six to read *Black Beauty* to my son, I had never read any horse fiction. I was a dog-book boy. Horse books were for girls. They were for the girls that the boys teased because they spent all their time talking and thinking about horses.

My preconception of the novel was that it would be a girl's book. After all, it was written by a woman, Anna Sewell. Or at least the original was, because I admit that when I first read *Black Beauty*, I didn't even read the version of *Black Beauty* she first published in 1877; I read the Illustrated Classic Edition, a modern version specially adapted for younger readers by Deidre S. Laiken, one that replaces much of Sewell's prose with pictures and subtly glosses hard words in the text. But you might say in my defense that I did get some form of the book instead of a video. At least I was reading.

I supposed that I would find *Black Beauty* centered on a teen or preteen girl protagonist who would love and care for a horse that would be threatened in some way. The horse would save her from danger and she would reciprocate by saving the horse from some other danger, most likely a rich uncaring stepuncle who would try to sell the horse to knackers to increase his store of filthy lucre. How I got such an idea, I don't know. As I said, I had never read any horse books. My amalgam of incorrect assumptions about the plot of *Black Beauty* seems to have filtered into my brain from extrapolations of the plots of dog books and movies, mixed with the occasional confused and inattentive glance at a TV set showing *National Velvet* or *The Black Stallion*.

My prejudices would make a standard, derivative scenario for a Hollywood large-animal picture. Yet as more experienced readers of *Black Beauty* know, my prejudices bear no resemblance at all to the text or plot of that novel, even to the Illustrated Classic version. In reading Sewell's novel, I met a text that disrupted my lazily assembled prejudices about, and against, girls' horse stories.

Briefly, then: the protagonist of *Black Beauty* is not a girl, but a horse. The horse is male, a colt who grows into a stallion. Black Beauty faces many dangers throughout the desultory episodic plot of the book and is saved from mortal danger at the end, but the plight and rescue are never maudlin or melodramatic. There is a lot of graphic violence in the book—not "cartoon" violence but stark cruelty dealt to horses by men and women. Most dramatically upsetting for the preconceptions of a 1990s reader, *Black Beauty* does not start from, or end at, the tableau of a family brought closer together by a central animal. The human families who own Black Beauty casually sell him and then disappear from the story. His own horse family and horse friends are scattered irretrievably in different directions by market forces. *Black Beauty* is anything but a "feel-good" book.

Such a reading encounter is shocking for the noninitiate who is used to the antics of Beethoven the dog or Andre the friendly seal. My childhood notions of animal stories for children were shaped by reading Albert Payson Terhune and watching countless hours of "Lassie" on television. These notions were reinforced by viewing more recent dog movies. *Black Beauty,* by departing so strongly from the formulas of all these texts that postdate it (an odd but accurate way of putting it) forced me to reexamine what was going on, what could be going on, in the animal stories that I knew best.

My initial reaction, as I lay reading *Black Beauty* to my drowsing son, matched what many of my children's literature students report on first reading a "classic" children's story. I asked myself, Should a child really be hearing this? My sentiment was related to a paradoxical tension in choosing reading for children. As a parent I want to provide something at once innocuous and provocative, both challenging and reassuring. *Black Beauty* was certainly provocative, but was it reassuring? Why had I chosen as bedtime reading this depiction of a hero's life as quite nasty, literally brutish, and presumptively short? Why had I chosen a text so imbued with the images of punishment that I had flinched at in Roald Dahl's *Boy?* Yet in fact I had not chosen this story. I had been guided to it by my common, culturally literate knowledge of what must be "good for children"—edifying, classic, tasteful.

So I cringed through page after page of horses whipped, reined up cruelly, overworked, poorly groomed, and broken in spirit. I become impatient with students who complain that a text is not suitable for children because its representations are too unpleasant, but I fell here into the same complaint. I had to ask why these *particular* representations of power and punishment were deemed suitable for children. I had to consider how power working across the body of an animal informed this children's classic.

Of course, *Black Beauty* became a "children's classic" through a process of juvenilizing that has affected so many animal stories. When it was published in 1877, the novel was addressed to adults as much as to children. Or, rather, it was addressed to as broad a readership as possible, so that it could be read not just by educated adults and children but also by those working-class adults who came most directly in contact with horses in their work. The simplified language and address that make the book suitable for a child's reading level are in part a function of Sewell's intention to address this book to a juvenilized audience of working-class adults.

The tone and language of *Black Beauty* may be at times simplistic, but the content of the book is not soft-pedaled. The novel deals explicitly, even grimly, with violence, pain, and death. Its barometer of what one can and cannot show children is remarkably different from the one that late 1990s culture would use, accounting for part of my shock at coming to the book as an adult reader. Or, rather, coming to it twice, because once I had finished Laiken's skillful and faithful abridgement, I went directly to the original—though I kept it to myself this time, so as not to risk traumatizing my child.

Perhaps the difference between the 1870s and the 1990s is not so much in the range of allowable subjects as in setting and context. In 1990s children's culture, we balance every endangerment with a rescue. Every villain gets a suitable comeuppance. Animal stories tend to work toward a family tableau—either the linking of a real human family around an animal or the establishment of an animal family that stands metaphorically for a human family.

No such tableau is allowed in *Black Beauty.* Sewell displays relentless indifference to her human characters as she focuses on the title protagonist and narrator. "The story of my life is the story of the people in it," says the narrator at the beginning of Caroline Thompson's 1994 film of the novel. That is a sentiment that Sewell's narrator neither utters nor shares. The novel decenters its people and leaves the viewer with plenty of human heroes and villains, but none who provides consistent plot interest. Thompson makes a very different move at the start of her film, asserting a human interest that Sewell fails to provide.

Black Beauty is episodic. The narrator changes his name, roles, and appearance as he ages and passes through the hands of many humans. The book works by keeping the reader engaged with the problems of the animal narrator. That very engagement is also the core of the book's narrative problem and the uncertainty of its direction toward its readers.

The novel is both directed toward children and *not* directed toward children. Its "reading level," to use a modern anachronism, is easy. The sentences are short, the episodes brief and self-contained. In these respects it resembles a present-day "chapter book" for intermediate readers or young adults. Yet one should note that its sentences are short and its images simple because the story is told by a *horse*. Having a horse as narrator cuts down the number of literary allusions and philosophical excursions that can be plausibly presented.

A continual refrain in the story is how Beauty, despite his command of English, cannot understand abstract human conversation. When the coachman John Manly first trains him, Beauty only half-grasps his meanings. Bound up with this half-understanding of language is the sensuality of intimate contact between horse and groom: "He used to make my mane and tail almost as smooth as a lady's hair, and he would talk to me a great deal; of course I did not understand all he said, but I learned more and more to know what he *meant,* and what he wanted me to do. I grew very fond of him, he was so gentle and kind, he seemed to know just how a horse feels, and when he cleaned me, he knew the tender places, and the ticklish places" (36). Is this paragraph for a child reader or an adult or both—or neither? The passage enacts its own complicated relation to its audience, an audience hardly expected, perhaps, to "understand all he says" either. A male narrator, given voice by a female author, is feminized in turn by the caresses of a male who is his (her?) perfect lover and groom at once. John Manly shows intuitive, complete knowledge of Beauty even as Beauty is unable to follow what John is saying. The horse surrenders to a wordless intimation of the groom's desires.

The mysteries of intimacy are beyond Beauty's linguistic powers; so are the mysteries of economics. Much later in the novel, when he is working as a cab horse, Beauty overhears conversations among horse owners and hack drivers who rent horses by the day. "As the horses did not belong to these men, the only thing they thought of was how to get their money out of them: first, to pay the master, and then to provide for their own living, and a dreadful time some of these horses had of it. Of course I understood but little, but it was often talked over on the stand" (173). By using an animal narrator, Sewell can selectively side-step political engagement. For this reason, the political stance of *Black Beauty* can be hard to identify. At times it seems like a Marxist critique of the way that labor is transformed into value; at others its equation of gentility with innate qualities of class and breeding marks it as an almost reactionary text.

Yet what is the point of interrogating the politics of *Black Beauty?* The novel can be read as a tract-like manifesto of animal rights, cataloging abuses that demand reform. The book is told in childish terms to make that point as unequivocally as possible. It may be reducible to a single sentence: "Don't mistreat horses." Such simplicity is problematic, however. The reader, whether adult or child, is asked to do two things at once: to identify with a horse and that horse's limited understanding and to listen to the book's author—though that author is severely withdrawn, given the limitations of the equine narrative. Such complications recall the double-address in Dahl's *Boy,* but in a form redoubled by the demands of animal narrative. Much more is at stake here than the beating of horses. Or, rather, the beating of horses becomes a place to talk about oppression of children and of women.

The first sentence of Sewell's *Black Beauty,* unlike that of Thompson's film, dives directly into narration: "The first place that I can well remember was . . . " (21). With these words Sewell assumes that the reader is interested in the story immediately. There is no explanatory preamble, no identification or self-naming. No "Call me Ishmael"; crucially, one can call the narrator anything one likes if one owns him. But the book does not begin, "I am a horse," either. There is no indication that the narrator is an animal until the third paragraph, and none that he is a horse until the fourth. The story simply begins by assuming that the reader has a reason for hearing it and by establishing a narrative relation between teller and reader before revealing the species of the teller.

The reason for telling or reading this story is an enigma. We learn quickly enough who the narrator of *Black Beauty* is, but a question never addressed is Who is the narratee? In Gerald Prince's theory of narratology, the "narratee"—as distinct from the actual implied *reader* —is the person to whom the narrative is told. The narratee can align fairly closely with the reader in much fiction, but is often a character in the story, as in epistolary fiction and fictions told as embedded narratives. The narratee of *Black Beauty* has several possible and shifting identities, but remains unrealized and provisional.

The provisional nature of the narratee in *Black Beauty*, the sense we get that we are not quite sure who's listening to this story, defines for me the uneasy relation the novel bears both to adult and to children's fiction. In strict terms, the novel is *not* the imagined narrative of a horse as interpreted through a human. It is the narrative of a horse in the first person, presented as if without interpretation. Strictly, then, *Black Beauty* has an absurd narrative situation. As Mr. Ed used to remind us, "No one can talk to a horse, of course." Except, of course, to Black Beauty; or, rather, he can talk to you.

Like Dickens's Pip or David Copperfield, Beauty tells his story initially from the perspective of an adult of indeterminate age looking back on his childhood. The novel begins from a colt's perspective as filtered through an older horse's accumulated experience. The motive for this telling is as unquestioned in this text as in any first-person human narration. Yet the sense of a narratee is vague. Is the listener to this equine memoir supposed to be a sort of horse therapist or horse confessor? Has the teller gone out to pasture on some sort of beastly Chautauqua circuit?

Like so many narratives that begin from a child's perspective, *Black Beauty* must supplement its childish perspective with the experience of adults. Its second chapter recounts a hunt that the colt can barely understand and must perceive largely through the explanatory narration of his mother and of other older horses. The narrative is consistently layered, never violating its various frames of a woman author, an adult male (horse) narrator, conveying faithfully the limits and perceptions of the colt that he was, including the perspective of the mare who is his early guide to perception.

There is always something lacking in Beauty's perspective. As a realistic horse, he can have no access to theoretical explanations, historical contexts, or human linguistic culture. He learns none of the rhymes, songs, or stories that fill out the juvenile perspective, let's say, of Stephen Dedalus in Joyce's *Portrait of the Artist as a Young Man.* As a narrator of severely limited perspective, Beauty seems to incorporate the limitations of perspective inherent to the child teller, and so to the child reader. Yet as with the boy David Copperfield, there is a constant feeling that the reader of the novel is privy to a slightly expanded range of perceptions, larger than that of the narrator himself. At this level, the implied *author* Anna Sewell, who stays withdrawn, shares with the human reader, child or adult, a kind of sliding scale of context that defines the impact of the horse's narrative.

The novel produces its meanings in part by putting its more speculative and philosophical passages beyond the ken of the narrator himself. When Beauty balks, for reasons that he himself cannot comprehend, at going over an unsafe bridge (62), his master and John Manly discuss this providential reluctance: "I could not understand much of what they said, but I found they thought, if I had gone on as the master wanted me, most likely the bridge would have given way under us. . . . Master said, God had given men reason, by which they could find out things for themselves, but He had given animals knowledge which did not depend on reason, and which was more prompt and perfect in its way" (62–63). It's not odd that Beauty understands little of this philosophy. I find it hard enough to follow myself. Nor, perhaps, are we supposed to trust this horse's ability to convey the particulars of an epistemological theory. The novel gives us a narrative situation in which many things are beyond the understanding of narrator, characters, readers, and maybe even the author herself. In this situation of strictly limited knowledges, the novel plays out a drama of punishment and its consequences.

Black Beauty is all about punishment. It is about the punishment of horses and how they are exploited at work. At another level that is not "hidden" but must remain explicitly inaccessible because of how the narrator's knowledge is situated, however, the novel is about physical punishment inflicted on women and children, punishments that maim and frustrate their lives.

As a colt, Beauty moves free and unencumbered. He is trained into adulthood by men who restrict his range of movement—as children are restrained at times—and strap limiting devices onto his body. For his whole adult life, until his lucky retirement in the final chapter, Beauty dreams of this childhood freedom and sometimes recaptures it for a few moments. His fall from grace is vividly described in physical terms: the bit in the mouth, the collar, the bridle: "Straps here and straps there, a bit in my mouth and blinkers over my eyes" (38).

Worst of all the torments, in the early days of Beauty's training, is the crupper: "A small saddle with a nasty stiff strap that went right under my tail; that was the crupper: I hated the crupper—to have my long tail doubled up and poked through that strap was almost as bad as the bit" (28). The crupper is just one item in the novel's catalog of horrors, and a small one. It is not as noisome as the bearing rein, which occupies several chapters later on. It's a realistic detail, not overstated. In the description of the crupper Sewell tries to get the reader to identify with an experience too often seen from the outside, unsympathetically: the discomfort inflicted on a domestic animal in the course of training it to conform to human needs.

Sewell does not argue here; she merely presents. Yet by presenting, she invites the reader to sympathize and to protest. Extraordinary in this passage, and in the text as a whole, which contains many such passages, is the physical nature of that sympathy. In the larger context of novel and audience, a Victorian woman writer is asking a reader, possibly a child reader, to imagine the pain of a leather strap drawn tight up under his or her rear end.

If we are not shocked by that image, it is because several distancing dynamics are at work: the dynamic of the children's story, where all is innocent and anything can be said, the dynamic of the animal story, which encourages us to maintain a distance between human and animal, and even the dynamic of the programmatic political text. *Black*

Beauty is about animal rights; it is not a piece of Victorian pornography about the agonies and ecstasies of leather. Yet what is it about, if it is not somehow about leather?

The impact of *Black Beauty* comes from its representation of the subjectivity of the animal in pain. The political referent of the book may be animal rights, and the book may actually have succeeded in persuading generations of children to ease the pain of animals. But the horse in *Black Beauty* is also what Elaine Scarry calls a "fulcrum," a way to mediate, among humans, ideas about pain: "Attention cannot stop at the object (the coat, the poem), for *the object is only a fulcrum or lever across which the force of creation moves back onto the human site* and remakes the makers. . . . The poet is working not to make the artifact (which is just the midpoint in the total action), but to remake human sentience; by means of the poem, he or she enters into and in some way alters the alive percipience of other persons" (307; emphasis Scarry's). Scarry's concept of the fulcrum comes from her magisterial work on the representation of suffering, *The Body in Pain,* a book that begins with an exploration of the problem of the unrepresentability of pain. Pain, according to Scarry, entails a "shattering of language" because "physical pain—unlike any other state of consciousness—has no referential content. It is not *of* or *for* anything. It is precisely because it takes no object that it, more than any other phenomenon, resists objectification in language" (5; emphasis Scarry's). Scarry sees some literary texts as venturing across the boundary into a world where language is shattered and pain is represented. We can see *Black Beauty* as one of those texts, though it is not often linked to the examples Scarry uses, like *Philoctetes* or Ingmar Bergman's film *Cries and Whispers.*

One reason for the unrepresentability of pain is that it is impossible to convey a true intersubjectivity of pain. Human pain is private, unreachable even by a committed and empathetic other. How much more, then, is the pain of an animal unrepresentable—or, as *Black Beauty* forces us to confront, the pain of a woman or a child, beings who are frequently coded as more animal than men are. Sewell connects women, children, and horses closely at several points and works through explicit comparisons of child abuse to trainers' maltreatment of young horses.

The most severe torment depicted in the story is inflicted by the "bearing rein," a device that compels horses to hold their heads up in the air while they pull a carriage. Since the horses cannot put their heads down to pull, they suffer agonies, particularly when going uphill. The mare Ginger has gotten her evil temper largely from being forced to wear the bearing rein by one of her owners, as she explains in chapter 8: "We were sold to a fashionable gentleman, and were sent up to London. I had been driven with a bearing rein by the dealer, and I hated it worse than anything else; but in this place we were reined far tighter; the coachman and his master thinking we looked more stylish so. We were often driven about in the Park and other fashionable places" (44–45). Fashion dictates the use of the rein, as does economics. Later, in chapter 22, Beauty's harnessmate Max asserts that the rein is used to make horses more attractive to potential buyers. Yet the rein is actually harmful because it shortens the working life of horses subjected to it. Sewell asks, What inspires such destructive "fashion"?

The mutilation of the body and its functions in the name of fashion is a constant theme in *Black Beauty*. In chapter 10, the docking of horses' and dogs' tails and the cropping of dogs' ears is given an explicitly human application by old Sir Oliver, a stallion whose own tail has been docked. He has lost a natural, functional flyswatter that way and gained a severe insight into the mechanisms of cruelty. He tells the story of a terrier bitch who has whelped five puppies. One day the puppies disappear, and then "poor Skye brought them back again, one by one in her mouth; not the happy little things that they were, but bleeding and crying pitifully; they had all had a piece of their tails cut off, and the soft flap of their pretty little ears was cut quite off. . . . They healed in time, and they forgot the pain, but the nice soft flap that of course was intended to protect the delicate part of their ears from dust and injury was gone for ever. Why don't they cut their own children's ears into points to make them look sharp?" (54). Fashion becomes a synonym for cruelty.

The implication of Sir Oliver's story is that people do not mutilate their children in the name of fashion. Yet the human characters who populate the England of *Black Beauty* are themselves a walking catalog of psychic trauma. One after another is in the grip of rage, alcoholism, deceit. One wonders how many of them have felt mistreatment as children. They pass through the novel inured to the suffering of others, both animal and human, and few of them manage to establish any real connections with the other human or animal characters.

The novel's women are more capricious and cruel than its men and follow fashion more slavishly. The mistress who owns Beauty and Ginger after they are sold from Birtwick (chap. 22) insists on the bearing rein. The too-spirited riding of Lady Anne (in chap. 23) leads to her mistreatment of the mare Lizzie and her fall. The mares in the novel are more mistreated than the male horses and develop worse tempers as a consequence. This parallel is not coincidental. In the novel both horses and people, as sexed species, are described with the same pronouns—pronouns that can shift reference oddly in midparagraph, as in chapter 10: "My mouth had never been spoiled, and I believe that was why the mistress preferred me to Ginger, although her paces were certainly as good. She used often to envy me, and said it was all the fault of breaking in, and the gag bit in London, that her mouth was not as perfect as mine" (52). In the second sentence of that passage, who used to envy Beauty? Ginger, one realizes afterward; when starting to read it, though, it's easy to think that the mistress is envious of Beauty, until one runs up against the image of the gag bit in the woman's own mouth and must change pronoun reference quickly.

Such pronoun confusion is not just a problem in the grammar of a single sentence. It is integral to the connections between animal and human made in the whole text. We confuse woman and mare, stallion and man, child and colt because horses stand in for people. Animals' pain gives voice to a human pain for which there is no plain prosaic human medium. The pain that Ginger feels when subjected to the bearing rein is directly related to her first mistress's social activity: "I chafed and fretted at the bits and rein; it was worse when we had to stand by the hour waiting for our mistress at some grand party or entertainment" (45). Her discomfort is perhaps of a piece with her mistress's own discomfort in fashionable clothing, with the tedium and display of human society.

"Horses have no relations," says Beauty (36). Like women, they pass from the hands of one man to another; their names are changed by their owners; they are dressed for social display. Like girls, they are broken early and forcefully into habits of patience and endurance. When Beauty's mother opines, "A horse never knows who may buy him, or who may drive him" (30), the reader may be invited to compare the fate of horses to the fate of the human heroines of many another Victorian novel, pressed into loveless or abusive marriages.

Ginger's experience parallels not only that of girls but also that of public school boys: "I was taken from my mother as soon as I was weaned, and put with a lot of other young colts" (40), a venue for corporal punishment and the breaking of wills like the one that the young Roald Dahl would experience decades later. Here, she is caught and broken; her absent mother is as unable to help her as the human mother of a boarding-school child: "One caught me by the forelock, another caught me by the nose, and held it so tight I could hardly draw my breath; then another took my under jaw in his hard hand and wrenched my mouth open, and so by force they got on the halter and the bar into my mouth; then one dragged me along by the halter, another flogging behind, and this was the first experience I had of men's kindness, it was all force" (40). The use of the inclusive term *men*—humans are always "men" in this novel—is another gendering factor. In this passage, a female refers to the kindness of "men" ironically, as a synonym for physical abuse. In all but its most literal form, this scene of horse-breaking is in effect a scene of rape, and of child rape at that.

Female riders can be capricious and careless, but males are cruel, and are cruel from childhood on. The pony Merrylegs looks carefully after the Birtwick girls, who ride him gently. But when it is the boys' turn, "they had each cut a great hazel stick for a riding whip, and laid it on a little too hard" (49). To Merrylegs's way of thinking, there is no innate malice in the boys; "they don't wish to be cruel" (49), but example turns them into abusers of animals. Perhaps there is an implicit suggestion that the boys are themselves whipped in the mention of the rod, that biblical emblem of corporal punishment.

A garrulous old ostler who cares for Beauty and Ginger in an early chapter claims that he can tell after only a few minutes' handling what kind of treatment a horse has had when young. The ostler repeats the novel's continual assertion that the formation of the young animal is the key to adult temperament. He also makes an explicit connection between animals and people, saying of horses, "Their tempers are mostly made when they are young. Bless you! they are like children, train 'em up in the way they should go, as the good book says, and when they are old they will not depart from it, if they have a chance, that is" (72). Such connections are too pervasive in *Black Beauty* to be mere offhand clinchings of a point about the ethics of animal handling. They point to a consistent outward direction of the text, its application toward human ethics and the rearing of children.

Black Beauty is a litany of abuses of animals. In the early chapters, Beauty and his various grooms can scarcely leave Birtwick Park without encountering some animal abuse that needs righting. The people of Birtwick are known in their neighborhood as animal-rights activists. John Manly refuses to help a boy who has been thrown after whipping a pony. Young Joe Green comes to manhood by informing on a man who has flogged horses. As a kind of chorus to these exploits, the Birtwick men keep up a running discussion of the best ways to treat animals and continually deplore the bad state of affairs at other stables.

A key scene in the development of the novel's rhetoric comes in chapters 18 and 19. Beauty, ridden hard in a bid to save his invalid mistress's life, takes ill when Joe Green doesn't put a blanket on him after his exertions. John Manly nurses Beauty back to health. John is severe with Joe and is taken to task by Joe's brother Tom for that severity. After all, Joe did not mean to harm Beauty. John responds that the unintended consequences of ignorance are as blameworthy as deliberate malice. Significantly, he cites as examples unintentional injuries done to children:

> If people can say, "Oh! I did not know, I did not mean any harm," they think it is all right. I suppose Martha Mulwash did not mean to kill that baby, when she dosed it with Dalby, and soothing syrups; but she did kill it, and was tried for manslaughter. . . . Bill Starkey . . . did not mean to frighten his brother into fits when he dressed up like a ghost, and ran after him in the moonlight; but he did; and that bright, handsome little fellow, that might have been the pride of any mother's heart, is just no better than an idiot, and never will be, if he live to be eighty years old. (87–88)

The incidents that John brings up—the inadvertently murderous nurse, the sham ghost—have a slapstick quality to them that doesn't allow the reader to take them quite seriously. By contrast, the injury to Beauty is *really* serious, John seems to argue. The dynamics are telling. In each case an injury that seems slightly comical, and is the result of no real malice, is shown to have terrible (if somewhat melodramatic) consequences. Maltreatment of a horse, or of a child, can seem trivial. But suddenly to see, in the projected figure of an eighty-year-old "idiot," the blighted chance of a young child is to connect the triviality of violence with its lasting effects.

Violence in *Black Beauty* is chronic, physical, and central to the text's moral concerns. The novel's violence is also sexualized. Yet while the moral and physical implications of violence are usually overt, the sexual nature of that violence remains unspoken. It must be teased out of the text by correspondences. Strapping and binding of the horses' bodies corresponds to the binding of women's bodies for sexual display. Horse breaking corresponds to rape. Docking of tails is possibly like circumcision—the cutting off of a functional but apparently inessential part of the body to meet demands of fashion. Circumcision was rare in Victorian England, but even this stray connection to male genital mutilation leads to another question: Why is there no scene of gelding in the novel?

This question is a variant on a theme already raised. Children's literature includes scenes of violence, often scenes of grisly violence, like the cropping of the puppies' ears in *Black Beauty,* with no excuse in the text or qualm on the part of the adult reader. But sex, in Victorian children's classics—and in some later ones like *The Secret Garden,* as we will see in chapter 5, is always elided. The lack of sex in a book like *Black Beauty* can even pose problems for late twentieth-century interpreters like Caroline Thompson. Her 1994 screenplay introduces a love subplot between Beauty and Ginger that is quite explicit (though not, of course, graphic). The friendship that unites Beauty and Ginger in Sewell's novel seems unlikely to a modern viewer, even to a child viewer, without some sexual element. Yet that sexual element is entirely lacking in the book.

Black Beauty is never bred, despite the admiration that some of his owners have for him. He is never gelded, either, despite the obvious impact such a scene would have as an example of the violence inflicted on the bodies of animals, the novel's great theme. No horse in the book refers at any time to a sexual experience; no mares are ever in foal, and there are no foaling scenes. (Again, Thompson's film, which shows the foaling of Beauty himself, updates and sexualizes Sewell's text.) The novel's reticence about the sex lives of these animals can hardly be attributed to general "Victorian" squeamishness. There is explicit violence in the novel, as we have seen; there is also a fairly blunt description of the dangers of excrement in an unclean stable (chap. 31).

Here, at least, I found that *Black Beauty* conformed to my preconceptions. I wasn't expecting sex in this Victorian animal story, and I didn't find any. But at the point I'd arrived at in my reading, such an omission seemed not innocent but rather like the concealing of an even less spoken dynamic than that of violence.

More than any other text, *Black Beauty* made me aware of the possibilities for reading children's literature and children's culture in terms of violence and power. It intrigues me that such a text, with its roots in the adult, political animal-rights beliefs of its author, should have been so easily accepted as a children's literature classic. Once sensitized by my experience of *Black Beauty* to the possibility that children's classics can function as statements about power and violence, I began to see the dynamics of power everywhere in children's culture, from venerable prose classics to ephemeral recent films. In part, of course, I had become Gadamer's hermeneut. I saw what I set out to see. But I think that readers will see these things along with me, starting from this flawed project of reading *Black Beauty*. I began to see these dynamics of power, as I will go on to explore in the next chapter, not just in the dramatic struggles of big animals in big-animal stories but also in the seemingly most benign venues: stories and movies about puppy dogs.

3

BEASTS:
DOG STORIES AND KIDS

One day, wandering into the family section of our local video store, I was overwhelmed by the animals around me. I thought I had entered some Borgesian menagerie. The beasts stretched out around me in a long winding catalog. Here were wolves: *The Call of the Wild, White Wolves.* Lots of horses, naturally: *Black Beauty, Black Stallion, Black Stallion Returns, My Friend Flicka, Lightning, Misty, Phar Lap.* (*Francis the Talking Mule,* however, is in our "classics" section. We have high standards of classicism in Arlington, Texas.) There were movies about water-going mammals of all sorts: a seal (*Andre*), *Flipper, Free Willy* (the original movie and its sequels), *Polar Bear King, Namu the Killer Whale* (wonderful film that: Lee Meriwether and Robert Lansing out-doing each other in expressionlessness), *Ring of Bright Water.* I saw large cats in *Clarence the Cross-Eyed Lion* and the lions of *Born Free.* Not many small cats, though either Milo or Otis is a cat, I have never been able to tell which. A deer movie, *The Yearling.* Bear movies like *Goldy* and *Goldy 2* and the Annaud bear which is just *The Bear.* Something called *Frog. Babe,* which, as the box says, is the *Citizen Kane* of talking pig movies. *The Amazing Panda Adventure.* Dinosaur movies including *Adventures in Dinosaur City* and *Prehysteria* (1, 2, and 3). Future historians reflecting on late twentieth-century culture may have to conclude that dinosaurs and humans were contemporaneous. There was a reindeer movie called *Prancer*. There were several primate movies, including *Born to Be Wild, Dunston Checks In, Monkey Trouble,* and *Ed,* Ed being a chimpanzee who plays major league baseball. And finally, at the bottom of the last shelf, *Watership Down,* or, as my sister-in-law calls it, *Bloody Rabbits.*

But the most popular animal for an animal movie is the dog, *Canis familiaris.* There was no end of these: *Beethoven, Benji* and *Benji the Hunter* and *For the Love of Benji* and *Benji's Very Own Christmas Story, Bingo, Where the Red Fern Grows, Far from Home, Fluke, Three Wishes* and *Old Yeller* and *The Shaggy Dog, Lassie* and *Courage of Lassie* and *Challenge to Lassie* and *Lassie Come Home* and *Balto* and *101 Dalmatians* twice (making 202) and I seriously lost count at this point. I went home that night and dreamt about packs of cuddly clever movie pets hounding me through the streets of my subdivision.

My attachment to fictional dogs began when I rode a bus to grade school and read dog novels to pass the time. My favorite dog author was Albert Payson Terhune. When I think of that time and that attachment now, it seems incongruous to me. Like Terhune, I lived in New Jersey. Unlike Terhune, who came of old Dutch and English stock and was a self-styled aristocrat, I was a scruffy ethnic mixed breed Slovak and Irish and German American, a recent arrival from inner-city Chicago, being sent to a Friends school to try to make me a little more Anglo than I had any realistic hope of becoming. I had no association with large dogs or large horses or any other trappings of the hunt country. We lived in the country all right, but we lived in a converted chicken coop on a tomato farm along a dirt path that had no name but was a reasonable facsimile of Tobacco Road. The only rural animals I routinely bonded with were pariah dogs, snapping turtles, and the occasional escaped pig from a dirt farm half-a-mile away.

But see the power of literature: just ten years later I started graduate school at Princeton, scruffy as ever but propelled into Terhune's circles by the sheer suggestive power of the poetry of American privilege—among other things. Just as English schoolchildren learn about heroic determination by reading about Scott of the Antarctic, I learned about American assumptions of entitlement and *noblesse oblige* by reading about Lad, the collie of the Place.

Lad (1919) was the book that propelled Terhune to fame. His biographer, Irving Litvag, notes that "by 1940, it had gone through more than seventy printings . . . and in 1975 was in its eighty-second printing. . . . More than fifteen years after initial publication, the book had sold over 250,000 copies" (113). It was still in print in the 1990s, but most readers would agree that *Lad* and Terhune's other dog stories have dated badly. Maybe it would be better to say that the mainstream of American discourse has shifted and left them isolated. This process has been relatively sudden. *Lad* represents a world not far removed from ours temporally, but very remote in terms of class and social dynamics.

Lad is about breeding in all senses: pedigree, an inborn sense of manners and behavior, and, elliptically, sex. The book conveys an ideology that fits the author's own standing in the American aristocracy. Bert Terhune was the son of Edward Payson Terhune (a scion of an old Dutch family) and the Virginian novelist Marion Harland, who was from an old colonial family. His second wife, Anice Stockton, the "Mistress" of the Lad stories, was a descendant of Richard Stockton, signer of the Declaration of Independence. The Lad stories justify the natural rights of the well-bred.

Lad is set at the Place, Terhune's fictionalized version of his North Jersey estate called Sunnybank. The Place is neither the family estate of colonial settlers nor the playground of a parvenu. The novel distinguishes clearly between the Master of the Place against the indigenous Jersey yeomanry on one side and the parvenu Hamilcar Q. Glure, the "Wall Street Farmer," on the other. In real life, Sunnybank was built by Terhune's parents on land that they purchased. In fiction, the Master's claim to the land becomes idealized. He has true title to it because of his class (finer than the country folk) and his deep devotion to the land (earthier than that of the book's parvenus). We get a peculiarly American sense of class and place. The dog hero of the stories becomes integral to the American aristocrat's possession of his or her rights.

The Place is the estate of a rich man and woman and is guarded by the huge collie named Lad. The Place seems to need this watchdog because it is threatened from all sides by the flotsam of the American polity: foreigners, thieves, "Negroes," "hobos," and "tramps" continually cross its grounds, usually to be treed, pinned down, or mauled by

Lad. (This is the same social detritus we'll meet in the next chapter, where it threatens the Hardy Boys.) The collie internalizes a set of distinctions concerning decorous access to the property: "Lad had learned in puppyhood the simple provisions of the Guest Law. He knew, for example, that no one openly approaching the house along the driveway from the furlong-distant highroad was to be molested. . . . On the other hand, the Law demanded the instant halting of all prowlers, or of anyone seeking to get to the house from road or lake by circuitous and stealthy means" (219). The Master enforces these distinctions because he fears transgressions and trespasses. The outer world, to him, is full of harness and tire thieves, orchard thieves, robbers and poachers, and worse. But with Lad on duty, "the women of my family are as safe here, day and night, as if I had a machine-gun company on guard" (230). Only the Master's preference for dogs seems to prevent him from resorting to military force.

Since *Lad* is a collection of previously published magazine stories, it lacks even the sparse pretensions to narrative direction that characterize *Black Beauty*. Reading along in *Lad*, one not only has no clue where it is going but also no clue why it is being told at all. It lacks an autobiographical frame to signal to the reader that this is the story of an individual's life, either human or canine. The stories in *Lad*, as Terhune backtracks to remind readers of events from other stories in the collection, reiterate attitudes about breeding, training, and instinct that highlight its significance as a text about animals and about children.

Lad is centered on competition, both formal (the dog show) and informal (combat). Almost in spite of himself, Lad wins ribbons in show after show. His sheer noble nature conquers the prejudices of the dog world in favor of more superficial qualities. (The real-life Lad was not even registered with the American Kennel Club. Litvag describes the dog show scenes as "pure fiction," 89.) Scenes of Lad's show triumphs are mixed about equally with scenes of his victories in battle against men and dogs.

In the course of the book, Lad fights the collie Knave (an episode I discuss at length later on), an invading "negro," a poisonous snake, a great mongrel dog, a thief, a bull, a sheep stealer, and two of the other dogs on The Place, including his son, Wolf, who has an extended combat in a different chapter with a different thief. These are not cartoon-violent combats. They are fights to the death, described intricately, with the tactics of dog fighting brought out in finical detail. The collie's strengths (huge thick coat, ability to slash and feint) and weaknesses (nearsightedness, tiny forelegs), its preferred methods of fighting, and its favorite death blows (severing the jugular, puncturing the spinal column at the nape of the neck, snapping the aforementioned tiny fore-leg) are mentioned over and over. Terhune glamorizes violence while insisting on control of violence by training and command.

Lad is what the narrative theorist F. K. Stanzel calls a "reflector-character." His subjectivity is presented by an external narration in the third person. Lad's perspective is not consistently the basis for the entire narrative, however. The reflection can just as easily be taken up by any of the human characters or by the impersonal voice of the narrator. This narrator is not specifically identified with the Master, though his perspective and values are identical to the Master's.

The narrative conditions of *Lad* are therefore complex. The narratee is clearly someone who is eager to learn more about the ways of dogs, and the narrator obliges that desire. But the animal's subjectivity is locked within an inaccessible consciousness. In *Black Beauty* the horse sometimes can't quite understand what people say and do. In *Lad* the humans who know this dog best are sometimes at a loss to account for his actions but have deliberate recourse to mythologies of atavism. Such mythologies keep the text focused on issues of inheritance and descent.

Lad has "the wisest and darkest and most sorrowful eyes in all dog-dom—eyes that gave the lie to folk who say no dog has a soul" (49). Lad is human-like, but better than human. Worshipful of his Master and Mistress, he is worshiped by them in turn. "If he'd known a little less he'd have been human," says the Master after one of Lad's astounding exploits (71). Lad is constructed as part noble savage. Prime among his noble savage qualities is an instinctive chivalrous behavior toward all female dogs, since "man is the only animal to maltreat the female of his kind" (58). As the humans of the story, and by implication the human readers, read their own behavior back through that of the champion collie, Terhune develops an ideology of noble instinct tempered by inflexible training—as a pattern for people as well as for dogs.

Lad is never beaten in training. His obedience to his Master's commands is preternaturally complete, but he has been brought to this obedience by firm and nonviolent handling, as the text repeats over and over. Instead of fear of retribution, the code known simply as the Law governs his actions. The Law is patriarchy at its most intuitive, commanding adherence to illogical demands of honor—as when, to prove a point in a legal hearing, the Master submits to having Lad whipped and himself kicked in the rear by his adversary, to prove some obscure point (275–79). Lad's innate reaction to both assaults is murderous fury, but his fury is checked in midspring by the Master's instructions. Perfect control of the living instrument, which obeys without question or delay, is the book's ideal. At some metaphorical distance, we can see here an ideal parent-child relationship: perfect obedience and submission to a master will, without the vulgarity of forcible coercion.

In *Lad* Terhune specifically decries the use of force and punishment in the rearing of young animals, and by extension, probably, in the rearing of human children. But Terhune recognizes the exasperation of dealing with a willful young creature: "Small wonder that many humans lose patience and temper during the process and idiotically resort to the whip, to the boot-toe and to bellowing—in which case the puppy is never decently educated, but emerges from the process with a cowed and broken spirit or with an incurable streak of meanness that renders him worthless" (83). The Master who can control himself and the young animal, welding both into a single demonstration of will, is the ideal of this text.

In one story (chap. 8, "The Gold Hat"), Lad is pitted in competition at a show against a champion collie who has been imported by the vulgar "Wall Street Farmer" Hamilcar Q. Glure. Glure sets the terms of the competition: it must involve control of the dogs' movements from a distance, as in a sheepdog trial. But Lad is at a great disadvantage since he has never worked sheep. Somehow he is coaxed, by the Mistress, around a simple course. When Glure proceeds to the course with his prize sheepdog, Lochinvar, he loses his own physical self-control, burning himself with a cigar and finally cursing and kicking the uncomprehending collie.

The point is made: the mere owner (the bad parent?) resorts to physical abuse. The loving Master (good parent?) exacts perfect obedience without any physical threat. The symbolic capital gained by such allegiance is perhaps more totally oppressive than that gained by threats because it demands a psychological surveillance that is nothing short of absolute. The expressed scorn for violence should hardly be interpreted as a liberating ideology. The ideology of *Lad* is comparable to that of the moderate Protestants that Philip Greven discusses in *Spare the Child*. Thinkers like the nineteenth-century minister Horace Bushnell, says Greven, "advocated a seemingly benign and kindly form of control, to bend rather than break a child's will. But his method was unlikely to create a genuine sense of autonomy in the child, or a sense of choice and responsibility. The child still had to accept the parent's will as the child's own" (88). A recurring situation in *Lad* exemplifies this acceptance, when time and again the bemused collie must accept his Master's orders, no matter how absurd or out of character, because the will of the Master is the one unquestionable guideline in life.

Lad is a parent too. The book contrasts his rearing of his son, Wolf, to the treatment accorded the pup by his mother, Lady—and, implicitly, to the rearing of Lad by the Master. Lady, to make a pun, is simply a bitch. She is "erratic" (57) and has "hair-trigger nerves" (77). Though she possesses mothering instincts that make no sense at all to Lad, "animal mothers early wear out their zealously self-sacrificing love for their young" (82). When distemper removes Lady temporarily from the scene, Lad must take over the parenting duties. Since he has no instinct for it, he goes about parenting in a rational way. His puppy care is entirely a social construct, not the mere bitch instinct of Lady, and, predictably, "Wolf grew to love his sire as he had never loved Lady. For the discipline and the firm kindliness of Lad were having their effect on his heart as well as on his manners. They struck a far deeper note within him than ever had Lady's alternating affection and crossness" (87).

Exceptions in this novel prove rules. Lad is subject, among other legislation, to the Guest Law. He must never under any circumstances act aggressively toward someone that the Master or Mistress identifies as a guest. Of course, like the Prime Directive on "Star Trek," the Guest Law is made to be broken for dramatic impact. In two separate incidents described in identical words, Lad "for the first time in . . . his blameless life" (88, 171) violates the Law by attacking a visitor to the Place. On both of these occasions, he has good reasons not immediately apparent to the Master.

The Master himself slips in obeying another prime directive: never hit a dog. This slippage, in the first Lad story, "His Mate," strikes a keynote for all the episodes that follow. "His Mate" introduced Lad to reading audiences when it was published in the January 1915 issue of *Red Book*. Lad and Lady are mates. He is the elder. She first came to the Place as a tiny puppy, and Lad protected her because of "the natural impulse of the thoroughbred—brute or human—to guard the helpless" (2). "He was Lady's life slave" (2). She is imperious toward him, holding him in thrall through an appeal that is obviously, but unspokenly, sexual.

Their domestic happiness is upset, however, when the Master takes in another male collie, Knave, as a boarder: "She turned to the all-conquering Knave in a keenness of attraction that was all but hypnotic" (8). There is something patently unrealistic in this love triangle. For one thing, Lady never seems to be in heat. Terhune's reticence about the facts of canine sexuality means that he cannot even allude to the estrus cycle. The story of jealousy among dogs therefore takes on the dimensions of a human courtly love triangle. "A Grail-knight in thought" (8), Lad "sadly withdrew from the unequal contest" (9). By the rules of the Place, he must not attack a guest, human or animal. Except, of course, when he *does*—but for dramatic purposes here Lad plays the wounded, withdrawn lover.

Lady has internalized the Law as well as Lad has. Just one beating has sufficed to instill reverence for the Law into her. It came when, as a puppy, she had damaged the stuffed bald eagle that "was the delight of the Master's heart" (5). The Master, with the Endangered Species Act still conveniently in the future, had himself shot this eagle for raiding his prize chickens, and in the complicated pecking order of interspecies dominance on the Place, the stuffed eagle symbolizes his mastery of wild and domestic animals alike. After this beating, Lady never misbehaves inside the house again.

The Master's pride in the eagle is also involved in the only beating he ever gives Lad. Knave mischievously enters the study, where Lady is recovering from an injury. He tears the eagle to bits, steals its head, and jumps out of the window. The Master comes in, sees the destroyed trophy, and begins to beat Lady once again for her misdeeds. Lad, who knows that Lady is innocent, growls at him. Immediately this show of resistance, not Lady's actual or presumed vandalism, becomes the focus of punishment. "The growl ceased. The orange-tawny collie stood erect. Down came the braided whiplash on Lad's shoulders—again over his loins, and yet again and again" (17). In a scene that is a twin for unjust school-flogging scenes in other children's books, Lad is chastised and his spirit broken. He starts to nurse a hatred, not for his Master, but for Knave, the ultimate cause of all the beatings.

The ensuing battle between Knave and Lad sets the tone for the rest of the stories. All sorts of competition finally reduce to combat, in the Terhune world. The formula for scores of subsequent dog fights is introduced in "His Mate." Knave tries to smash Lad's foreleg. Furrows and slashes and rents are ripped in the dogs' coats, sending down trickles of hot blood. Knave gets his teeth around the base of Lad's skull, "and holding him thus helpless, he proceeded to grit and grind his tight-clenched teeth in the slow, relentless motion that must soon or late eat down to and sever the spinal cord" (22). With Lady's help, Lad reverses the hold and sinks his own sharp teeth into Knave's throat. Finally, Knave is vanquished and runs off the Place.

The final tableau of the story is not about the dogs, however, but about what happens to the Master when he comes upon this battle, too late to prevent it. Lad sees the Master holding the eagle's missing head, the proof that Knave, not Lady, had destroyed the stuffed eagle. When he sees Lad, the Master breaks down, admitting his own mistake: "Oh Lad! Laddie! I'm so sorry. So sorry! You're—you're more of a man than I am, old friend. I'll make it up to you, somehow!" (25).

The entire scene is predicated on the mangling of the eagle. Nowhere does the story suggest that the problem may be, not the misattributed blame for the eagle's destruction, but the Master's own unreasonable attachment to the bird. The right of the Master to punish the dog that has chewed up the eagle is not disputed; the pathos of his repentance comes from his having chosen the wrong dog to beat. The Master's affection for a grown-up toy is presented as a natural motive for his cruelty toward the helpless dogs.

Lad is full of justifications of the Master's actions and rules as reasonable and functional. The text is full of doglore, true or false.[1] The main precepts of the Law—never to attack domestic animals or human guests, to tolerate whatever the Master tolerates, to guard the house, chase wild animals, and behave well when indoors—seem self-evident and are upheld on both sides with mutual respect. But when the dogs attack an object on which the Master places a sentimental value, any amount of violence toward them is seen as justifiable.

In effect, the Master himself has never grown up. "His Mate" is a rueful and coded admission that all Law is founded in children's jealousies. A jealous god to his worshipers, the Master turns little child when a favorite thing gets broken. By extension, the whole category of the Law seems to proceed from the Master's childish fixation on having his own way. All of the impositions of this Law, and perhaps any law, come from the desire to order what in the long run cannot be perfectly ordered: the chances and conflicting desires of everyday life.

The reiterations of the Law in *Lad* come to resemble not so much the necessary scaffolding of a series of magazine stories slapped awkwardly together as the insistent efforts of a will to impose itself. The Master's will is imposed by repetition, a rhythm that comes to feel natural, but which carries the threat of merciless force behind it. Behind *that* force is no higher law but only the blind rage of a child who cannot get exactly what he wants.

One cannot be sure what Terhune thought of evolutionary theory. *Lad* is not exactly a venue for the higher intellectual debates of its day. However, Lad's obedience to the Law is explained not just in terms of conditioning but also in terms of heredity: "Years of training and centuries of ancestry had taught him to understand every spoken wish of the Master's" (7). Since *Lad* connects animal breeding with human breeding as often as possible, a higher justification of the Master's whims arises. These layings-down of the Law are posited as inbred in the Master's own evolutionary makeup. They have been selected for in his own breeding. Recall that it is the "natural impulse of the thoroughbred—brute or human—to guard the helpless" (2). A thoroughbred himself, the Master has certain race characteristics that are ingrained in his blood.

40

This kind of seat-of-the-pants evolutionary theorizing helps explain the persistent references in *Lad* to atavism. Collies, the book tells us, are domesticated wolves: "A collie has a strain of wolf in his queer brain" (45). This kinship allows Lad advantages in combat that no other kind of dog could obtain and even leads him to understand how to recover from the bite of a poisonous snake (73). Lad's son—named, unsurprisingly, Wolf—inherits this strain and exhibits, even as a puppy, the fighting instincts of a wolf: "Wolf dived for Lad's white forelegs, gnawing happily at them with a playfully unconscious throwback to his wolf ancestors who sought thus to disable an enemy by breaking the foreleg bone. For all seemingly aimless puppy-play had its origin in some ancestral custom" (81–82). The collies of the Place are therefore not just pets or working animals, but a continual display of the power of primitive humans over the forces of wolfish nature.

One might assume that *Lad* and its successors by Terhune have always been children's novels. The 1990s marketing of these books is almost entirely as juveniles. But the books made their early progress as adult best-sellers, and even as critically acclaimed adult fiction. Litvag cites correspondence between Terhune and his old college professor Brander Matthews in which Matthews, in 1924, tells Terhune how much pleasure the *Lad* stories have given him (39). It is difficult to conceive of Matthews, one of the founding figures in modern American literary nationalism, making children's books his main reading, even leisure reading. Matthews apparently did not think of Terhune's books as being for children; they were self-evidently "serious" fiction.

Dutton and other publishers of Terhune's dog fiction marketed the books as general fiction, and the stories that continued to fuel Terhune's books appeared in the major general-interest magazines of the twenties: the *Saturday Evening Post*, the *Ladies' Home Journal*, the *Atlantic Monthly*, and many others.

In midcentury, however, the primary venue for circulation of Terhune's animal books was the children's list at Grosset and Dunlap: "For many years some fifteen titles were published as children's books by Grosset & Dunlap under licensing arrangements with the original publishers. The figures show that by the end of 1970, the Grosset & Dunlap editions had sold a total of more than 650,000 copies" (Litvag 287). Litvag makes no comment on this peculiar transformation, apparently thinking that none is needed. A set of books that was read mostly by adults in the twenties and thirties had become, by the fifties and sixties, a children's series, for no better reason than that it was about animals. Lacking the canonical cachet of Jack London and the connections that his animal fiction has with his decidedly adult stories about the northern wilderness, the Terhune books ceased to lead even the double existence of London's dog books and have become entirely juvenilized.

Books like Terhune's and London's slip into the sphere of children's literature in an ideologically purposeful if often unconscious way. The dynamics that these texts represent are often those of violence, breaking of wills, and sexual reticence. As muted, potentially wild, unformed beings, human children are confused with animals in our society. The fate of many books about animals, even when written for adults, is that they are given to children.

Such a dynamic becomes self-sustaining. When we make a movie for children, in turn, it seems natural for it to include lots of animals. At times the distinctions blur altogether. "We're all pretty much the same," says Eddie Murphy's Dr. Dolittle of humans and animals at the conclusion of Betty Thomas's 1998 film. Murphy's Dolittle-for-the-nineties learns to connect better with his children by listening to animals, just as he learns to be a better people doctor by becoming a veterinarian in midcareer.

Movie dogs are fascinating because they go two ways at once. Malleable fictional creatures, dogs can be both big and small: puppy and giant, cuddly and fierce, at work and at play. They are at the same time surrogate parents and surrogate children. In a key scene from Brian Levant's film *Beethoven* (1992), the hapless father (played by Charles Grodin) must decide whether to have his Saint Bernard put down. As he stares at the grown dog in its kennel, he visualizes the dog alternating between its adult appearance and the puppy that he remembers. More than most animals, a dog remains childlike even as it grows to the prodigious size of a Saint Bernard. Grodin's character is thinking of destroying Beethoven because the dog may be too wild and vicious to control, but his fear of the violent potential of the dog is inextricable from his sense of its infant cuddliness.

We can learn about nineties anxieties about power, children, and families from a close watching of some midnineties dog movies. Such films, like the adult-to-child transformation movies that I discuss in chapter 6, blur distinctions between categories. In so doing they heighten issues that might remain unspoken if the films were all-human dramas. By means of a magical, transformational, or preternaturally aware dog, one can represent dynamics that one cannot represent in human dramas. Because these dog movies are specifically marketed to children—or to the "family" audience presumed to be watching and reacting as a unit—they implicate kids as audience in a way that much commentary about the family—for example, political discourse or self-help books—specifically does not.

The following discussion of recent dog films and dog stories is not an argument but a description, a "thick" description in which I attempt to pick out threads of cultural address in the movies and to show their potential status as elements of cultural discourse. I don't think that the disparate writers and directors of these pictures have a concerted message or that studio heads are impressing an ideology on the public. I conceive of Hollywood not as some sort of Althusserian Ideological State Apparatus but as an uncontemplative mechanism for reflecting cultural commonplaces not usually available to analysis. The makers of these films take certain things for granted because most Americans also take such things for granted: ideas about the family, the status of children, the nature of power.

Dog movies are such a long-standing genre that the newer ones inevitably comment on the earlier ones. Daniel Petrie's 1994 *Lassie* is not so much *Lassie* as meta-*Lassie*. The movie opens by enlisting itself in Lassie nostalgia. The Turner kids are watching "Lassie" on TV. The little girl, Jennifer, loves to watch the dog story. Her elder brother, Matt, opines that "Lassie," along with Santa Claus and other sentimental American favorites, sucks. Matt is cynical in part because he can remember their dead mother well and Jennifer cannot. Matt is having a harder time accepting his father's remarriage. The sentimentality of the dog story on TV grates on his nerves.

Reversing the demographic trend of the entire twentieth century, Jennifer and Matt, along with the rest of the Turner family, move away from urban Baltimore to remote rural Virginia—specifically, to Franklin Falls, population 148. On their way to their new home, they come across a collie whose owner has died in a truck crash. Against the father's better judgment they adopt the collie and name it Lassie.

From this point on the movie both is and isn't a Lassie movie. Unlike the long tradition of Lassie narratives that dates back to Eric Knight's 1938 original short story, it does not stay focused on its title character. The dog disappears from many scenes, as the movie centers strongly on the Turners and their problems. They have many. Their relocation is dubiously motivated (like so many in the Goosebumps series of children's books, as we'll see in chapter 4). Vague business prospects bring Matt and Jennifer's father, a contractor, to Virginia. More emotionally significant is that he is bringing his children and his second wife back to the childhood home of the children's mother. This dead mother, Anne Collins, is the force that holds the reconstituted Turner family on the Collins homestead in Virginia.

This scene of widowing and remarriage shows, by transference, a persistent nineties concern with divorce. The challenge of remaking a divorced family around a stepmother is written over with nostalgia for the challenge of surviving widowhood. The 1994 *Lassie* yearns for an erasure of the rupture caused by the mother's absence. By representing that absence as death, the picture brings an older set of values— the values of fairy tale and of "till death do us part"—into an era in which the vast majority of reconstituted families are voluntarily reconstituted by divorce and remarriage. By placing the newly made-up family in the extended family of the first wife/mother, the film erases the original absence and loss. A family—archetypally, *the* American family—is made whole again.

The picture goes further, reabsorbing the family back into the countryside. The original loss was the removal of Anne Collins, the dead mother, from her family homestead. Lassie engineers the family's rediscovery of Anne's attachment to her native soil. The son, Matt, is the most disaffected of the Turners. He has nowhere to skateboard in the heartland, so he spends most of his time lying in bed listening to his Walkman and wishing he were in Baltimore. At least, that is, until Lassie steals the Walkman and leads Matt on a chase around the homestead, where Matt discovers such things as his mother's diary (which reveals her deep love of sheep ranching and her longing to own a collie named Lassie) and his mother's initials carved into her favorite tree.

The 1994 manifestation of Lassie is all dogs to all people. She does the usual Lassie things, like rescuing people and sheep. In a scene that is almost daring in its own triteness, Lassie tries to alert the family to the sheepnaping of their entire flock. "What is it, girl?" asks Matt. "Where's our sheep?" In another bit of doggy bravado that recalls Terhune's Lad, this Lassie takes on a wolf that has materialized in unlikely fashion in nineties Virginia to menace Matt. This new Lassie also has her paw on the pulse of the family's emotional life. Aside from merely rescuing them from mortal danger and preserving their livelihood, Lassie tries, in her silent but sensitive way, to get them in touch with themselves. As if to reverse the well-known cartoon in which a drowning man yells, "Lassie, get help" and in the next panel we see Lassie on an analyst's couch, the new Lassie herself acts as therapist, helping to reintegrate the family emotionally into middle America.

She becomes not just pet and pal but a stand-in for the departed mother. The main plot of the film involves a feud between the Collins-Turner clan and the Garlands, their sheep-herding rivals. The Garlands live in a stuff-crammed parvenus' house, treating the ecosystem and their neighbors with contempt. By contrast, the Collins place is homespun and humble. They assemble their sheep pens in a music-video-like scene to the strains of "Forever Young." In the climactic scene the Turner-Collinses and the Garlands struggle for some reason in a waterfall, and Lassie, after saving all the humans concerned, plunges over the falls and disappears.

In the next scene, Matt is despondent and complains, "We didn't even get to bury her." For a split-second, we think that he is talking about his mother. As in *Black Beauty*, the gendered pronoun allows for a slip between animal and human referents. But his father sets the antecedents (almost) straight: "It's hard to imagine now, but we'll get you another one just as good." Which is exactly what he had done after the loss of Matt's mother, of course. Matt, trying to sort out his emotions toward all the females in his life, carves LASSIE on the same tree into which his mother had carved her initials. It goes without saying that the unburied Lassie is also undead and comes home, a bit wet but otherwise in good form, to an overjoyed Matt. The family finally makes peace with their neighbors and themselves. Who needs to come to terms with a stepmother, really, when a loyal dog is close at hand?

Lassie and other nineties dogs are primarily not wolves or even beasts, but people. They stand in for people and take upon themselves, as all-absorbent surrogates, the emotional energy of the family unit. Not satisfied to stop at the cute catchphrase "dogs are people too," recent dog movies start from the premise that dogs are people first and foremost—people with quaint tendencies, like digging in the garden and drinking from the toilet, but people all the same.

Eric Knight's original story, expanded into the 1940 novel *Lassie Come-Home,* is distinctly centered on the animal as animal, just as Terhune's *Lad* stresses the distance between human and animal consciousness. As Knight's collie makes her famous journey across Scotland to come home, the narrator of *Lassie Come-Home* waxes philosophical about this distinction: "[Lassie] could not base her conduct on the past experience of others of her kind, which is another human method. . . . Every animal must meet each new experience as if it had never faced his kind before in the history of the world" (98). By contrast, the 1994 film avatar of Lassie is not only a reasoning problem solver but also a repository of human knowledge. She knows the secrets of Anne Collins's past. In some ways this Lassie is neither a human nor a dog, but an angel. The genre of dog movie in the nineties segues at one margin into that other popular recent genre, the angel movie.

We will see more dog angels in *Fluke* near the end of this chapter. For the moment, I'd like to keep considering the humanization of dogs, apparent in the 1989 Tom Hanks comedy *Turner and Hooch.* Hanks, who reappears in the boundary-blurring film *Big* in chapter 6, plays Scott Turner, a neurotically tidy small-town detective. When an old man is murdered, Turner must try to track the killers with the help of the only witness—the old man's dog, Hooch. The film does not know whether it wants to be a screwball comedy or a sentimental melodrama. The generic confusion is built on some interesting interspecies confusion.

In the screwball part of the picture, Hooch and Turner are an odd couple, sharing a house that Turner cleans and Hooch messes up. They are also a parody of partners in other detective movies, clowning together as they sit in the front seat of Turner's car during a stakeout scene that recalls dozens of movies and TV shows—except that one partner here is a great slobbering dog.

Turner, slightly prissy and independent, is afraid of commitment in a relationship. He does not have a girlfriend until he has to find a vet for Hooch. Then, he starts to see the town's new vet, a woman who uses Turner's ambivalent relationship with Hooch as an entry into her own relationship with the detective. Turner resists the relationship, even bounding out of bed to track down more criminals. But ultimately, when Hooch is killed in the climactic shootout—*really* killed, violating the summer movie commandment never to kill the dog—Turner becomes emotional for the first time in the film, weeping over the death of his partner. Only then can he let go of his dream of working on a big-city police force. He marries the vet and stays in the small village to raise puppies and kids.

We expect our dogs to do so much! Given these two films alone, it would seem that Americans of the nineties wanted our dogs to be pets, farm workers, bodyguards, best friends, surrogates, therapists, and murder witnesses. The most celebrated dog novel of the nineties, Phyllis Naylor's *Shiloh,* is another intriguing example of this dynamic. This Newbery Medal winner is in many ways a reworking of themes and plot ideas from Eric Knight's *Lassie Come-Home.* In *Shiloh,* as in Knight's story, a young boy develops an attachment to a dog. Also as in *Lassie Come-Home,* the dog is someone else's property, and the boy's family, poor but honest, keeps returning the dog to its rightful owner even as the dog keeps escaping back to be with the boy.

The similarities extend to the character of the boy's father. In both books, he is a model of probity who tries to train his son to accept responsibility rather than succumb to dog-loving sentiment. The similarities extend to the scenes of escape and return, which in several places are mirror images. But Naylor's *Shiloh* imitates little of the emotional dynamic of Knight's story. *Lassie Come-Home* is a *dog's* story, told from the dog's point of view. The long central section offers Lassie's journey from her own perspective. Lassie's view alternates with those of human reflector-characters, but is always foregrounded. It is an animal adventure. In *Shiloh,* however, we do not see the beagle Shiloh except when the eleven-year-old Marty is in contact with him. When Shiloh wanders free or is in the keeping of the abusive Judd Travers, we lose contact with him and follow instead Marty's drama of longing and loss.

Shiloh is Marty's story. *Lassie Come-Home* is never Joe Carraclough's. The great heart and miraculous persistence of Knight's collie are explained to the reader in purely animal terms. In *Shiloh,* however, the loyalty of the beagle comes to be seen in affective human terms. Shiloh becomes the brother that Marty lacks, the male friend that he has never been able to make in isolated, rural West Virginia. Shiloh's history of abuse at the hands of Travers parallels Marty's own emotional hunger.

In Dale Rosenbloom's 1997 film version of *Shiloh,* the dog-beating Judd Travers explains his cruelty: "Animals were put here for us. They ain' got no other purpose or feelin's." Marty, in both book and film, insists that animals do have feelings, feelings identical to those of humans. Though Shiloh never talks (unlike the humanized animals of *Dr. Dolittle* and *Charlotte's Web*), he clearly responds affectively to Marty's emotional life. *Shiloh* is a successor to E. B. White's *Charlotte's Web* (1952) in equating humans with people in a blurry way. In both White's work and Naylor's, less imaginative adults see animals as different from people, as having a purely economic relation to human society. Sometimes, they are just human food. A child (Marty or Fern), raised in a rural setting where this human-animal distinction underpins traditional culture, begins to break away from the ideologies that surround him or her—in effect, to assimilate to the upper-class condition of Terhune's Master—by seeing the dog (or pig) as a human companion.[2]

Naylor's West Virginia is a tough, uncompromising place. Marty's family is hard-working but chronically poor. When Marty tries to earn money to buy Shiloh from Judd, he has no prospects except collecting old cans and bottles. His mother is stretched to her limit with housework and has no hope of getting a paying job. Marty's father supplements his postal worker's income by shooting small game for the family table. Though Marty and his folks are decent and sensitive people, they are no animal-rights activists. Their marginal economic status precludes any high principled stance against killing animals or eating meat.

Rosenbloom's film version of *Shiloh* reverses the economic implications of the novel. The economic horizons of the novel are suddenly opened up and made (relatively) limitless. Marty does odd jobs and accumulates money quickly. This turns the struggle with Judd over Shiloh into a conflict more emotional than economic. In Naylor's book, it would be a terrible stretch for the family to feed Shiloh. Even if they could buy him, he would take food off their table. In the film, Marty's mother gets a job as a beautician and kick-starts her own business as a manufacturer of cosmetics. In the novel, the family lives in a four-room house, a homestead that has seen few improvements since pioneer days. In Rosenbloom's movie, the house is a stunning showplace of hardwoods, elegant color schemes, and tasteful appointments. It has two stories and must be at least five thousand square feet.

At the same time that the film inverts the economic direction of the book, it alters the power dynamics of human-animal relations. Nearly everyone in Naylor's book kills animals. Marty is reluctant to hunt, but he has a gun and carries it prominently—a feature of his character that is greatly reduced in the film. In the film Marty's father never hunts. Even Judd Travers is turned into a bit of a softy. In the climactic scene in *Shiloh,* Marty catches Judd taking game out of season, thereby gaining an advantage over him. In the book, Marty sees Judd killing a doe; in the film, he finds Judd trapping a rabbit—and in a humane trap at that. When Marty faces down Judd in the movie, he also frees the rabbit from the humane trap—so that we are spared even the suggestion of animal death.

The film's lack of blood sport cannot be because of film censorship and ratings. *Shiloh* would probably have a PG rating with or without the suggestion of animal death. The film is geared to the same audience as the book, so there's no age-level justification for the change. There seems, instead, to be a different cultural work attempted in Rosenbloom's *Shiloh,* a work that places it in line with other kids' dog films and apart from Naylor's book (which in other respects it follows "faithfully"). Naylor represents a moment of crossing-over, when the boy Marty realizes that he must act in Huck Finn–like fashion against the prevailing mores of his society. He transgresses. Rosenbloom's film, however, represents a culture in which the gulf between animals and humans has been bridged before the story begins. The force of the film's ideology is to blur all distinctions between humans and animals. Judd Travers becomes an outsider, not a piece of the social fabric, as in the novel. He speaks in the movie for the lonely view that there might, after all, be some difference between people and dogs.

In other movies, that difference all but disappears. In *Beethoven,* a dog is not only accepted as part of a single human family but also takes on the mission of resolving perceived contemporary crises in the American family in general. The Newtons, the family that adopts Beethoven, face a common plight in American films of the nineties: the American Dream has gone sour for them. Alice (Bonnie Hunt) and George (Charles Grodin) have a lovely home and three children. However, they work too hard trying to attract investors for their car air freshener business. Their ambitions are destructive to their happiness. At the same time, a wicked veterinarian (played by Dean Jones) is trying to abduct neighborhood dogs, including Beethoven, so that he can perform gruesome experiments on them at the behest of a munitions company.

Beethoven is a strange, conflicted movie. It brims over with family values and earnest suburban work ethic. Every moment of it works at some implicit level to reinforce the values of capitalist corporate America, but at the same time its quite explicit message is to portray the evils of corporate America, the villainy of big companies, the tawdriness of venture capitalists, and the soul- and family-destroying effects of hard work in pursuit of financial payoff.

Yet somehow it all makes sense, and it seems to make sense because the conflicting ideologies of the film are mediated through the character of a big dog. Beethoven, the Saint Bernard of the title, is a malleable ideological symbol. He is child and adult at once, as in the scene described above in which George sees him simultaneously as puppy and adult dog. Beethoven stands for order and disorder, force and vulnerability, threat and reassurance. Since the central image of the movie is constructed in such ambivalent terms, the surrounding political ambivalence of the movie seems positively to cohere around it. We fear the potential violence of the big, destructive dog, just as we fear unleashed capitalism. But in the final tableau, both dog and capital are just big fluffy puppies after all.

Because he begins the film as a puppy, Beethoven stands in, initially, for children. This is odd because the Newtons already have three children, ages five through twelve: Ryce, Ted, and Emily, girl-boy-girl, one cuter than the next. Yet the Newton family seems too well-planned, too perfect. They lack organic spontaneity. George, like Tom Hanks's Turner, is a neat and straitlaced man who can't stand the thought of a big slobbery dog invading his home. The Newtons live in a big, beautifully decorated California house that is oddly like Marty's house in the film *Shiloh.* Like that home—and like Scott Turner's home in *Turner and Hooch*—the living space has never experienced the slightest disorder before the title dog invades it.

This procession of immaculate interior spaces is disturbing. The immediate cause of all this clean is just an army of set decorators, but the unrealistic tidiness has an ideological impact. All these ultra-clean lives cry out for a dog. The Newtons in *Beethoven* have assembled their complement of children without mess, diapers, dirt, or strewn toys—possibly, without sex itself. When Beethoven arrives on the scene, the Newton household experiences for the first time the miry entanglements of real physical life.

Beethoven is the catalyst for sexual awakenings among the Newton clan. Twelve-year-old Ryce is self-conscious around boys. The boys she knows prefer older girls until Ryce starts hanging around with her enormous new puppy, who is distinctly cool and draws the guys' attention to her. Beethoven's role in helping Ryce into adolescence is minor compared with the role he plays in getting George Newton to loosen up. George is considerate at heart, but has become a neurotic shell of himself because of business worries. The veiled implication is that he has also become sexually unresponsive, seeing his wife, Alice, as a business partner, not a lover.

George and Alice display little affection in the movie, but one night George comes into bed and responds amorously to someone he thinks is Alice licking and nuzzling him. It's Beethoven, of course. When George learns that he's been sexually aroused by a dog, he responds in phobic panic. But the point has been made despite the disclaiming effect of George's panic. He needs loosening up in every sense, and Beethoven is the pet/companion/lover who can answer perfectly to his shifting needs.

As Alice will say in a later scene, "Beethoven made this house real. He put the dance in it." He is the perfect surrogate for all desires. In a film in which the dominant mode is confusion of boundaries, Beethoven's dual role as substitute child and sexual surrogate would be confusing enough, even without his other jobs as procurer and "dance" director. The film suggests that the Newtons have failed by failing to live through their children. They should, perhaps, be channeling desires through and toward their kids. It takes a dog to show them the proper method for mixing parental affection and sexuality. In doing so, Beethoven provides the "dance," that strange mix of desire and disinhibition that reorients the Newtons' lives away from mere economic functionalism.

While Beethoven is catalyzing the Newtons' newfound anarchy, he is under threat from a sinister corporate villain, the veterinarian who wants to test a new kind of ammunition on him. To pry the dog away from the family, the vet tells them that they must watch for signs of aggression on the dog's part. George explains to Alice that they have to watch Beethoven for incipient "weirdness." "Weirdness?" she asks. "What should I watch for, hon? Wearing my clothes around the house?" Like parents who watch their sons anxiously for signs of latent homosexuality, the Newtons fret about their dog's state of adjustment to the norm. The male dog's wearing George's clothes would be wacky; his wearing Alice's would be a symptom of something truly off-balance.

As Beethoven comes under threat from corporate predators, the Newtons are threatened by their own corporate longings. Under pressure from George, Alice accompanies him to a meeting with potential investors. The children are left behind in the care of the most neurotic parent's most nightmarish stereotype of the baby-sitter from hell. She is hideous, sexually frustrated, and vampish. She doubles as the "featured performer Saturday nights at The Padded Zebra." While she caterwauls away at the piano, little Emily promptly walks into the swimming pool, where she begins to drown but is saved, naturally, by Beethoven.

Unlike the slimy investors, who sneer, "We have a *career*" when asked if they have children, Alice Newton realizes, after the near-loss of Emily, that "what these children need is their mother." Yet she has been unable to surrender to the maternal instinct in herself until she sees her daughter pulled out of the swimming pool by the great lumbering male dog who now turns out to be a better sitter—and perhaps, even, a better mother?—than any of the film's human women.

Beethoven is apparently a critique of the desire to have things both ways. You can't have kids and a career too, the movie tells us. You had better choose in favor of your family. Capitalism is ugly. The desire to succeed is ugly. The desire to make money destroys. Yet the alternative to becoming an entrepreneur is—what, exactly? If the Newtons opt out of the rat race, how will they live? At the end of *Beethoven,* they are in dog heaven. Beethoven and the dogs that the Newtons have freed from the evil veterinarian join them in the conjugal bedroom for a final tableau. They have chosen in favor of warm mammalian values instead of the silicon coldness of spreadsheets or the chemical camouflage of their air fresheners.

Yet man cannot live by dog food alone. The option that *Beethoven* advocates—to choose the humanity that is somehow best represented by a Saint Bernard—depends on unspoken and unseen economic resources. Let's give up business success, indeed. Then we can fall back on our gorgeous home, limitless assets, and general good looks in order to earn our living.

Despite the efforts of its enormous hero to hold all these contradictions in suspension, *Beethoven* is ideologically unsatisfying. So the film has a sequel. The image of a big dog uniting a family in the face of the distractions of capital is not realistically satisfying. That only happens in the movies. In real life, we would have . . . another movie.

Beethoven's 2nd (1994) is the lesser movie. Much of it is taken up with Ryce's budding sexuality and a subplot of Saint Bernard puppies running around escaping from bad guys in a very *101 Dalmatians* way. This sequel (like so many sequels, it is less a continuation than an instant remake) realizes that the resolution of its precursor is specious. As *Beethoven's 2nd* opens, George is at it again, grasping for an even bigger air freshener breakthrough. Alice is back at work, leaving her family anchorless. There are now several dogs: Beethoven, his mate (a pedigree Saint Bernard; no miscegenation for this dog movie), and their puppies. They are called into service again to act as surrogate children for the neglected Newton children and as role models for the negligent Newton parents.

Hollywood never remembers its past and is always doomed to repeat it. Family values are in permanent crisis. The sequel series reveals its own cynicism about the rosy tableaux of its own endings. As a genre, dog movies reveal a pressing anxiety that the contemporary human is not human enough and must be grafted somehow onto a dog to realize his or her humanity.

Such is the theme of Carlo Carlei's *Fluke* (1995). *Fluke* has as protagonist a man who actually becomes a dog. He dies and is reincarnated as a puppy. It's a cross between *Topper* and *Lassie*. But it is neither a screwball comedy nor a warm family picture. Instead, it's a dark and uncertain narrative, filled with unreliabilities and misdirections. If anything, its primary model is Hitchcock. *Fluke* is less sentimental than it is Gothic, and in these Gothic depths we can see one limit, perhaps, of the cinematic uses of dogs.

Fluke is really Tom Johnson (Matthew Modine), who has been killed in the opening scene of the film—perhaps driven purposely off the road by another driver? The resolution of that initial mystery takes quite a while, however, because before we learn the truth about Tom Johnson's death, Tom must first be reincarnated as a dog, take up with a street person who names him Fluke, be instructed in doggy street life by an African American reincarnated as a dog named Rumbo, and wander *Homeward Bound*–like across the American landscape to find his human family again.

He's a man-dog on a mission. His family seems to be in terrible danger, a danger that Fluke intuits more than consciously understands. The other driver of the opening scene is hanging around his family, posing some vague threat to them. Fluke thinks that he has to return and save them. When Fluke shows up at the Johnson house, it is a home that puts even the gorgeous dwellings of other nineties dog movies to shame. It is a suburban palace on several acres, with enormous bedrooms, a housekeeper, and a drop-dead beautiful decorating scheme. Sensing a strange kinship with the smelly pariah dog Fluke, the Johnsons take him in and bathe him, and he proceeds to put some dance into their lives.

The widow puts Fluke to bed in a closet. Possessed by the desire to relearn this house and this family, Fluke escapes at night and takes a slow tour of the premises. He tucks in his sleeping son, Brian. Then, he heads for his widow's bedroom and lies down on the conjugal bed, where she wakes next morning to find a dog in her dead husband's place.

The dogs in other contemporary dog films always have something potentially puppyish about them and easily slip into the role of surrogate child. Fluke, though, is distinctly an adult human in dog guise. Since there's no human father present, Fluke takes on many of the roles of father. He spends quality time with his son. "Playing with Brian—doing things I never had time for when I was a man—made me realize how precious every moment is," says Fluke in the voiceover that offers a running commentary on the film's action.

Tom Johnson could never be a human while he was a human; he can only begin to be fully human as a dog. (We will see this pattern again in chapter 6, in which men never become men until they become boys again.) Like George Newton in *Beethoven*, Tom has been a cipher as a person, a mere economic function. As a dog, he is a better father and a more attentive husband.[3] Fluke finds some of Tom's old clothes and dresses up in them. His widow finds him in the clothes and starts to caress him, in what is easily the picture's kinkiest scene. Then the family—Mom, Junior, and dog—take off for a family road trip in an old convertible.

The blithe adoption of a fully human emotional life by a big dog raises intense problems for current ideologies of the family. As in *Beethoven*, some of these problems are economic. We learn that Tom Johnson has burnt himself out in pursuit of professional success. With Tom dead, however, the considerable rewards of his business success are available to the Johnsons and their new dog without any of the sacrifices. Whether Tom was lavishly insured or had built up a huge nest egg is unarticulated. The main point seems to be that if the breadwinner suddenly becomes a dog, he can be fed, clothed (literally), and catered to emotionally without any worries. Life continues as comfortably as before, minus all the stress. It really is a dog's life.

The film presents a fully human role in a family emotional life, and in a marital relationship, as dog's work. When he finally stops to smell the roses—or sniff the hydrants?—along the way, Tom/Fluke relaxes into a nurturing and emotionally fulfilled humanity. A dog's life parallels a child's in many ways, if both are fortunate: food is assured, beds are warm, and affection is free. By nominating a dog as the most appropriate model for adult humans, these films implicitly advocate a more childish orientation for adult emotional life. Such an orientation may be uncritical and politically quietist. It may abandon all emotional responsibility. If you cannot relate to your wife and kids, these films tell us, just lie down on the rug and chew up somebody's slipper. Things will be all right.

Or not. As disquieting as the more placid moments of *Fluke* are, the climax of the mystery plot is still more unsettling. Here, the Hitchcock elements come into play. Jeff, the man who had apparently run Tom off the road in the first scene, starts to hang around the Johnson family more regularly. Fluke "knows" that Jeff is a murderer. He attacks Jeff. The Johnsons in turn throw Fluke out of their house. But Brian is so emotionally involved with Fluke that he runs away. Fluke gets Jeff where he wants him—back behind the wheel of a moving car—and proceeds to maul him, forcing him off the road. Jeff survives and is lucid enough to explain to Fluke that he must save Brian, who is now alone in a cemetery during a snowfall that builds into a plot-enhancing blizzard. Fluke saves the boy. He then realizes that Jeff is wholly innocent. It was *Tom,* not Jeff, who had murderous intent on the night of the fatal crash. Tom and Jeff were business partners, and Jeff was the idealist of the pair. Irate at Jeff for proposing beneficent but unprofitable projects, Tom had tried to run him off the road.

Like any good dog, Fluke is sorry for his misbehavior. After rescuing Brian, Fluke turns tail and leaves the Johnsons, realizing that they will be happiest if Jeff takes his place among them. "I didn't know how to live as a man," Fluke muses, "and I didn't know how to live as a dog." Instead, he goes off to live as a street dog, aided by Rumbo, who has been reincarnated as a squirrel.

The principal effect that these recent dog movies have on the viewer, taken as a whole, is confusion. They engage no coherent ideology, even internally. Something is amiss in the American family, and dogs can save us—that's as consistent as it gets. Betty Thomas's *Dr. Dolittle* (1998) rounds out the decade. Its plot is by now almost identifiable as an archetype. A husband and father is pressed too hard in the name of financial success, ready to sell out to investors, egged on by his venal partner (played by Oliver Platt, who also played one of the dognappers in *Beethoven*). The husband/father gets in touch with his animal side and becomes a better husband, father, doctor, citizen, and human being. He foregoes considerable corporate wealth to live off his considerable private wealth. A final tableau full of people and animals ensues.

These animals are anything but cute. They are all about power, anxiety, and conflicted feelings toward children. Kids who watch these movies may well tune out everything but the animal slapstick and the endangerment-and-rescue sequences. These dog films do not indoctrinate children as much as they display grown-up anxiety. But I wonder about the cumulative effect of seeing, in film after film, that money isn't everything as long as you have a lot of money; that the best way to cope emotionally is to live as a dog.

NOTES

1. Among the false lore, Litvag cites Terhune's belief that rabies was exceptionally rare (205–7). Terhune's position, says Litvag, inspired many dog owners foolishly to resist vaccination.

2. Much the same thing happens in Chris Noonan's film *Babe* (1995), except that the function of the child is taken by a rejuvenated adult, Farmer Hoggett.

3. A similar plot motif arrived for Christmas 1998 at the heart of Troy Miller's film *Jack Frost*. Michael Keaton plays the title character. He is a charming but dysfunctional dad who is killed in a car wreck. He returns to become the best dad ever—in the form of an animatronic snowman.

4

Goosebumps:
What Was Series Fiction Doing
in the 1990s?

I grew up collecting and reading series novels. I really liked Dig Allen Space Explorer, the Kid from Tomkinsville, and TV tie-ins like the novelized versions of "Get Smart" and "The Man from U.N.C.L.E." Most precious of all, I read and collected the Hardy Boys books. I had a complete set, which I kept up-to-date until I outgrew them—though in important ways, I have never outgrown them (Morris, "Returning").

My memories of grade school book collecting came back to me vividly as I watched my son, as a first and second grader, collect R. L. Stine's Goosebumps series. The most immediate connection was the physical appeal of collecting a uniform set of objects. Textual experience is important, of course. We would not collect these books if we didn't enjoy reading them. But textual experience is only partial. Just as important is accumulating the set, feeling the weight of the books, comparing their same-but-different covers.

The Hardy Boys books, in the 1960s, were published with hard blue covers. A growing list of all the titles in the series was printed on the back of each book along with the crucial name of the very next book to be published in the series. An exciting illustration of Frank and Joe Hardy meeting some peril appeared on the front of each. Goosebumps books, in the 1990s, were published in paperback, with a *faux*-gruesome illustration of a beastie on the front and the same illustration on the back, above some copy about the contents. Every other month, the books had tear-out trading cards and bookmarks bound into the middle. Every book had a joke on the front cover, a small ad or two for some spin-off product or the Goosebumps TV show, and an injunction not to miss the next book in the series. I think that children would agree with me that the revelation of the next series title is probably the best thing about getting the new book each month.

But it isn't the covers that matter most when you're collecting a series; it's the *spines*. The blue spine of the Hardy Boys series, with portraits of Frank and Joe, or the multicolored spine of a Goosebumps book, with the trademark dripping letters, make the whole effect of the series. Best of all is the effect produced by stacking one spine after another after another on your bookshelf, with the numbers in perfect order—that is as close as a young book collector can get to heaven.

To ask what the children's series novel was doing in the nineties entails asking what it was doing in the decades before. How much was the series in the nineties of a piece with previous conventions in the form? Where did it innovate, where did it extrapolate trends? I can't comprehensively study this issue here. Instead, I will look at how the issue touches me most directly. I will compare the Goosebumps series, which affected me strongly as a parent, with an example from two series that affected me as a child—the first Hardy Boys series of the twenties and thirties and the radical reworking of that series into the books that I loved in the sixties.

The Hardy Boys and Goosebumps series share a particular vision of America. In both cases, it is a white America, where the default-value American is a white youngster who confronts corruption in the body politic. In the Hardy Boys novels, the corruption consists of crooks, rogues, and ne'er-do-wells. In the Goosebumps series, the problem is hideous manifestations of the occult. The America presented in these series is becoming blander and more generic all the time, even as a nominally progressive political consciousness shows up in later and later forms of the series.

The original Hardy Boys titles began their run in the late twenties. In the late fifties and early sixties, the series continued to add new entries at the end, but did not drop the earlier titles. Instead, the early titles survived as newly rewritten versions of themselves. At first, the rewritten titles began with an acknowledgment of their status, claiming that author Franklin W. Dixon had revised them to bring them into touch with today's modern science of detection: "In this new story, based on the original of the same title," the overleaf of the title pages said, "Mr. Dixon has incorporated the most up-to-date methods used by police and private detectives" (F. W. Dixon, *Chums* vi).

But it seems clear that a concern for accuracy in criminological technique was the least of his worries. For one thing, of course, "Mr. Dixon" (unlike R. L. Stine) did not exist. He is and always was the corporate fabrication of the series creator, Edward Stratemeyer. The books themselves are written by various ghost writers who are sworn to secrecy about their identities (see "Tex W. Dixon"). For another thing, the advances in sleuthing amount to updated transportation and gadget choices. The boys travel in planes instead of trains in the newer books and have more technological paraphernalia, but their preferred investigative method in both originals and rewrites is to wander into the bad guys' hideout and look for "clues" until the bad guys find them and commence a fistfight.

The main function of the rewriting in the series is to remove racist material. In the twenties and thirties titles, the Hardy Boys live in a decidedly multicultural, but stratified, America: the boys, Anglo-American, are the upper crust of the social order. Most good hard-working Americans of every economic class, in the originals, are also Anglo-American, as are many of the bad guys. But the novels are shot through with comic and villainous types who represent, in caricature, other American ethnic groups.

Hunting for Hidden Gold (1928; rewritten 1963) is the fifth novel in the original series and the first in which the boys venture beyond the confines of their native Bayport, a city on the Atlantic Coast that is sort of Boston but not really. The 1928 original has a strong sense of region: "We've never been more than two hundred miles from home," says Joe Hardy (1). They are boys of the Northeast, adept at ice-skating and other New Englandy recreations. Their father, the famous private detective Fenton Hardy, is investigating a desperate gang of toughs in Montana, and so exotic is that Western locale that to the whole Hardy family it seems like he has gone off to the dark side of the moon.

The boys find plenty to keep them busy in the Northeast. In fact, while they are out skating they get lost in the woods near Bayport and come upon a cabin buried in an avalanche. The cabin's occupant turns out to be a genuine Montana prospector. He is a victim of the same gang of robbers that Fenton Hardy is tracking down out West. With the penchant for coincidence that the series is chronically prey to, this misplaced sourdough enchains the boys in a string of adventures.

The plot is unimportant, however. Striking in this twenties evocation of the United States is its cultural and social geography. In between avalanches, the boys engage in less dangerous activities, like sledding. Their sledding is cut short, however, by the interference of Officer Con Riley, policeman and killjoy. Riley, a stickler for the letter of obscure ordinances, forbids them from sledding in a public park (42–46).

When Riley interrupts the young people's fun, they get back at him by luring him into an ambush and pelting him with snowballs. The assembled Hardys and their friends pummel Riley unmercifully with the snowy spheres (I am slipping into the idiom of the series here myself). But an ethnic dynamic is at work. The Hardys and their friends the Shaws, the Mortons, and the Hoopers are a cross-section of WASPy America. If they aren't Mayflower descendants, they might as well be. Con Riley is, on the other hand, the stereotypical Irish-American cop: buffoonish, self-important, prone to outsmarting himself. The Anglo-American teenagers smack him with snowballs and impunity. As long as they hurt his pride but not his person, he seems powerless to retaliate.

The 1928 version of *Hunting for Hidden Gold* never explicitly calls Riley Irish. His name is a giveaway, of course, but there is no other explicit signal of his ethnic identity. Both the text and the implied reader take for granted the stock humorousness of the Irish cop. This is an America so shot through with ethnic stereotype that the stereotypes don't even have to be underlined. A name, an attitude, an occupation can be the trigger for a whole automatic series of slurs.

The anti-Irishness of the text is mild compared to its racism. The 1928 version has several "negro" characters who disappear completely from the 1963 revision. When the boys take a train for Montana, the porter speaks in an eye-dialect that immediately types him as black, even though his color is not identified. In the 1928 novel's logic, his color probably doesn't have to be identified. If he's a railway porter he must be black. He obliges the reader by saying things like, "All ready, sah, jes' as yoh asked" (64). This porter shuffles about for several pages, condescended to by a conductor who speaks in unmarked Standard English, is presumably white, and solves problems over which the porter has been able only to wring his hands (65–68).

A few pages further on, the boys are waylaid by "toughs," but "an enormous negro" comes to their aid, declaring of the toughs, "You's the speeders what run oveh mah chickens!" (77). This "enormous" and beneficent "negro" is helpful, but fixated on the usual stage-Negro concerns with cheap foodstuffs and paltry possessions. He is foolish-wise, telling the boys, "Ef yoh wait deah foh a train foh Chicago yoh'll wait yeahs and yeahs, and even den yoh won't get no train" (78). Frank Hardy wins him over completely by "slipping a five-dollar bill into the hands of the big driver, who beamed with gratification" (80).

This novel verges on carnival, a carnival run for the benefit and amusement of the central privileged group. The ground rules of this carnival are too well-known to have to be spelled out for white child readers, who (the author assumes) will have been schooled from infancy about the leverage these "humorous" caricatures make available to their own privileged position. That the books might be read by black or by white ethnic children seems not to have crossed the minds of series creators. Or maybe the assumption is that nonprivileged children reading these books should become ashamed of their own identities and seek to shed them.

As he rescues the boys from the toughs, the enormous driver shouts after the fleeing scoundrels, "White trash!" (78). Here's another country heard from, a fault line between quality and trash. How would a poor white kid feel reading this book in 1928, or since? The incongruity of my question points to another social dynamic revealed in these texts. No one, however oppressed, it seems, identifies with the appellation "white trash." No one can be offended by the hurling of such an abusive term, because poor white Americans (in the author's implicit logic) are in a continuous state of assimilation. White readers try to distance themselves from "trash" and never seek to forge positive identifications with working-class, rural, undereducated, or oppressed white Americans. Nobody identifies with Judd Travers in *Shiloh*, either; the whole novel is a guide for escaping his fate.

By contrast, in the 1963 version of *Hunting for Hidden Gold* the American ethnic landscape is suddenly airbrushed clean. Everything is sparkling, even stray linguistic details. Instead of striking out for Lucky Bottom, Montana, as in 1928, the Boys head for "Lucky Lode" (5–6). Evidently this change removes the slightest hook for a childish smutty thought to catch at. Montana in the 1963 version is superficially more colorful, more "Western" than in the 1928 version. In 1928, the boys capture a prosaic bunch of crooks by unremarkable methods, basically by walking around trying to locate them. In 1963, they ride around on horses and encounter gunfighters, ghost towns, tommy-knockers, and spectral pianola playing. Instead of the gritty matter-of-fact West of 1928, which is of a piece with the rest of the culture in the book despite its remoteness, the West of 1963 is a place you can reach in a few hours by airplane but which has been gussied up and Disney-fied. It's cartoon exotic.

I will not speculate at length about the reasons for the changes in the texts. Various factors combined to compel the revisions, including the need to reach a wider audience of readers and the need to play to the sharpened sensibilities of white readers in an era of civil rights consciousness. The long-term effect of the changes has been dramatic, however. In just thirty-five years, social discourse in America changed so decisively that the 1928 version of the Hardy Boys was felt to be hopelessly out of date. Thirty-five years further on, the 1963 version of *Hunting for Hidden Gold* was still in print and going strong. It seems barely to have dated at all. The revision has been poised for longevity by the strategic removal of nearly every social reference except for the dead-plain neutral terms of generic family, generic city, generic airport.

As the Hardy Boys moved across the American midcentury, covering the tracks of their origins in ethnic burlesque, a later series started from the conditions evolved in the sixties Hardy Boys novels. As we move to Goosebumps, we encounter a fictional America where all but the barest markers of social location have been boiled away at the outset. In their stead we find a construction of America even weirder than the monsters that lurk beneath its sinks and in the cabins of its loathsome summer camps.

R. L. Stine's Goosebumps novels were, in the midnineties, the bestselling American books of any kind. "Sales stand at 4.5 million books monthly," says a marketing report from late 1996 (Warner 38). In 1995, the year that the Goosebumps series held a near-stranglehold on the children's book market, the scale of its dominance was difficult to comprehend. *Publishers Weekly's* annual review of children's book sales for 1995 reported:

> The first 27 paperback backlist titles on our list are all Goosebumps.
> The phenomenon is even more astounding when the sales figures are added up. Scholastic sold 19,125,700 copies of Goosebumps frontlist titles in 1995, and 12,906,800 backlist titles, for a grand total of 32,032,500 copies sold. (Roback S24)

As high as their sales were, the Goosebumps books were only the leading edge of their own marketing phenomenon, which in turn was only the main entry in a mobilization of children's publishing to produce, and then to meet, demand for scary kids' stories.

In 1995–96, Goosebumps novels were everywhere and on everything. The marketplace was saturated with images related to the books and their trademarks. Bernhard Warner reports that "over the past year [1996] the apparel line alone has generated, by some estimates, more than $40 million in sales. Some 40 licensees have combined to create a powerful mix of toys, multimedia titles, a top-rated children's television show, audio books via Disney, and video cassettes that have made the property a year-round revenue generator rather than just a Halloween phenomenon" (38). Reports on merchandising tie-ins in *Publishers Weekly* conveyed a sense of the Willy Wonka–like proportions of the Goosebumps industry, as if hordes of Oompa-Loompas were at work somewhere to produce the necessary stuff: "Six million Goosebumps toys will be given away with Taco Bell Kids Meals between September 23 and November 1 [1996]. . . . A series of three 20–page mini-books by Stine, collectively called the Goosebumps Thrillogy, will be packaged in 32 million bags of Doritos" ("Children's Bookbag").

Somewhere in my house is one of those toys, a glow-in-the-dark chattering skull on friction-driven wheels. Somewhere too is one of those minibooks, delivered from its salty womb of MSG and cool ranch flavor to provide minutes of fun for the whole family. If statistics are correct, similar objects are somewhere in your home too—maybe everywhere.

Yet one really got a sense of the impact of Goosebumps by visiting the bookstore. Though one didn't even have to go that far. Goosebumps books were sold in supermarkets, gift shops, discount stores, and toy stores and through direct catalog sales and traveling book fairs in schools. "For many independent book fair operators, the series has become a rallying point, defining a certain type of book fair" (Rosen 135). Goosebumps functioned for fair operators either as the mainstay of their sales or as the one product line they were determined *not* to carry.

My son and I bought these books at chain superstores and independent bookstores (including Kramerbooks & Afterwords in Washington D.C., where we no doubt unwittingly rubbed elbows with Monica Lewinsky on her shopping rounds). We bought them at Target in suburban Fort Worth, at a knickknack shop on the eastern shore of the Chesapeake Bay, in the large bookstores of downtown Chicago, in a discount supermarket in Bristol, Tennessee. Sometimes, we bought them secondhand, but such coups were rare at the peak of interest in the novels in 1996 and 1997. At the height of the series, kids didn't let their parents get rid of these books. The Book Rack near my home in Arlington, Texas, carries a huge selection of traded-in children's books, including vast tiers of Sweet Valley High that lard the lean earth of the prairie strip mall as they accumulate. In 1997, the Goosebumps books available in the Book Rack consisted of three or four beat-up copies kept by the front register, and they disappeared daily.

In new bookstores in the midnineties, the prominence of the Goosebumps novels was, as their characters would say, "awesome." The success of the series was made vivid in a marketing writer's description of finding Goosebumps books in the only bookstore serving the elderly of Catalina Island: "A large display merchandised *Goosebumps* books together with glow-in-the-dark boxer shorts. When questioned, the store owner remarked that customers frequently seek out the books when their grandchildren come to visit" (Benezra 48). (In case you are wondering, we have the boxer shorts too, scored at a Borders in Dallas after a frantic scene at a school book fair that had sold out of its allotment. They still glow after many washings.)

If thus Catalina, how much more the superstores of child-stocked suburbs? Goosebumps books anchored the children's sections of these retailers, with rack after rack of the series novels, their various spin-offs, and their various accessories (boxed toy sets and other novelties) stacked around. Audio books and video cassettes extended the experience into other media, with the occasional board game threatening to turn Goosebumps from a series into a lifestyle.

Series novels exemplify that endless Darwinian struggle of retail: the competition for shelf space. As a series grows, it crowds nonseries titles out of the way. My local Barnes & Noble, like many of these stores, has entire sections, six feet high and from four to six feet wide, devoted to Nancy Drew, the Hardy Boys, or the Babysitters Club. The Goosebumps series at its peak of Darwinian fitness merited two such sections, with many titles turned cover-out to grab attention. Before and after that peak (reached in mid-1996), the Goosebumps shelves featured mostly the spines of the books, shelved more matter-of-factly. Growing at the rate of two or three titles a month—the one-per-month flagship titles written by R. L. Stine himself plus the ghosted accessory titles like Give Yourself Goosebumps, Goosebumps Presents TV books, postcard books, Scare-a-Day calendars, and such like—the series threatened to expand, like one of its own creepy burgeoning substances, to take over the entire store. Then, gradually, like an alien microbe exposed to some insalubrious earth substance, it shrank back into a smaller and smaller niche.

One constraint on the aggrandizement of Goosebumps novels was competition for the same niche in the bookstore ecology. Sally Lodge catalogued various "knockoffs" that rose to do battle with the original:

Sisters Annette and Gina Cascone (who use the pen name of A. G. Cascone) have contracts to write 17 Deadtime Stories, which will be published monthly through December 1997 [by Troll]. . . . Shivers titles [from River Publishing] are . . . written by a team of authors under the pseudonym of

M. D. Spenser, the series has 2.5 million copies of its inaugural 12 titles, released in September [1996], in print. . . . Among Bantam's entries in the kids' horror genre are the Graveyard School series by Tom B. Stone and the Choose Your Own Nightmare series. . . . Random House Children's Publishing . . . is taking a classic tack with its newly renamed Random House Chillers Line. . . . At Harper Paperbacks . . . is Betsy Haynes, whose Bone Chillers, launched in Spring '94, now has 12 titles and 1.5 million copies in print. . . . Taking a different [sic] approach . . . is Avon's Spinetinglers series, whose 16 releases have been created by various writers, though all carry the pseudonym M. T. Coffin. . . . Aladdin last spring [1996] issued the first in its Scaredy Cats series. . . . Grosset & Dunlap president Jane O'Connor also opted to start up a series for younger readers. . . . Aimed at children six to eight, Eek! Stories to Make You Shriek will include eight volumes by Spring '97. (25–26)

They were really all out there, sometimes springing up out of a dump to horrify you as you rolled your supermarket cart around the corner of an aisle. But as Paula Kempf, manager of a Maryland Borders, reported, children were just as good at adults when it came to telling a knockoff from the real thing: "Kids head straight for the Goosebumps display and don't look to the right or the left at any other series" (Lodge 26).

Then, just past the height of their popularity, the Goosebumps books were gone. The series closed with *Monster Blood 4* (number 62) in December 1997. It started over again in January 1998 as a knockoff of itself with a new book 1, *Cry of the Cat*. Like a bedraggled phoenix, the series rose out of its self-cancellation and took the form of Goosebumps Series 2000. In most ways, the second series was the same—same monthly publication routine, similar format, similar content, some of the old sequel threads carrying over into the new series. But by being the same, it also wasn't the same—much like New Coke supplanting Coca-Cola. You had to start collecting all over at number 1. You had the vague suspicion in the back of your mind that Stine had stopped writing the books and had turned them over to ghosts—a suspicion that is unfounded, but is aggravated by the series taking on the guise of an imitation of itself.

The detumescence of Goosebumps left my son and me bemused. It points to a key dynamic of the juvenile series. The series is ephemeral, and it is always with us. The series is dead; long live the series. The actual long-term cultural impact of the Goosebumps series, despite its millions upon millions of units sold, may be next to nothing. The books may be slightly more treasured than Pet Rocks, but they will soon clog the used bookstores like so many juvenile series before them. As paperback-only titles, they will be more ephemeral in the long run than the Tom Swifts and Nancy Drews one can still find holding up shelves at antique malls. But some series or other—Sweet Valley High the day before yesterday, Goosebumps yesterday, Animorphs or something stranger tomorrow—is central to children's culture at any given moment. It is a rite of passage, an obligate stage in the ontogeny of the adult reader. What I want to understand here is the particular nature of that stage for the juvenile readers of the nineties.

R. L. Stine is a writer of considerable talent, a talent perhaps best seen in short stories like "Strained Peas," "How I Won My Bat," and "Click" from the collection *Tales to Give You Goosebumps* (1994)—sardonic little tales that can stand with the best things from a more highbrow juvenile horror writer like Australia's Paul Jennings. It's true that in a series of over sixty monthly novels there are some dogs here and there (not just the spectral kind). There are quite a few cases of Goosebumps novels imitating themselves. But, highbrow literature professor that I am, I have more than once been caught up in a Goosebumps novel even after reading my child to sleep.

The Goosebumps series is above all a formula. One novel is pretty much like the next. Every one has to be just different enough to offer a modest justification for its separate existence, but not too different. The paradoxes involved in such a relentless fulfillment of formula illustrate the terms of the conventionality of culture industries discussed by Theodor Adorno and Max Horkheimer. "The constant pressure to produce new effects (which must conform to the old pattern) serves merely as another rule to increase the power of the conventions when any single effect threatens to slip through the net. Every detail is so firmly stamped with sameness that nothing can appear which is not marked at birth, or does not meet with approval at first sight" (35). In late twentieth-century American society, this sameness in cultural representations produces a children's literature that reflects what Paul Monette calls "the peculiarly American obsession that everyone be the same, once the pot has melted down" (30). Despite occasional references to other ethnicities and cultures, the central characters in the Goosebumps formula are always white, middle-class, unmarked Americans. Their adventures are the controlled and processed dark side of white America, the bad dream that the culture industry has so that we don't have to have it, geared to a third-grade reading level and rated PG.

What happens in the typical Goosebumps novel (which is to say, in every Goosebumps novel)? A twelve-year-old child tells the story.[1] He or she (about half the narrators are of each sex) has a ten- or eleven-year-old sibling. The younger brother or sister is annoying, makes lame jokes, and generally embarrasses the narrator. The narrator has been relocated to a new home, a new city, or maybe sent to stay with indifferent or eccentric relatives. His or her parents are for some reason absent: dead, divorced, workaholic, off on business, just plain distracted, or obsessed with some aspect of the occult. For whatever reason, the parents don't pay much attention to the narrator.

The narrator develops problems that cry out for attention. He or she finds a strange object, explores a mysterious empty house, discovers a weird substance, meets an eldritch new playmate, or senses the presence of a monster. The younger sibling tags along and compounds the trouble. The trouble deepens and becomes desperate, but the adults in the story are indifferent to the children's plight or actively hostile to them. Finally the children are sucked, sooner or later, into an alternate dimension filled with surreal horrors, where everything goes wrong. Some unlikely plot twist saves them from this trouble, and order is restored. Then, on the final page of the final chapter, the trouble reappears in a slightly altered form: the magic talisman resurfaces, the monsters regroup for another attack. The "happy" ending—what one might call the return to stasis—is revealed to be a dream or a misprision or a temporary respite. We are sent back by a twisty path to the original horror.

That plot fits nearly every Goosebumps novel. The novels run from 110 to 140 pages, but have become somewhat shorter in the later volumes in the series. The chapters are short. There are many of them, twenty-five to thirty in each book. The sentences are short and the paragraphs are short too, sometimes only one short sentence long. (The chapters, paragraphs, and sentences have become shorter in the later volumes too.) Each chapter ends with a terrifying situation: a fright, a menacing attack, a dilemma from which there seems to be no escape, a horrifying realization that . . .

This cliffhanger is resolved in the opening sentences of the following chapter. The quality of the cliffhangers changes as each novel progresses. In the early chapters, the cliffhangers are invariably false. The novel always begins with a dream, prank, "gotcha" (the word the younger sibling invariably utters when some phony scary trick has worked), or just plain mistake that renders harmless the first fright (or first several frights) of the book. As the novel goes on, the cliffhangers become more difficult to resolve. The twist ending is in a sense the ultimate cliffhanger, perhaps promising a sequel. Several of the novels have developed into series-within-the-series of sequels.

Goosebumps sequels, like *Beethoven's 2nd,* are not so much continuations of an ongoing story as instant remakes of the same story. The same characters meet a very similar nemesis in an identical plot situation. *Say Cheese and Die—Again!* (number 44, 1996) gives us the same terrifying photos that come to life; *Monster Blood 2* (number 18, 1994) and *Monster Blood 3* (number 29, 1995) and *Monster Blood 4* (number 62, 1997) give us more of that icky magic goo; *The Haunted Mask 2* (number 36, 1995) involves another haunted mask; and so on. Within the formulas of the series industry, the sequel allows for cloning of the original plot devices.

After the end of the final chapter, before the endsheets on which various Goosebumps paraphernalia are advertised, comes a thrilling preview of the next book in the series, several chapters long. Goosebumps novels never exist as individuals but are marked within their own pages as elements of a series. Goosebumps books resist closure. Even the final series entry offered a preview of the successor series. There are no happily-ever-afters here, or even sad farewells. There is only the literary equivalent of that twentieth-century mantra: "Tune in again next time."

Goosebumps books are never illustrated, except for one highly stylized cover picture on each book. The cover illustrations of the original series were done by Tim Jacobus, who gained celebrity in his own right as a result. Jacobus's pictures served as icons in the marketing campaigns that promoted the books. The covers do not closely render scenes from the stories. Only rarely do they reveal the protagonists of the books. The cover of number 6, *Let's Get Invisible* (1993), showing the narrator, Max, as he gazes in horror into the magic mirror that will turn him invisible, is an exception. Usually, the illustrations depict monsters of some kind or only parts of the child hero (his feet, as on number 52, *How I Learned To Fly* [1997], his torso underwater, on number 19, *Deep Trouble* [1994]). Sometimes, and doubly scary, they show only *part* of the *monster.*

The functional reason for this lack of illustration might go like this: horror is scarier if you use your imagination than if you have a loathsome creature like King Jellyjam shown to you. "I can imagine the characters and places in my mind to look how I want," says one child reader (Rud 23). The lack of illustrations also entails a reading dynamic. If a reader has no idea what the hero is supposed to look like, it can be easier to identify with that hero.[2] Not only are the scary bits scarier if you have to imagine them, but the familiar bits become more familiar if they're not fully drawn, either.

Boy narrators alternate with girl narrators from book to book. Within a given book, a boy narrator is likely to have a girl for a best friend, and vice versa. When a group of friends is the focus of part of a story, it's usually a mixed-sex group. Furthermore, the characters don't do things that are particularly stereotyped by gender. Here is a great contrast with both the twenties and the sixties Hardy Boys series. In those earlier books, sexual segregation is total. The boys share their adventures only with their masculine "chums." They venture into the company of girls only for innocuous dates or for the odd day of recreational sledding. In Goosebumps novels, however, both sexes share the scary adventures. They play similar sports and participate in similar school activities. Neither boys nor girls lock onto gender-specific role models.

In at least one case, the narrator's gender remains unspecified throughout an entire Goosebumps novel. *The Scarecrow Walks at Midnight* (number 20, 1994) is told by a twelve year old named Jodie who has an eleven-year-old brother named Mark. Jodie has long blond hair (1), but that is the extent of the physical description the narrator offers. Jodie's best friend back home is named Shawna (61). Jodie wears "faded denim cutoffs" and "a sleeveless blue T-shirt" (67). None of these details helps definitively to specify Jodie's sex, and at no point in its 122 pages does the novel use a gender pronoun in relation to Jodie or have the narrator make a gendered self-reference.

What should one make of this indeterminate gender situation? In some books for younger children, like Dr. Seuss's *Green Eggs and Ham,* the characters are constructed entirely without gender. An ambiguous name makes for easy gender cross-identification in a picture book like Anna Grossnickle Hines's *Daddy Makes the Best Spaghetti* (1986). Hines's book conveys a progressive message that gender doesn't matter in child-care and work roles. In *Spaghetti,* a young child named Corey, who has longish red hair and indeterminate preschool clothing, is actually pictured on each page but remains gender unspecific.

One way to read *The Scarecrow Walks at Midnight,* then, might be to see it as a progressive, ambi-gendered text. Whether deliberately or not (the result is the same regardless of the author's intention), the text allows readers of either gender to identify readily with its narrator. We might choose to celebrate *Scarecrow* as a kind of tour de force of gender neutrality. Or we might see the book as a culmination of an ideological trend that is neither progressive nor liberating in terms of gender.

There are good reasons for hesitating to claim *The Scarecrow Walks at Midnight* as a progressive text. The novel's villain is a retarded man named Stanley. The narrator pokes fun at Stanley even while being scared of him. Stanley makes silly remarks and can't do things competently. Stanley unleashes the scarecrow monsters who terrorize the narrator's family when he reads magic spells out of an old book that he cannot understand and then is incompetent to control them. A novel that would portray Jodie's indeterminate gender as politically positive would presumably not resort to such a crude stereotype of a disabled man to provide its terrors.

Every other character in *Scarecrow,* in fact, reinforces gender stereotypes, unlike the caring cooking dad and the office-working mom of Hines's *Spaghetti.* Jodie's grandfather is competent, wise, and full of stories, the grandmother is sentimental and bakes all day, eleven-year-old Mark is highly strung and full of boyish mischief, and Stanley's son Sticks, a little older than Jodie, is a figure of power and male decisiveness, a gaunt, laconic figure Jodie can't quite place as good or evil (he turns out to be good). Stanley is a cliché of bearish retarded male power who recalls Lennie in John Steinbeck's *Of Mice and Men,* without any of the dignity.

The construction of genderless Jodie is significant as the limit of a trend present in other Goosebumps books. Difference is systematically drained out of the characters, to the point where a character ends up lacking even those most basic of defining linguistic features, gender pronouns. Difference is avoided rather than discussed or critiqued, avoided rather than carnivalized in the manner of the early Hardy Boys books. This tendency to remove distinctive features that might prevent readers from identifying with the characters is an ideology of avoidance.

The narrators of Goosebumps novels, with their spare self-descriptions and their lack of typed behaviors, construct a liberal sense of self, in two senses of the word *liberal.* One is a neutral, gender-blind sense in which distinctions between male and female are inappropriate or meaningless. Gender does not matter in these Goosebumps stories because it is an irrelevant concept. Boys and girls do exactly the same things, participate in mixed-sex groups, and inhabit a world where there are no gender barriers.

The second sense of *liberal* is the classical one, in which the individual economic agent participates in the market and in politics free from limitation by qualities that might constrain his or her scope for choice. In pure marketing terms, you can sell more books if you can sell them to boys and to girls too. Goosebumps novels say that America is a place where men and women are economically and socially interchangeable, because it is a place where boys and girls have an equal chance to be scared out of their living wits by evil ventriloquist dummies.

Men and women are interchangeable, these stories tell us; but they are interchangeable within social and psychological orders that deny the existence of history. In no Goosebumps book is any current gender equality predicated on a consciousness of historical gender roles, much less on any kind of feminist struggle against historical constructions of separate gendered spheres. We simply take for granted a current America where men and women have an equal right to consume and produce the stuff of culture. And then we don't discuss it any further. It is no wonder that the most stereotypical of gender roles, as in *The Scarecrow Walks at Midnight,* are always ready to reemerge in the middle of the weak gender clearances of the text.

The Goosebumps novels are as free from religious markers as they are from gender markers. Everything in the books is secular. The characters never go to church. They never go to a synagogue, either, even though Stine discusses his own Jewish childhood in his memoir (written with Joe Arthur) *It Came from Ohio!* (1997). Church activities, even church *buildings,* are unrealistically absent from the communities. Those monsters that might have some potential for religious construction—vampires, for instance, or werewolves—are relentlessly secular. (In number 5, *The Curse of the Mummy's Tomb* [1993], the usual mummy movie cult is depicted, but it is totally stylized, bears no resemblance to any possible world religion, and is set in a picture-postcard version of Egypt.) The draining of religion from Goosebumps stories presents a disturbing tendency. It is as if no potentially divisive topic could possibly be raised within the world of these fictions. If Stine could avoid gender and race as easily as he can avoid religion—by sheer force of silence—he might be tempted to do so.

The neutrality of the social world of Goosebumps extends uneasily to questions of race and ethnicity. The narrator is almost always white. The narrator's friends sometimes include African-American and Hispanic children. In number 48, *Attack of the Jack-o'-Lanterns* (1996), the narrator, Drew, has another of those unspecific names that allows us to forget her gender for pages at a time. Drew's nemeses are Tabby and Lee, best friends who torment Drew at Halloween time. Tabby is a white girl. "Lee is African-American, and he sort of struts when he walks and acts real cool, like the rappers on MTV videos" (4). That's the extent of Lee's role as an exemplar of African-American culture. For the rest of the novel, he becomes indistinguishable from the other child characters, all of whom are white or presumptively white.

Attack of the Jack-o'-Lanterns takes place in the same blank suburban setting as so many of the other Goosebumps stories do. (In fact, one of the nicer touches in the book is when the children, out trick-or-treating, pass into an alternate universe that is a suburb even *more* blank and uniform than the one they actually live in.) There is nothing like an African-American community in the novel. Lee's ethnicity is for the most part completely irrelevant to his character; he might as well be from any hyphenated- and long-assimilated white ethnic group. It becomes hard to remember that Lee is black, just as it's hard to remember that Drew is a girl. Still, one becomes uneasy in the later chapters, when the children are terrorized by spectral jack-o'-lantern creatures: "I saw Lee step back in fear. His knees seemed to buckle, and he nearly dropped the trick-or-treat bag" (81). Or, a few chapters later, when "Lee still gripped the other pumpkin head between his hands. But he dropped it when the jagged mouth began to move" (86), Lee begins to take on elements of that racist archetype, the "Negro" scared of "haunts."

In number 56, *The Curse of Camp Cold Lake* (1997), the narrator, Sarah, has a bunkmate named Briana, who is named as African American. Like Lee, she is given one quick ethnic marker: "She shook her head so hard, the beads in her cornrows rattled against each other" (6). After that, Briana is not marked as black for the rest of the story. Though she plays a major role, first saving the narrator from a ghost and then, in the twist ending, revealing that she herself is a ghost, her color becomes invisible—as indeed does her gender and everything except her plot function. Such invisibilities are due in part to the exigencies of quickly written series fiction. Even at their best, Goosebumps books are not really notable for character development. But there is also something more socially significant at work here: a denial of diversity.

Hispanic characters in the Goosebumps series are even less visible.[3] Freddy Martinez, the narrator of number 49, *Vampire Breath* (1996), is generically Hispanic. He and his best friend, Cara Simonetti, "both have wavy black hair, dark eyes, and round faces" (3)—that is the extent of their supposed non-Anglo characteristics. As the story progresses, Freddy finds a vampire in his basement and at the end of the book, the twist is that he and his parents have really been Eastern European vampires all along, a conclusion that somewhat dampens any hope of seeing *Vampire Breath* as a positive image of *la raza*.

As with the books' construction of gender, these racial and ethnic images are not progressive in any way. They constitute a superficial tokenism that conveys the idea that the history of race matters even less than the history of gender. The communities portrayed in the Goosebumps novels are places where all the marked American identities are like peel-off labels stuck onto stock white characters. The texts, now and then, refer to nonwhite people, gesturing vaguely at things that they cannot be allowed to express.

Sex is one of those things. An interesting feature of the series is the number of best-friend pairs who are boy and girl: Freddy and Cara in *Vampire Breath*, Zackie and Alex in number 55, *The Blob That Ate Everyone* (1997), Cooper and Fergie in number 32, *The Barking Ghost* (1995), Greg and Shari in *Say Cheese and Die—Again!* Clark and Gretchen (who are step-siblings) in number 46, *How to Kill a Monster* (1996), Gabe and Sari (cousins) in *The Curse of the Mummy's Tomb*. These pairs of friends are always twelve years old, as old as they can plausibly be without being sexually mature. Therefore they act and think and talk almost like adults and have a lot of freedom from adult supervision. But their relationships are never even protosexual.

If you think back to when you were twelve—or indeed, if you happen to be twelve and reading this—this lack of sexuality in the Goosebumps series will strike you as one of its falsest notes. Twelve (or even earlier) is the age when ignorance, innocence, and curiosity drive people to think persistently about the sexuality that some of them are entering and all will be involved in soon. Yet like many series books, certainly like both manifestations of the Hardy Boys, Goosebumps novels simply don't mention this growing sexuality. Mild and asexual ploys to get the attention of someone of the opposite sex sometimes enter the plots— *How I Learned to Fly* is an example—but there is no realistic portrayal of preteen attitudes about sex.

The characters in Goosebumps stories are balanced, perpetually, in novel after novel, on the cusp of an adulthood they never quite reach. There is a constant stream of twelve-year-old protagonists on tap in the series. The protagonists in some of the sequels age to a ripe old thirteen, but they never escape their serial preadolescence. The standard-issue protagonist of the Goosebumps series remains frozen at age twelve. One can see that eternal twelve year old as the projection of an *adult* desire to retain a core self unthreatened by sexuality, family responsibility, or work.

Goosebumps books deliver not so much a picture of twelve year olds as a powerful fantasy for eight and nine year olds (the core target audience for the series) that also includes elements of fantasy for thirty-eight and thirty-nine year olds. This fantasy, extrapolating the concerns that one has when nine to the greater freedom and independence of a twelve-year-old hero, is akin to the dynamic of most genre fiction, in which we unprepossessing adults read about heroes who are spies, detectives, cowboys, or athletes and imagine ourselves in their bodies. The location of the children's series at the border between childhood and puberty is a backward-looking fantasy, too. Many adults, particularly those from comfortable suburban homes, remember the step into puberty as a fall from self-containment into a world of problematic responsibility. In children's series fiction, the fantasy reaches back to confer power on that moment of autonomy and to let an adult reader live again in the singular heroism of being twelve. It's almost as good as becoming a dog.

This fantasy is extended to the Goosebumps heroes. Children who in one way or another lack the structure, the emotional support, and the organic interdependence of a family become protagonists in miniature versions of adult genre fiction. Harassed by siblings, misunderstood by parents, ignored by daffier relatives, these protagonists strike out into a world of horrors. Sometimes they find a pal of the opposite sex with whom they forge a nuclear partnership that remains comfortably asexual and cannot threaten to become a new family in its own right. The individuals' freedom, and their essential purposelessness, are preserved.

Such alienation is of course archetypal in children's stories. In being thrown onto their own resources, the child heroes of series fiction are not much different from the children who win out over adult enemies in fairy tales. There is a strong fairy tale appeal in Goosebumps stories, complete with the uncanny magic that works for or against the hero. But Goosebumps books lack fairy tale rites of passage into adult responsibilities. They resemble other series like the Hardy Boys in which the protagonists are eternally young. Nor does any Goosebumps hero inherit half a kingdom upon marrying a prince or princess. Another thing that distinguishes Goosebumps stories from the fairy tales of the Grimm brothers, let's say, is the commitment to banal settings. Rather than represent some fantastic realm in the middle distance, the Goosebumps books are set here and now, albeit a washed-out here and now, located in the blanker than blank suburbs of *Attack of the Jack-o'-Lanterns*.

The main factor in the alienation of Goosebumps protagonists is the alienation of their parents. These parents are upper middle class and provide for Goosebumps children the basic accoutrements of suburban life: their own rooms, their own stuff (electronics, bikes, and major toys), their own pocket money to buy haunted masks and Monster Blood. But these parents provide the trappings of suburbia at the cost of a sense of community. Frequently the setting for a Goosebumps novel is a family relocation. When the family moves to a new house it is sure, of course, to be haunted.

"Josh and I hated our new house" is the sentence that begins the whole series (*Welcome to Dead House* 1). Their new house is not in fact new. It is a legacy from their shadowy Uncle Charles and located in a town called Dark Falls. Why the parents in the story have taken on this unpromising item of real estate is never quite clear. Josh and Amanda's dad had "been looking for an excuse to quit his boring office job and devote all of his time to his writing career. This house—absolutely free—would be just the excuse he needed" (4). It's a flimsy excuse, because Dad could just sell the place and invest the proceeds. Of course, since the house turns out to be the abode of the living dead, he might not have been able to find a buyer.

Like this dad, parents in Goosebumps novels are distracted professionals or harried business people. They have economic objectives that are opaque to their children, who see their behavior as a sort of impatient indifference. For the purposes of the series narratives, only the children's perspectives exist—another resemblance to fairy tales. Pursuing their blurry goals, the parents uproot the children from the communities they're accustomed to, or dash off on business, while leaving the children in someone else's care or shipping them off to camp or to their grandparents' house for the summer.

So, Evan has to stay with his eccentric Aunt Kathryn when his father is suddenly "transferred to Atlanta" (5) in number 3, *Monster Blood* (1992). Stripped of context, that commonest of American corporate phrases, "transferred to Atlanta," takes on weird, evocative resonances. The transfer is never explained, never given narrative reality. Why Evan must stay behind while his mother and father leave for Atlanta is never clear. Cooper, in *The Barking Ghost,* sees the fact of relocation like an awful sentence when his family leaves Boston: "I had no choice. We were moving. Mom's new job landed us in Maine, and there was nothing I could do about it" (4). In number 59, *The Haunted School* (1997), Tommy finds himself relocated because his father has remarried and asks, "Can you imagine what it's like to suddenly have a new school, a new house, and a new mom?" (2). Even less motivated is the relocation in number 53, *Chicken Chicken* (1997), when the parents

> dreamed of leaving the city for good and living on a farm near a small country town. . . . The whole town is three blocks long. We have a cute little farm with a cute little farmhouse. And even though Mom and Dad are computer programmers—not farmers—we have a backyard full of chickens.
> *Cluck. Cluck.* That's *their* dream. (2)

In *How to Kill a Monster,* "Mom and Dad had some kind of work emergency in Atlanta" (1), so Gretchen and Clark have to stay with their grandparents, who also have a voracious monster staying with them. In number 51, *Beware, the Snowman* (1997), Jaclyn has to move from Chicago, where she starred in sports and had many school friends, to a village on the Arctic Circle called Sherpia. "Why did we have to move from the United States to this tiny, frozen mountain village? . . . What kind of name is Sherpia? Can you *imagine* moving from Chicago to *Sherpia?*" (3–4).

Frankly, no. That relocation is probably the weakest in the entire series. The pattern of displacement, however, means several things in the Goosebumps world. In functional terms, the relocation of the family and the displacement of the child enable the isolation that drives the adventure plot. The new home is haunted, the new village is full of weird creatures, and the spooky events begin.

These relocations are also a realistic feature of corporate American life. Kids do have to move when their parents get transferred, and the sudden break with old friends and homes is traumatic. One can read the ensuing scary situations as a reflection of the difficulties of coping with a sudden move. In *Monster Blood* Evan's mother realizes that "he needs to learn how to get along under difficult circumstances. You know, moving to Atlanta, leaving all his friends behind" (5). Cooper, in *The Barking Ghost*, misses his friends in Boston terribly and has no way to make new ones. He eventually befriends a mysterious girl named Fergie and is turned, along with her, into a spectral chipmunk.

Well, I said that these plots were projections of anxieties, not that they made any sense. The sense that these anxious relocations, sometimes coupled with abandonments, make is more ideological than mimetic. But it's not the psychological sense of the fairy tale alienation, the young hero against the world of Joseph Campbell's formulation. In the Goosebumps novels alienations like leaving home and friends behind are the normal postmodern condition. Under these conditions, the child's task is to master the distortions inflicted on his or her life rather than return to the older, familiar situation, even a better version of that situation (as in the fairy tale or mythic return). Goosebumps stories rarely end with the status quo reasserted. Though the child may long throughout for his or her old home—Chicago, Boston, anywhere that is *not* Sherpia—the novels are far more likely to end with the child mastering the new situation than being restored to the old one. At least until the twisty ending, when all is thrown into uncertainty again.

The Goosebumps kid accepts the changing ground rules of the American corporate landscape and flourishes in the entrepreneurial field that that landscape provides. Goosebumps child characters make instant new best friends, learn new neighborhoods, and slay the demons that assail them. Or at least they cope with the permanent anxiety of their disrupted existence, out of balance forever in a land of horrors, after the twist ending.

The archetypal Goosebumps move is a move out of the city. I can't imagine that even the Atlanta-bound white corporate types of *Monster Blood* are moving to the inner city. More likely, they are bound for the antiseptic housing estates of Marietta or someplace even whiter. Goosebumps parents pack their kids off to the Maine woods, to European forests, to remote summer camps, to Dark Falls, to the swamps of southern Georgia, to chicken farms in Goshen Falls, to Sherpia. Somewhere here is an anxiety over, or even an odd nostalgia for, American white flight in the twentieth century. Life will somehow be better out in those wide open spaces, but for the children, at first, life becomes simply terrifying. Knocked free from their moorings in stable urban communities, these families cannot return to their homes, physically or emotionally. Horrors confront them on both sides. In the suburbs, the theme parks are full of monsters out of control, the lawn gnomes are enchanted evil trolls, the trick-or-treaters are aliens from space who eat children. Back in urban settings, the old houses are full of malevolent objects like haunted cameras or antique lamps that turn you invisible and drag you into a parallel dimension. The venerable school building is undermined with secret underground passageways or sealed-off tomblike wings and is haunted by the Phantom of the Auditorium.

The space between city and suburb is narrow, but it is the one that the Goosebumps plots and characters aim for. These books celebrate the conventions of repetitive mass society, packaged as *home,* a home without traditions, memories, or knowledge, where the dominant cultural style is annoying your parents, where the occasional child older than twelve is imagined, like Rich in number 24, *Phantom of the Auditorium* (1994), as someone who "spends most of his life being grounded" (4). In number 6, *Let's Get Invisible!* (1993), Mom (they never have *names,* these parents) fixes lunch for the narrator and his pals: "Canned chicken noodle soup and peanut-butter-and-jelly sandwiches" (40). She disapproves vigorously of the cool haircut that Zack, the narrator's friend, has gotten at Quick Cuts, but tries to feed Zack chocolate cupcakes all the same, for dessert. Of such rare and soul-destroying moments is the novels' only sense of home constructed. One would almost prefer to surrender and become fodder for the Blob That Ate Everyone.

Of all the sinister venues in the Goosebumps stories, the epitome of horror is the evil summer camp, a staple of the series from its second year (1993) with the publication of number 9, *Welcome to Camp Nightmare.* More camp novels appeared in 1995 (number 33, *The Horror at Camp Jellyjam*), 1996 (number 45, *Ghost Camp*), 1997 (number 56, *The Curse of Camp Cold Lake*), and in Goosebumps Series 2000 in 1998 (number 8, *Fright Camp*), each time in early summer, to take advantage of the seasonal connection. (I detect no puns here, by the way. These are not campy camps.)

Goosebumps novels were popular from their introduction, but the publication of *The Horror at Camp Jellyjam* in July 1995 marked a quantum leap in the visibility and popularity of the series.[4] In its first six-and-a-half months on sale, *Jellyjam* sold 1,354,700 copies. It was the year's top paperback children's bestseller, outsold among children's books overall only by two hardcover versions of Disney's *Pocahontas* (Roback S26; see *Disney's Pocahontas;* Ingoglia). Marketing efforts featured the cover of the book, with its grinning, *Mad Magazine*–like caricature of a camp counselor (a picture corresponding to no scene or character in the book). This picture of summer camp gone mad is central to the whole cultural work of the Goosebumps series.

Kids in Goosebumps stories rarely want to go to camp. Alex in *Ghost Camp* wants to study music instead of going to Camp Spirit Moon, even before he realizes that his fellow campers are all undead zombies. Jaclyn in *The Curse of Camp Cold Lake* speaks for many Goosebumps protagonists: "I don't like to be outdoors. I *hate* the feeling of grass brushing against my ankles. I don't even like to touch trees. And I certainly don't like getting wet" (1). These children of indoor climate-controlled spaces are served up their worst nightmares by being sent to camp.

The kids in *The Horror at Camp Jellyjam* aren't even shipped off. On vacation, the narrator, Wendy, and her brother, Elliott, are riding in a trailer that comes unhitched from their parents' car. The trailer rolls down a hillside and stops outside King Jellyjam's Sports Camp. The parents *disappear.* Only 114 pages later do the children see the parents again. The parents explain vaguely, "The police checked everywhere, trying to find you two" (126). They are as distracted as any child who has been entrusted with a responsibility and instead wandered off to play. Here we have the ultimate distillation of summer camp. Without warning, your parents vanish, leaving you out in the woods at the mercy of sadistic counselors.

Camp Jellyjam is an evil venue. A children's sports camp where the essence of the experience is competition, a ritual pitting of the skills of children against one another, it is a parent-free world for the testing of children. The counselors incessantly repeat the camp catchphrase, "Only the Best," as they exhort the children to win races and games and collect King Coins, the prizes for winning.

The competitions in Camp Jellyjam don't really involve adults at all, even in the sense that the abandoned children are somehow angry at their parents or determined to succeed in spite of them. Instead, they express a curious resignation, as if nothing thicker than a trailer hitch had ever connected Wendy and Elliott to their mom and dad. Suddenly landed with a crash in an inexplicable workplace, Wendy and Elliott barely register surprise. Instead, they set about the pointless task of winning sports events and collecting King Coins.

That occupation is more sinister than it seems, because the reward for success—collecting six King Coins—is to be honored in the Winners Walk. At this ceremony, the winners are abducted and made to serve the hideous slime monster King Jellyjam in his underground lair. This noisome, ravening beast is continuously washed and fed by captive children and occasionally turns over, shaking the ground on which the camp is built. King Jellyjam could be iconic for success in capitalist enterprises generally—the amassing of pointless achievements leading to greater and greater service to a blind unreasoning monster—if indeed he were sufficiently elaborated to mean much of anything. For the purposes of the novel he's just another scary creature.

The tone of this novel helps define the cultural gesture of the entire Goosebumps series. Far from being robust characters who enjoy adventure, Wendy and Elliott are detached and distant. Elliott so immerses himself in winning King Coins that he loses all personality. He seems to forget that he has been deserted by his parents and is being held prisoner. Wendy is more resistant, but still untroubled by the demands made on her to fit into the Jellyjam routine. One could imagine several different types of affect for the novel's bizarre situation, ranging from nonstop panic and efforts to escape all the way to embracing the zany camp atmosphere in an attempt to declare freedom from their parents' boring lives. None of these alternatives is even posited. The children of Jellyjam are spiritless suburban creatures whose all-child venue strangely recapitulates the texture of the adult world outside. Wendy and Elliott have fallen out of a stereotypical family vacation into a vacation from that vacation, which turns out to be a rehearsal for corporate America.

The parents are similarly bland and ineffectual. They do not know what is best for children. They are intellectually and emotionally lazy and are generally helpless to solve the children's problems. In the relatively weak way Goosebumps stories represent struggles for power in adult-child relationships, at least on some grounds the children seem to win. By being cut adrift from parents and triumphing over their own problems, the children reconstitute (though almost always temporarily, given the necessity for that twisty ending) a world where balances are reasserted. The children gain power through recognizing that their parents cannot and do not maintain such balances by themselves.

Unlike those in the archetypal children's story, the adults in these novels are not so much oppressors to be vanquished or role models to emulate as they are twelve year olds themselves. The recurrent settings and resolutions of Goosebumps novels relentlessly co-opt representations of children in the service of reasserting the anti-intellectualism, self-absorption, and greed of both kinds of twelve year olds as normal. The adults are as peremptory, as fixated, as *immature* as the children.

I am not sure what children "get out" of these books—or any books, for that matter. I know, for instance, that my own son, at ages six through eight, read these books, or had them read to him, with an all-consuming attention. I have described children's reading tastes as addictions (*Making the Team* 169). Perhaps a child's devotion to a favorite set of books is a wholesome direction of addictive tendencies. Perhaps not. Perhaps all that will come out of reading Goosebumps novels is a mindless, soul-deadening consumerism.

Gary Cross discusses action figures and playsets of the eighties and nineties, but his comments apply equally well to children's series fiction: "When toys lost their connection to the experience and expectation of parents, they entered a realm of ever-changing fantasy. Indeed, the parent's gift to the child became not the learning of the future or even the sharing of a joy of childhood. Parents instead granted children the right to participate in a play world of constant change without much guidance or impact from adults. The events of the 1980s did not bring this change by themselves. But they seemed to have closed the door on the past" (227). Books don't work the same way. They wear out less easily than toys, and many literary cultures can co-exist in a single present moment. But series novels of any period are less about the communication of cherished cultural values than about an escape from cultural communication. Recent series novels are just getting better at providing such an escape and linking that escape back to a brisk trade in merchandise.

Goosebumps novels present a world that is alienated, cut off, blank, and fantastic. It doesn't arouse my ire; it's hard to get excited over it as either bad or good. It is a world that beyond a certain point I do not enter. My son has moved beyond Goosebumps Series 2000. He reads the inexplicable kid-SF series Animorphs to himself, when he is not constructing action worlds on the floor by himself out of action figures. How can I manage, surround, engage in such play or such reading? Was my own reading of the Hardy Boys series much different? If the content changes while the form remains the same, is series fiction anything but a filter for culture, a filter that affects us generation after generation in much the same way no matter what attitudes and ideologies it happens to trap?

The dynamic of reading and collecting may ultimately be of more cultural importance than anything in the "content" of these series. The way we buy and save these books may effectively be their content. But at the same time we can study what the filters trap and what they don't: what we tell ourselves and are afraid to tell ourselves. Classics like *The Secret Garden* and *Peter Pan,* my next subject, tell us richer stories. They make culture rather then merely record it as it passes. But they too are intricately connected to the same dynamics of power and desire. Whatever the material setting, we cannot escape these dynamics when we encounter children's cultures.

Notes

1. Some initial volumes in the series, including number 2, *Stay Out of the Basement* (1992), number 3, *Monster Blood* (1992), and a few others, are told in the third person. They have as their principal reflector-characters twelve year olds similar to the ones who narrate the other series novels. First-person narration becomes the invariable rule later in the series.

2. At least one entry in the series plays with its own lack of identifying illustrations or descriptions. Number 57, *My Best Friend Is Invisible* (1997), presents a typical Goosebumps family described with the usual neutral economy of detail. At the end of the novel, the twist is that they have been five-eyed many-limbed and tentacled creatures all along. They think that humans are disgusting monsters. The complete blandness of the narrative allows for such a twist, which is no twist at all because the world of monsters is conceived of as identical to American suburbia.

3. Several of the Goosebumps titles have been translated into Spanish and marketed under the series title Escalofríos in the United States. These books, starting with *Bienvenidos a la casa de la muerte* (Welcome to Dead House, 1995) are not adaptations of the originals to Spanish-language cultural settings, but instead are mechanical, phrase-by-phrase renditions of the English originals. (So mechanical are the Spanish versions that no translator credit is given.)

4. Since the books are always released a few weeks before their publication date, this volume went on sale in June 1995.

5

IMPOSSIBILITIES:
THE SECRET GARDEN AND PETER PAN

I never read *The Secret Garden* when I was a boy; in fact, I never read it (as I never read *Black Beauty*) until I was in my thirties. Even today, I'm not sure many boys read this book. I am therefore an outsider to reading *The Secret Garden*, especially in the sense that so many women now report to me: that the book was a crucial reading experience for them when they were growing up, that they read it more times than they can remember. But if I must always remain excluded, in some sense, from *The Secret Garden*, the opposite is true of its contemporary, *Peter Pan*. He is the most paradoxical of role models, but I can say this with complete accuracy: I grew up with Peter Pan.

One could object that Jacqueline Rose, in *The Case of Peter Pan or the Impossibility of Children's Fiction*, has said just about everything that can or needs to be said about *Peter Pan*, its sexual confusions, and its impossibility as children's culture. But as Rose makes clear, "*Peter Pan* was both never written and, paradoxically, has never ceased to be written" (6). James M. Barrie provided the story idea for the hit show, a cross between play and pantomime, that opened in London in 1904. He never published a definitive version of the story, which exists in several different prose versions and one dramatic version that was published only in 1928. Barrie also franchised the writing of versions of *Peter Pan* out to other writers, a practice that persists as the story is regenerated around the framework of Barrie's characters and settings. *Peter Pan* has been recreated in this way continually from its first appearance as an episode in Barrie's 1902 novel, *The Little White Bird*, to the 1992 Steven Spielberg film *Hook* and beyond.

Rose draws her examples of *Peter Pan* from English culture. I will focus here on one cherished American adaptation, the 1954 Broadway musical starring Mary Martin—what Didier Deutsch calls "the only real *Peter Pan.*" (Walt Disney's 1953 cartoon version [directed by Hamilton Luske, Clyde Geronimi, and Wilfred Jackson] is better known in the United States, but much less problematic. Its use of animation leaves it less able to tease out the subtleties of the drama as played by live actors.) The 1954 stage play, perpetuated as a 1960 NBC television production and now immortal on videotape and CD, epitomizes the generative, collaborative nature of *Peter Pan*—a play that can't even end properly unless the audience helps resuscitate Tinker Bell. To read the credits on the versions in print is to try to find an author, or even an author function, in vain. The 1954 cast recording and the 1960 video credits attribute the work as follows. Richard Halliday is listed as presenting Edwin Lester's production of a version of James M. Barrie's play, directed and staged by Jerome Robbins and adapted by Robbins for television, where it was directed by Vincent J. Donehue, with lyrics by Carolyn Leigh and music by Moose Charlap, and additional music by Jule Styne and additional lyrics by Betty Comden and Adolph Green. If you don't see yourself listed, it's probably because I didn't include the fine print. The show refutes the *auteur* theory. At some deep level, we all wrote *Peter Pan*.

Rose defines the impossibility of children's literature:

> Children's fiction is impossible, not in the sense that it cannot be written (that would be nonsense), but in that it hangs on an impossibility, one which it rarely ventures to speak. This is the impossible relation between adult and child. Children's fiction is clearly about that relation, but it has the remarkable characteristic of being about something which it hardly ever talks of. . . .
>
> There is, in one sense, no body of literature which rests so openly on an acknowledged difference, a rupture almost, between writer and ad-

dressee. Children's fiction sets up the child as an outsider to its own process, and then aims, unashamedly, to take the child *in*. (1–2)

These kinds of impossibility—rupture, inadmissibility of being what it purports to be about, evasion of blatant concerns—are central to both *The Secret Garden* and *Peter Pan*. In each case, the text is an appropriation by an adult of a territory that is supposed to belong to a child. Each text proposes a place that belongs to children alone—the Garden, Never Land. It shows children who desperately want to invite adults into this place, and adults who take an unseemly interest in invading it.

Both texts are balanced on the cusp between children's and adult entertainment. The American *Peter Pan* was a Broadway musical. In its translation to TV it confronted children and parents together as families, inviting a companionate viewing that makes more problematic some already problematic features of the production. *The Secret Garden* is a young adult novel that remains one of the children's classics most consistently chosen, adapted, or abridged by adults for children. *The Secret Garden* was one of the "Touchstones" chosen by the canon committee of the Children's Literature Association in the early 1980s. *Peter Pan* was not, though that omission may be due to the problems of identifying a definitive text. *Peter Pan* is also a work originally directed to adults and continuously redirected toward children. It remains the kind of text that adults continue to reinterpret for children, as if waving a plea for recognition of a problem in the children's faces. As Rose remarks, "The problem is not, therefore, J. M. Barrie's—it is ours. Ours to the extent that we are undoubtedly implicated in the status which *Peter Pan* has acquired as the ultimate fetish of childhood" (4).

The Secret Garden and the 1960 version of *Peter Pan* are insistently and nervously about adults' relations to children, specifically both the sexual and nonerotically romantic relations that these texts dare not talk about. I am not suggesting at all that either text is about genital desire for children by adults, that these are somehow overlooked manuals of pederasty or even of unhealthy physical closeness. Nor do these texts engage, in any way that I or probably any adult critic can perceive, the actual eroticism of children. Paradoxically but rightly, the expression of an appeal to juvenile sexual interest can be the fantasy of only the most adult of fictions, as in the maunderings of the insane writer Fenig in Don DeLillo's novel *Great Jones Street:* "I'm not just writing pornography about kids. I'm writing pornography for kids" (51). Fenig attempts to write erotica in the language of the nursery. As with most of DeLillo's characters, a hopeless missing of connections between language and reality dooms his projects to failure.

The Secret Garden and *Peter Pan* are neither pornography nor erotica, whether about or for kids. They encode adult desire and anxiety at a level that never becomes overtly erotic and is in any case never concerned with genital acts or even with the preliminaries to love that are staples of young adult romance. The sexuality and desire they explore can perhaps be best illustrated with reference to another children's classic that is about the nature of desire, Roald Dahl's *Charlie and the Chocolate Factory* (1963).

Charlie explicitly shows us an adult's seduction of a child. Willy Wonka tests and teases Charlie Bucket. In the film *Willy Wonka and the Chocolate Factory* (1971) the test is in part one of probity. Charlie passes when he doesn't deliver the secrets of the Everlasting Gobstopper to Wonka's competitor, Slugworth. In the novel, the Gobstopper test does not appear. The test is purely one of Charlie's imagination and malleability. Willy Wonka says, "A grownup won't listen to me; he won't learn. He will try to do things his own way and not mine. So I have to have a child. I want a good sensible loving child, one to whom I can tell all my most precious candy-making secrets—while I am still alive" (157). This is a relation of power, but mediated by love and persuasion. It is cathective, not coercive. There's nothing of the stick and everything of the carrot in Mr. Wonka's approach—or, one should say, everything of the Luminous Lolly.

Wonka works out his seduction of Charlie across an endless array of candy, a catalog of oral pleasure. Dahl being Dahl, the double entendres are everywhere, and the list of things one can do with sweets is stunningly prurient: sucking, licking, wriggling, exploding, swimming in pools of lemonade, and of course "MAGIC HAND-FUDGE— WHEN YOU HOLD IT IN YOUR HAND, YOU TASTE IT IN YOUR MOUTH" (128). But the most erotic descriptions of candy eating in the novel are not graphically suggestive of sexual acts, and indeed are more deeply connected to desire and more poignant. Charlie's Grandpa Joe describes "little feathery sweets that melt away deliciously the moment you put them between your lips" (14). These sweets recall the pleasure Charlie takes in chocolate, a pleasure so intense that he does not really eat a Wonka bar but only tastes it slightly every day, so that he "would make his ten-cent bar of birthday chocolate last him for more than a month" (9).

Charlie's desire to prolong the intensity of the chocolate act is magnified in the story of the prince who commissions Willy Wonka to build him a palace of chocolate (15–17). Wonka advises the prince to eat his chocolate house as quickly as possible, but the prince refuses even to nibble, wanting to preserve the indefinite deferral of his pleasure. On the next hot day, of course, the palace melts, and the Prince wakes "to find himself swimming around in a huge brown sticky lake of chocolate" (17), the wet dream to end all wet dreams.

We should all be so lucky. But in *Charlie and the Chocolate Factory*, the central disparity between the experienced seducer Mr. Wonka and innocents like Charlie Bucket and the prince is framed in terms of an attitude toward time. Wonka promises a pleasure that can be prolonged infinitely, crystallized in the gums that never lose their flavor and in the Everlasting Gobstopper, a candy that is always about to be, but never quite ever is, perfected. The sober reality of any candy is its disappearance. Grandpa Joe explains the appeal of Wonka's "most secret" sweets: "He can make lovely blue birds' eggs with black spots on them, and when you put one of them in your mouth, it gradually gets smaller and smaller until suddenly there is nothing left except a tiny little pink sugary baby bird sitting on the tip of your tongue" (14). We become voyeurs of the primal scene of candy. The eggs give birth, a birth contingent on the evocation and extinction of a pleasure partly characterized by amorphous sensuality and partly by a recognition of the necessity of change. These pleasures don't last, something that the greedy children who compete with Charlie for a lifetime supply of sweets cannot understand.

The Secret Garden and the 1960 *Peter Pan* draw me into this concern with the intensity of transient pleasure. These texts too concern eating, growing, waiting, and trying to fix the moment so that it will not transpire. The moment must transpire, as each work realizes to its own heartbreak, but that only makes its appeal more magnetic. There is something in these appeals that allows them to be shown to children, even insisted upon as wholesome reading for children, without ever being quite explained to those children. In both texts, as in *Charlie,* adults try to fix their relationship with children in an eternal present, marked by unconditional devotion from the child and unflagging care from the adult. Unlike the Goosebumps books, where the point is that everybody stays and is really essentially twelve their whole lives, the world in balance in *The Secret Garden* and *Peter Pan* is a world where adults meet children who don't grow up. Theirs is the perfectly desirable beauty, the fulcrum of a perfect balance.

In a way, then, though I assert the detachment of the following reading of *The Secret Garden,* I am engaged as an adult reader in its mysteries. *The Secret Garden* speaks from a historical moment when heterosexual love, and the origin of every person in heterosexual love, cannot be directly spoken. We recapitulate such moments in our own growth as persons; there is always some moment when the truth of our existence is both known and not known. Our desire, perhaps, and the reason this text touches me so deeply, is to hold that moment of uncertainty in stasis, to refuse to surrender to it. We cannot hold the moment. We can only read about doing it.

Readers often feel that the best parts of Frances Hodgson Burnett's *The Secret Garden* (1911) come early on. Mary Lennox, in these early chapters when she is the novel's sole protagonist, is an engaging heroine whose flaws make her even more attractive to readers. Later, when the focus of the story shifts onto making a suitable heir out of the hysterical Colin Craven, the novel seems to lose its energy. Some adults who haven't read the novel in years tell me that they can't remember the second half or the ending, a pattern also noted by the critic Elizabeth Lennox Keyser.

Barbara Wall sees this imbalance as the product of imbalances in narrative technique: "In the best parts of *The Secret Garden* . . . the 'great gulf' was bridged by the use of a narrator who cared more to engage the interest of children than to maintain an overt adult presence or to provide a level for adult readers" (177). In keeping with her thesis that children's literature evolves historically toward unembarrassed single address to the child, Wall sees the success of *The Secret Garden* as a success of single address and its failures as a matter of looking over its shoulder at adult readers.

Yet if we think about the earlier chapters of *The Secret Garden,* when Wall would have it that no adults are implied as listening, it can be unsettling to think of that particular narrator alone with one's children. *The Secret Garden* is elaborately sexual, without directly invoking the sexuality of Mary Lennox. The appeal of the garden as shorthand for the unseen workings of women's sexuality is so pervasive that Nancy Friday could borrow the title of the novel for her 1973 collection of women's sexual fantasies without making any explicit reference to Burnett. It was not even that Friday perpetrated an irreverent seventies joke at the expense of a children's book. Rather, it was as if the sexual undercurrents of the novel were so well understood that the only possible title for a book about what women think during sex, but won't tell their lovers, must use the phrase *Secret Garden.*

The main plot of *The Secret Garden* actually does not involve eroticism. Orphaned in India by the death of her parents in an epidemic, nine-year-old Mary Lennox is brought to Misselthwaite Manor, the Yorkshire home of her reclusive uncle, Archibald Craven. Here she is left to her own emotional devices in the vast "queer" house and its extensive gardens. She renovates one of the gardens, the long-abandoned "secret" garden, with the help of Dickon, boy of the moors and general lover of nature. Then she discovers that there is another child in the house. It is Craven's son, Colin, bedridden for no physical reason. He is as emotionally starved as she is. Mary befriends Colin, invigorates him by taking him out to the garden, and reconciles him to his long-detached neglectful father. At the end of the novel, the final tableau is that father's embrace of his son.

This plot, condensed into one paragraph, is not very appealing. There's no action. The book has little political point except a blanket conservatism that sees class and race distinctions as immutable. The smooth continuance of patriarchal aristocracy is its highest value. Central plot events include taking extra helpings of food and doing stretching exercises in order to grow. It is not, on the face of it, the recipe for a children's classic.

Read simply as a children's text, wrapped in the mantle of classic status, *The Secret Garden* raises more questions than critics can answer. Heather Murray points to shifts in tone and narratorial perspective and to even more disquieting questions of political thematics, asking, "What are we to make of a woman-authored text which so validates the *status quo*, which erases the presence of the lower-class boy of the moors, and so disposes of its heroine?" (40). Lissa Paul concurs in questioning the novel's politics, but concludes that a novel published in 1911 couldn't well have ended differently. Its "female quest," in Paul's reading, "fizzles out" (162), and the quest becomes that of young Colin for his rightful inheritance to be acknowledged. In Paul's terms, the plot is a *plot*, a reinforcement of patriarchy by insidious means.

Paul's ascription of the ideologies of *The Secret Garden* to its original time and place is both correct and necessary. This resolution, however, leaves another in its wake: how does a novel that so validates the status quo of 1911 continue to have such appeal in the 1990s, in the memories and reading experiences of women who work actively against the kind of patriarchy that the novel upholds?

The internal conflicts of *The Secret Garden* are ones that may be explained partially by employing Susan K. Harris's sense of "exploratory fiction." As charted in her 1990 book, *Nineteenth-Century American Women's Novels: Interpretative Strategies,* Harris's notion of "exploratory" fiction takes into account multiple strategies of reading and rhetoric in the nineteenth-century fiction so often dismissed in the twentieth century as "sentimental" or "domestic." In Harris's analysis, novels that strongly present patriarchal values often work to question them rather than to argue for them. Unlike late eighteenth- and early nineteenth-century "didactic" fiction, which uses engaging first-person narrators and foregrounds the explicit development of thematics, "exploratory" fictions like Augusta Evans Wilson's *St. Elmo* and Susan Warner's *Queechy* portray educated, competent women and then disavow their education and their competence. Exploratory novels typically feature withdrawn narrators and disjunctions of perspective and tone like those seen in *The Secret Garden.*

When read as an exploratory text, *The Secret Garden* makes more sense. Its narrative features are typical of the genre. It also exhibits another structural feature common to exploratory fictions: the ending that continues, as it were, beyond an ending. Mary's story properly closes with her rehabilitation of the garden. The novel continues on to rehabilitate Colin too, but that second plot movement does not cancel the first. The novel is both a story of a girl's power and the subjection of that power to the interests of a boy. The two movements are equally strong. They appeal to differently interested readers. The appeal of Mary's resourcefulness is challenged by the subsequent subordination of her power to the task of rebuilding Colin's position. But perhaps Mary's independence is not erased—particularly if readers tend to remember her longer than they remember Colin coming into his own.

Identifying *The Secret Garden* as exploratory may help account for some of its appeal. Exploratory texts are notoriously plastic in the hands of readers. Lacking the explicit programmatic themes of didactic fiction, these novels allow their multiple addressees to reconstitute them in multiple ways. Generations following Burnett's publication of the novel have taken advantage of the indirections inherent in the text.

These indirections are persistently erotic. *The Secret Garden* is about desire—not sexual desire, at first, but the desire for a home. "She doesn't know where home is!" taunts Mary's playmate Basil near the beginning of the story (14). Mary begins the book deprived not only of her parents but also of a national and cultural identity. She has grown up as a daughter of empire, accustomed to the deference of Indian servants. The novel posits Mary's early upbringing as a problem, as a maladjustment to the conditions of life that she will have to face back in England. Her task—her "quest," in Lissa Paul's terms, though it is a curiously static quest—is to become integrated into a new home.

From the start, Mary's quest is not to become independent. She must establish domestic relationships and lock herself into family connections. Her situation resembles that of many other girl heroines in literature, from Ellen Montgomery in Warner's *The Wide, Wide World*

(1850) to Harriet M. Welsch in Louise Fitzhugh's *Harriet the Spy* (1964). Physically or emotionally abandoned by her family, the heroine tries to become embedded in other personal relations—the same relations that most boy heroes, like Huckleberry Finn, are trying to flee.

Mary's quest is paradoxical, since incorporation into the Craven family must come at her own expense. She finds herself by subordinating herself to Colin's interests. It's a Victorian conclusion for an exploratory fiction. *The Secret Garden* resembles *The Wide, Wide World*, in which Ellen must finally submit to the tutelage of John Humphreys, much more than it resembles *Harriet the Spy*, in which Harriet's dream of being a writer is finally supported by her once-distant parents. As in all exploratory fictions, outcome matters less than process. The romance of the entire novel lies in the process of the early chapters. Burnett's is a plastic, multiply directed text that continues to be available to contemporary idioms of reading.

Mary grows into her new home by means of a complex of dynamics: learning how to hold her body, to speak a new native language, to cultivate the garden. In India she had been dressed by servants. In Yorkshire it is clear that she cannot get along with her English servant, Martha, unless she does more things for herself: "It had not been the custom that Mistress Mary should do anything but stand and allow herself to be dressed like a doll, but before she was ready for breakfast she began to suspect that her life at Misselthwaite Manor would end by teaching her a number of things quite new to her—things such as putting on her own shoes and stockings, and picking up things she let fall" (30–31). *The Secret Garden,* however, is no *Captains Courageous.* In Rudyard Kipling's 1897 novel, young Harvey Cheyne, son of a millionaire, is suddenly thrust into the role of ship's boy by accident. He must abandon his class prejudices against physical labor to win the trust of the other sailors. But Mary does not need to work alongside her servants to earn their trust. All she has to do is rethink her management of servants, to make the appropriate demands on them while bearing herself appropriately. In this respect, the novel lies much closer to Burnett's own *Little Lord Fauntleroy* (1886), in which an outcast child must recenter a decaying aristocratic household on himself. Fauntleroy and Mary, unlike Harvey, succeed by gaining the properly coded allegiance of the household servants, not by winning their respect as equals.

The novel is uncertain about the value of Mary's effort to relate to Martha. After the abrupt awakening described above, there is an immediate qualification of Mary's new relation to her maid: "If Martha had been a well-trained fine young lady's maid she would have been more subservient and respectful and would have known that it was her business to brush hair, and button boots, and pick things up and lay them away. She was, however, only an untrained Yorkshire rustic" (31). The deficiency in the relation between Mary and Martha is ascribed not entirely to Mary's caprice, but also to Martha's shortcomings. This qualification, which comes from some withdrawn narrative perspective unknown to Mary, but not quite that of an "authorial" first person, suggests that if Mary had been given better service in England she might have continued rather as she was in India, spoiled and helpless. Missing is any suggestion that such a suggestion is ironic. Mary is better off by learning to help herself. The circumstances that force her to help herself are seen, however, as the result of an unfortunate accident.

As Mary must learn to manage her body properly in relation to other bodies, so she must learn to move her body properly. The stiff unplayful girl gets a skipping-rope from Martha to loosen her body and make it more girlish. The text codes the rope as quintessentially English. Mary has never even seen one before. Martha asks, "Does tha' mean that they've not got skippin'-ropes in India, for all they've got elephants and tigers and camels? No wonder most of 'em's black" (65). This racist little non sequitur indicates that the whole force of the episode is the acculturation of Mary, coupled with the vigorous coding of everything not English as "black," including presumptively neutral things like toys. Mary's inability to skip rope is not really a racial failure but a class failure. Aloof from other children, she has never learned their games. But by making Mary's lack into a marker not of class but of race, the novel manages to blame the class gulfs of colonialism on the subject peoples, not on class society. Whatever their differences, the text appears to say, English children all skip alike.

Mary's skipping is crucial to the plot, since when she goes outside with her new rope she finds the entrance to the secret garden. It is also crucial—in its own way, as important as the garden—in defining a new physical relation of her body to other bodies. Caught in a sort of akinesia of her own privilege, Mary is propelled into movement by her delight in the rhythms of Martha's skipping. When she sees Martha demonstrate skipping technique, Mary comes alive, like one of Oliver Sacks's postencephalitic patients awakening. In her excitement, Mary exemplifies Sacks's insight that "it is only an ever-changing, melodic, and *living* play of forces which can recall living beings into their own living being" (349).

The skipping-rope defines the moment when the relationship between Martha and Mary verges on the erotic. In gratitude, Mary shakes Martha's hand stiffly. Impulsively, the servant tells her:

> "If tha'd been our 'Lizabeth Ellen tha'd have given me a kiss."
> Mary looked stiffer than ever.
> "Do you want me to kiss you?"
> Martha laughed again.
> "Nay, not me," she answered. "If tha' was different, p'raps tha'd want to thysel'. But tha' isn't." (66–67)

How different? we might ask. It is as delicate a moment as one would find in any coming-out novel, this suggestion that a kiss might occur if the situation were different: if Mary were older, more in tune with her own desires. Of course such a kiss would be "innocent," a kiss of exultant gratitude. But in the novel's multiple address, the kiss cannot be separated from its erotic connotation. A kiss is still a kiss.

The moment passes. Mary's desires are redirected toward her newfound garden. But we see a parallel path not taken, into a different enactment of physical need. The moment, like most of these early moments between Mary and Martha, is also one of a dramatic contrast in language. Martha's Yorkshire dialect is coded as the language of direct emotional expression. Mary's featureless standard dialect is seen as stilted. She is integrated into her new home by language as well as by physical interaction. Martha's commentary throughout, in dialect, is directed less at Mary than at the reader, providing a foil for the direction of Mary's growth and the reader's identification with that growth. Martha talks at us in order to talk Mary into herself.

When they first meet, Martha speaks two dialects, but Mary is able to use only standard dialect, though she does readily accept the existence of other dialects because of her experience in multilingual Indian culture. Martha, however, is self-conscious about her nonstandard English. She comprehends standard, though she can barely restrain her Yorkshire exuberance when Mary asks her what the phrase "Nowt o' th' soart" means: "'There now,' she said. 'I've talked broad Yorkshire again like Mrs. Medlock says I mustn't. "Nowt o' th'soart" means "nothin'-of-the-sort,"' slowly and carefully, 'but it takes so long to say it'" (57). The text, in reporting Martha's speech, walks a line between approval and derision. Even Martha's most careful effort is subtly marked as substandard: "nothin'" for "nothing." Yet the energy of Martha's remark "it takes so long to say it" turns an issue of dialectal difference into one of moral comparison. Martha's reluctance to use the more "proper" phrase is not laziness but its reverse, an impulsive linguistic attitude that is of a piece with her other Yorkshire speech qualities of frankness and concreteness.

For a long time Mary is shut up in her own dialect, understanding Yorkshire passively but making little effort to produce it. Having learned to dress herself and to skip easily enough, she finds that Yorkshire demands more effort. She learns, perhaps, that to speak is to remake the whole of herself, both consciousness and instinct, while her physical renewals were merely liberations of an instinctual self. The impulse that finally drives her to speak Yorkshire comes from her desire to awaken Colin as she herself has been wakened by Martha and Dickon. Having tested her Yorkshire on Dickon and been approved, she goes in to sit next to Colin's bed. He smells her body, finding it unusually "cool and warm and sweet," and asks, "What is it you smell of?" (161). She replies in dialect: "It's th' wind from th'moor. . . . It's the springtime an' out o'doors an' sunshine as smells so graidely" (161).

Colin is puzzled. He asks Mary what she is talking about. Her reply is crucial: "'I'm givin' thee a bit o'Yorkshire. . . . I canna' talk as graidely as Dickon an' Martha can but tha' sees I can shape it a bit. Doesn't tha' understand a bit o' Yorkshire when tha' hears it? An' tha' a Yorkshire lad thysel' bred an' born! Eh! I wonder tha'rt not ashamed o' thy face'" (161). The sensuality of the scene intensifies as it centers on language. Mary teasingly insists on her own linguistic power. Just as Martha has brought her out by speaking "broadly" and suggesting that the abandon of a kiss might lie in the same direction as lingual fluency, so Mary practices the same kind of seduction on Colin.

Mary's newfound fluency is so astonishing that Mrs. Medlock, the stuffy housekeeper, slips into Yorkshire when she overhears Mary. "Speaking rather broad Yorkshire herself because there was no one to hear her," Mrs. Medlock marvels at the event (162). Mrs. Medlock's slip into dialect suggests a defining role for Yorkshire in the novel's linguistic dynamics. The dialect is not a comic counterpoint to standard. It's not an analogue, therefore, to the imitations of African-American dialogue in the stories of Joel Chandler Harris or to Finley Peter Dunne's comic Irishman Mr. Dooley. Yorkshire is the unconscious native tongue of every character in *The Secret Garden*. Or if it isn't, as with Colin, it should be. Dialect becomes an approach to inner truth of expression, against which the use of standard seems effete.

In reading the development of Mary's physical self-sufficiency and her ability to tap into Yorkshire dialect, I am trying to come to a sort of accommodation with the text of *The Secret Garden*. This is what, for me, the text neutrally represents. It can be instructive to test such readings against differing interpretations. The 1993 film version of *The Secret Garden*, directed by Agnieszka Holland, is such an interpretation. Distinctly a version for the midnineties, the film features different elements from those in the novel and in the preceding Hollywood version (directed by Fred M. Wilcox in 1949).

The 1949 film follows Burnett in emphasizing Mary's acquisition of dialect. It also makes the final tableau belong exclusively to Colin and his father. Holland and screenwriter Caroline Thompson (who also wrote the screenplay for the 1994 version of *Black Beauty*) tone down the "broader" Yorkshire dialect. They include Mary and Dickon—and the whole Misselthwaite community—in the final rapprochement between Colin and his father. In the 1993 film, all the servants of Misselthwaite surround the Craven men in the cinematic equivalent of a group hug as they stride together up to the manor. The scene is an elaboration of the ending of the novel, where the servants react in surprise to seeing father and son walking together (256). It is in stark contrast to the 1949 interpretation, in which father and son embrace in the closed garden as the movie ends.

These interpretive choices in the 1993 version, like the decision to kill off Mary Lennox's parents in a sudden earthquake rather than in an epidemic, seem to be politically motivated. The inclusive final tableau, the partial erasure of speech differences between the privileged characters and their servants, the substitution of a random disaster for the outbreak of cholera (which might have implied failures in Indian sanitation) all serve to avoid racism and classism. More telling, however, is the spin that the 1993 film gives to the erotic elements of the novel. This spin is a way of seeing both the sexuality of Burnett's *Secret Garden* and its lack of sexuality—in short, of seeing its impossibility.

The opening credits of Holland's 1993 *Secret Garden* are shown over a stylized scene of Mary Lennox being dressed by her Indian servants. The scene emphasizes the body of actress Kate Maberly (who plays Mary). It highlights the control that Mary and her attendants exert over her body as they force it into compliance with the customs of the master-servant relationship. The scene represents a ritual ignored by the 1949 film. The dressing ritual is present only by implication in Burnett's text. In the novel, we know that Mary has been dressed by servants in India because she is surprised at *not* being dressed by her English maid. This dressing is never directly described in the book.

It is impossible to say whether Mary's body is eroticized in the opening frames of Holland's film. The scene recalls, cinematically, the disturbing transformations enacted on Debra Winger's body in another early nineties East-meets-West film, *The Sheltering Sky* by Bernardo Bertolucci. Yet it is presented virtually without comment, as an opportunistic cinematic effect. The 1993 film does go on, however, to develop an erotic context for the cultivation of the garden. Or rather, one should say, the film acknowledges that there is an erotic context present, a context suppressed in the 1949 film and the 1911 book.

The plot of Burnett's novel is centered on a romantic triangle that it cannot bring itself to acknowledge as potentially erotic. Young as they are, the characters show an evident attraction to one another. Dickon and Colin are rivals for Mary's attentions. Neither of them wins her. There is no romantic resolution, and as in *Charlie and the Chocolate Factory,* the pairing of a boy with a suitable father is the real romance at the ending. But the two boys compete to spend time with her, though in the novel there is a curious dampening-down of this competition. The relaxation of tension is not entirely ascribable to Dickon's knowing his place as a peasant boy and surrendering the *droit de seigneur* to Colin. For one thing, the novel's Colin seems uninterested in his *droit.* Burnett's characters are emphatically not young adult romance proto-types. They are kids playing together.

In Holland's film, though, the children have obvious romantic attach-ments and jealousies. Dickon and Mary join hands during one scene in the garden, in a way that is unmistakably romantic. Colin is upset at Mary's attachment to Dickon, an attachment that he sees as threaten-ing his own burgeoning relationship with her. These romance elements are grafted onto the text of the novel that would seem without them to be inexplicable—or worse, just coy—to a nineties audience. In much the same way, we have seen how Thompson's 1994 *Black Beauty* screen-play invents a romantic subtext for Beauty and Ginger that is absent from Sewell's novel. It is as if the screenwriter senses a collective "oh, come on" from the audience if a situation so full of erotic potential were allowed to go precisely the nowhere that the Victorian author takes it.

Nowhere in the 1993 *Secret Garden* is the development of an erotic potential taken as far as in the alteration of one detail from the novel. In the novel, Mr. Craven explains his family relationship to Mary Len-nox succinctly: "Captain Lennox was my wife's brother and I am their daughter's guardian" (17). In the Holland film, Mary's mother is instead the dead Mrs. Craven's twin sister. This change in detail, small enough to pass as arbitrary, is a response to a pattern latent in the text of the novel itself: the fascination, ultimately sexual, that Mrs. Craven holds for Mary Lennox.

Though the initial dressing scene in Holland's *Secret Garden* may not be overtly erotic, a later scene surely is. When Mr. Craven meets Mary in the 1993 film, he has a Yeatsian moment. Like the narrator of "Among School Children," he suddenly feels that "She stands before me as a

living child." Maddened by his grief over his wife's death ten years earlier, he is now maddened again by the appearance of a girl who recalls
her own mother, that wife's double. Unlike Burnett's Mr. Craven and
the Craven played by Herbert Marshall in the 1949 film, who are melancholy and detached in their grief, John Lynch's 1993 Craven is eroti-
cally obsessed, longing like a Poe character for the reincarnation of his
dead lover. Hence he is a distinct sexual threat to Mary, a threat that
must be defused. She defuses it, possibly, by offering Colin to Mr. Craven instead of herself.

In the novel (and in the 1949 film), Mary finds the key to the secret
garden buried in the soil of the Misselthwaite grounds. In the 1993 film,
she finds it in her aunt's sealed boudoir, a room that has been left in a
welter after her death, like the forbidden wing of the Beast's castle in
various film treatments of *Beauty and the Beast*. This room is full of
souvenirs of Mary's aunt as a young, vital, sexual woman. It has been
left as it was when she died—in futile hope, perhaps, of her resurrec-
tion. The change is sumptuously dramatic. After all, there's nothing
particularly piquant about digging up an old key out of the dirt. The
scene also makes explicit an interpretation performed by Holland and
Thompson, a reading that sees Mary's fascination with the sexuality of
Mrs. Craven as the figurative key to the development of the garden—
and of the core of Mary's identity.

This is an interpretation, not an imposition of a theme. The novel *The
Secret Garden* allows the identification of aunt and niece without
specifically authorizing that interpretation. When Mary first comes to
Misselthwaite, the house and grounds conceal a mystery of sexuality,
birth and death. Mrs. Craven has been dead for ten years. There is a
garden on the grounds, locked and hidden by walls, that has been sealed
for ten years. A woman who loved roses died ten years ago. The secret
garden is full of rosebushes. It is also the place where a robin and his
mate nest. Nobody is supposed to talk about the garden, or go near it,
though naturally *everybody* talks about the garden, and nearly everybody ends up going there. The house is full of mysterious cries at night,
cries that Martha dismisses as the wind "wuthering" around the house.
When you hear the word "wuthering" on a Yorkshire moor, you have
license to suspect Brontëan erotic mysteries. The cries are revealed to

be those of a hysterically ill ten-year-old boy, despised by his father and left for paralyzed. More hideous yet, the garden is not just a place that Mrs. Craven loved, but the location of her sexual encounters with Mr. Craven and the place of her death.

Burnett's text doesn't say that Mr. and Mrs. Craven made love in the garden. Martha says only, "It was Mrs. Craven's garden that she had made when first they were married an' she just loved it, an' they used to 'tend the flowers themselves. An' none of the gardeners was ever let to go in. Him an' her used to go in an' shut th' door an' stay there hours an' hours, readin' and talkin'" (45). The point is made, though narrator and narratee may conspire to ignore it, that the secret garden was literally the Cravens' paradise, their sexual *hortus conclusus*. When a tree limb that "she made roses grow over" (45–46) collapses while she is sitting on it, Mrs. Craven is fatally injured. The garden is then sealed off, though it remains present in the narratives of the Misselthwaite household. Martha cannot possibly remember this ten-year-old story for herself, but has imbibed knowledge of it from the traditions of the place.

Colin Craven is ten years old. The accident in the garden coincides with his birth. Left unanswered in the novel is whether Mrs. Craven dies *in* childbirth or just *after* childbirth. Does the branch fall when she is pregnant, precipitating Colin's delivery and killing her, or is she killed after his birth? Since there are no witnesses but Mr. Craven, the circumstances of her death are murky. (This gap in the story allows a weird subplot in the 1949 film, in which the children briefly suspect Mr. Craven of murdering his wife.) His wild reactions to her death allow of other interpretations, too: that his impregnating her led (in his mind) to her death; that postpartum intercourse led (in his mind) to her death; that the whole sexual relationship, with the eroticism of the walled-off rose garden, led (in his mind—it's all in his mind, actually) to her death; that Colin has killed her during his birth; that her own sensuality has brought her death upon her.

It's heady stuff for a ten-year-old girl to contemplate. Old enough to be conscious of sexuality but too young to experience it, Mary Lennox is fascinated by the story of her dead aunt. She is determined to explore the mysteries of the garden despite any prohibitions. To discover the garden is to unravel the mystery of Colin's birth. More important, to discover the garden is to discover her own future as a sexually mature woman. Marriage and childbearing may have been distant rumors to her, but the prospect of a bloody death in the garden of married love concentrates her mind wonderfully on finding some explanation for those rumors.

Mary's fascination with the garden, and with its connection to her aunt's death, support the interpretation that Holland offers, of a close connection both physically and spiritually between the dead woman and the girl. The eerie twinship of Mary's mother and aunt in the film is shorthand for this connection. The connection is worked out in the garden, which stands for the sexuality that Mary shares with Mrs. Craven and also denies the sexuality they share, in a tension of affirmation and negation.

The secret garden, as Nancy Friday intuited in borrowing the phrase for her title, is one of the most intensely sexual places in literature, an extended and lingering catalog of pent-up flows, blossomings, and urgings-forth from the earth. It is also intensely asexual. Burnett never once connects its vegetable erotics with the drives of its human caretakers. But what erotics they are! "'When it looks a bit greenish an' juicy like that, it's wick,' [Dickon] explained. 'When th' inside is dry an' breaks easy, like this here piece I've cut off, it's done for. There's a big root here as all this live wood sprung out of, an' if th' old wood's cut off an' it's dug round, an' took care of there'll be—' he stopped and lifted his face to look up at the climbing and hanging sprays above him—'there'll be a fountain o' roses here this summer'" (94). The garden, like Mary herself, is only apparently stiff and sterile. It comes to life under Dickon's hands and Dickon's knife, his gentleness and power combined.

Their reinvigoration of the garden has elements of courtship. They "like" each other, as they confess (98). They trust each other with the secret of the place: "'If tha' was a missel thrush an' showed me where thy nest was, does tha' think I'd tell any one? Not me,' he said. 'Tha' art as safe as a missel thrush'" (99). But that is as far as it goes. Their dialogue foreshadows the most famous awakening of a standard-speaking woman by a dialectal man, the affair between Mellors and Connie in D. H. Lawrence's *Lady Chatterley's Lover*. The best-kept secret of the garden, its metaphoric connections to the pleasures and generative powers of sex, remains unspoken.

The novel *The Secret Garden* is in a tension unresolvable in either erotic or childish terms. It is a song neither of innocence nor of experience. The novel works because it maintains a balance between the erotic and the nonerotic that refuses to collapse. It's post-Victorian situation enables a neither-nor quality that could exist only at a precise historical moment. Earlier on—say, at the time of *Black Beauty*—the suggestions of eroticism might have been suppressed altogether. Later, as in so much young adult fiction since the 1970s, the sexuality might be openly erotic. In Burnett's novel, sex and childhood are curiously fused. The erotic qualities of the garden are not just tacked onto a whimsical tale of childhood secrets. The deep innocence of Mary's childish delight in the garden is not a mere papering-over of deeper drives. Both forces co-exist. They create the texture of the novel between them.

The novel folds into the story of Colin's reconciliation (or pure conciliation, since they have never had a relationship) with his father. That plot has its own erotics, which I will not examine here. The novel heads in a male-bonding direction because it has explored a girl's sexual identification with a grown woman as far along the way as it can without making its interests explicit. Homosocial love is a safer territory. To go further with Mary would lead her to contemplate the experience of Mrs. Craven, to begin to acknowledge her own oneness with her aunt's body. *The Secret Garden* would turn into something like Elizabeth Bishop's great poem, still more than fifty years in the future, "In the Waiting Room." There, the nearly seven-year-old Elizabeth realizes suddenly her profound empathy with the embodied experience of her aunt: "Why should I be my aunt, / or me, or anyone?" It is one thing for an adult poem to drag a girl into a terrifying identification with a woman and quite another for a 1911 children's novel to follow such a course.

Burnett began her career as a writer of adult magazine tales about erotic fascination. Tales in her first collection, *Surly Tim and Other Stories* (1877), reveal her fascination with sexual secrets. Tim, the protagonist of the title story, marries a soldier's widow but loses her when the soldier reappears. A marriage is the front for an erotic quadrangle in "Le monsieur de la petite dame." Smethurstses is the name of a traveling waxworks whose owner has seen his lover go off with an upper-class man and then has taken her back after she's been rejected. On "One Day at Arle" a woman marries a suitor only after he tells her lies about her lover's infidelities. In "Lodusky" a woman writes to her lover about a rural beauty, causing her lover to abandon her for the beauty. "Seth" focuses on a woman who, dressed as a man, pursues a gentleman to America from England and becomes the lover of a rough female mill worker as she pursues the hopeless dream of marrying the gentleman. In her adult fiction, Burnett pursued themes of sexual longing and indirection. The triangles and squares of relationship in *The Secret Garden* are of a piece with her adult fiction. At the same time, they are sundered from it.

The conventions of *The Secret Garden* as exploratory children's fiction, as fiction in which, as it were, everything must be said while nothing is spoken, are frozen in superb tension by the surface innocence of the text. But, to follow Jacqueline Rose's contention, *The Secret Garden* "was only ever innocent to the extent that it told a different story: that [Mary's] innocence was protested in exact measure to the burden of repression which [she] had, from the outset, been expected to bear" (xi). I have altered that quotation only to substitute Mary Lennox's name and pronoun for those of Peter Pan. For if *The Secret Garden* is the polished essence of the sexualized children's classic, *Peter Pan* is its expressionistic nightmare.

When I was four or five years old, before I started school, my mother had a routine. To get through her housework, she would sit me down in the morning in front of reruns of sitcoms: "The Donna Reed Show," "Father Knows Best." In the afternoon, the soaps would come on, and I couldn't sit still for them, so she would sit me in front of the phonograph and put stacks of show tune albums on the changer. I would listen as, one by one, the first acts of musicals fell onto the turntable. *The Music Man, Gypsy, Camelot, The King and I,* and *Destry* would in turn strike up, get halfway through their scores, and fade out. Then, with a flick of the hand as she passed the record player, my mother would turn the stack over and, one by one, the second acts would play: *Destry, The King and I, Camelot, Gypsy, The Music Man.* Her tastes ran to some eccentric things, and as a result I still sometimes wake up in the middle of the night humming tunes from *Take Me Along* or *New Girl in Town.*

Of all the records that my mother played, my favorite was *Peter Pan* with Mary Martin. It was the one that got played the most, to drug me into uncomplaining compliance with the demands of housework. Mopping, vacuuming, washing, hanging, sprinkling, and ironing went on around me as I stared at the grooves of *Peter Pan* spinning by. I remember the LP, which may still be sitting in my parents' basement: a warped and undulating thing, in a frayed green sleeve, its glassine sheath long gone, scratched and given to a skip here and there. Its uneven way of turning on the table gave its rhythms a special quality of verve.

Every year, we would watch *Peter Pan* on our TV, a snowy little black-and-white set that delivered a smudgy Tinker Bell and minuscule pirates. My memory of the show, in grainy black and white, is so authoritative that I was shocked to find a few years ago that *Peter Pan* was in color. A color drab and washed-out by 1990s standards, it's true, but one that must have seemed riotous in that early world of gray-scale video images.

Watching the same show come round year after year in the cycle of seasons, I did not understand then—as children do today, with VCRs that show them perfect iterations of dramas on command—that the story of *Peter Pan* never changed. So my memories of watching the show are memories of anxiety: would the children be able to fly? What would Captain Hook do to Wendy when he kidnapped her? And most distressing, would Tinker Bell be saved from death this time? Did America still believe in fairies? I can still feel myself squirming in my pajamas at the suspense of it all.

That's ironic, right?—that a text whose central image is the fixity of its ungrowing hero could be, for a real growing child, the focus of so much uncertainty about its textual stability. It seems preposterous to me in my late thirties that I once took the danger and suspense of *Peter Pan* so seriously. *The Wizard of Oz*, now, there is a scary movie. To hear Margaret Hamilton's laugh is as frightening when you're forty as when you were eight. *Peter Pan,* however, is a burlesque of its own roots in pantomime. Its villain is a queenish, inept pirate. Its hero is a grown woman in tights pretending to be a boy. Its moment of greatest pathos is when Tinker Bell nearly "dies"; but Tinker Bell is no more than a shuttered followspot and doesn't have a coherent character note or relation to the plot until she throws herself in front of Peter's poisoned medicine. I repeat these responses now, involuntarily. I shudder at the sight of Tink draining the poison, almost leap with joy when Pan, the Avenger, appears in the rigging of the *Jolly Roger* to take on Captain Hook.

This is the film, the music I come back to thirty years later, and try to make sense of as an academic reader of *Peter Pan* and its meanings. I cannot make sense of these artifacts. They affect me as no adult literature or film possibly could. When I think of the most profoundly affecting book I have come to as an adult—an easy choice, Proust's *A la recherche du temps perdu*—I rehearse for myself its greatest scenes: the narrator scrambling out of his bedroom to intercept his mother for a goodnight kiss, the duchess of Guermantes retrieving her red shoes as Swann calmly announces that he is dying. I find myself in depth after depth, responding at every level that the text allows. But even though Proust pushes every button on me, his text is as nothing to that first moment in the nursery when the enormous shutters fly open and Peter flies into the room, looking for his shadow.

I feel impelled to account for the affective response I feel in the face of *Peter Pan.* It's not to indulge myself by talking about my childhood, but to test the power of *Peter Pan* as a cultural artifact and to make contact with readers who may feel a similar affect in themselves. Suspense is the strongest of my memories, then. But many children's adventure stories are suspenseful. Next strongest, and more significant, is my memory, and my continued feeling, of confusion.

I am confused because Peter Pan is not a boy but a woman. Peter Pan has been played by a woman since the very first productions of the play (Garber 165–66). In the 1960 video, from the moment that Peter flies through the window, the character is simultaneously boy and woman. As David Van Leer puts it, Martin's great showstopper is "[S/he] Gotta Crow" (162). Martin's Peter always inhabits both genders at once. Walt Disney, in 1952, sidestepped this problem in his animated *Peter Pan* by having Peter drawn as a boy. Disney's version has always been signally boring to me, lacking any character interest. The Mary Martin version generates its impact by getting into severe gender trouble.

On TV, the contradictions of Martin's version of Peter are continuous. On the LP, the contradiction was at once less and greater: less, because there was no visual Peter to signal "boy" while the voice said "woman," but greater, because that boy was unmistakably the same person who was Maria singing "My Favorite Things" on one of the other records in the stack. Then, of course, offering another turn of the screw, she/he disguises her/himself as a woman for the "Mysterious Lady" number and sings in a soprano register, immediately turning Captain Hook from a lecherous pederast into a smitten heterosexual. I cannot for the life of me figure out what these characters *want.*

I wonder if children in the nineties have a more fluid sense of gender than I did as a child of the sixties. I imagine that they might. Turning on *Peter Pan* now, after an evening of watching k. d. lang or Dennis Rodman on TV, it seems more of a piece with the surrounding culture: "Ah!" one imagines the average third grader saying, "more cross-dressing!" In the sixties, when we turned on *Peter Pan,* it was in the context of "My Three Sons" and "The Dick Van Dyke Show." On TV men had short hair, straight narrow ties, serious expressions, and pipes. Women had flouncy skirts (except for Laura Petrie, of course, who was allowed to don her scandalous capri pants once per episode), lifted and pointed breasts, elaborate foundation garments, plucked eyebrows, and coiffed hair. And they were kind of ditzy, as if they shouldn't be trusted with sharp objects or sums of money over ten dollars.

It wasn't so much, either, that this was TV, and we were all laughing at it from the other side of a culture that had survived such categories, as we do now watching the same shows on Nick at Nite, or did in the seventies watching "Happy Days." The humor of "Happy Days" lay in the absurdity of the represented past, evoked not in nostalgia but to reinforce the viewer's sense of hipness at having outlived that past. No, for a kid in the early and midsixties, the representations of the tube were an ideal pattern, not a safely contained reality. My father *did* have narrow ties and gompy-looking eyeglasses. My mother had bras and girdles and garter belts and elaborate unspeakable rituals of leg waxing, hair curling, and makeup.

Men like my grandfather drank highballs and talked baseball together. Women like my grandmother—well, they drank highballs too, but they did it in such different clothes! and never together with the men. Parties at my grandparents' house, in Aurora, Illinois, 1964, enforced a sexual segregation that would be the envy of any Islamic republic: the men on the porch in shirtsleeves talking about work, the women in the air-cooled living room discussing upholstering and recipes. And that was when the sexes, so to speak, got together. In the rest of their spare time, my grandparents gravitated to opposite ends of their property, getting as far away from each other as they could: Grandma in her basement, putting piles and piles of wet clothes through a great wringer, building forearm strength I will never attain; Grandpa in the workshop he'd built himself behind the garage, like an alternate dwelling, refinishing ghastly old furniture, sorting bits of hardware into old coffee cans on the theory that a guy could use something like that some day.

Peter Pan would have had trouble fitting in had she/he swooped through the shutters of those houses. But she/he was invited into the television set once a year, spring cleaning or no. One watches Mary Martin in the role now and is astounded. Her hair is short, her figure not much disguised at all—not overly curved, but hard to accept as a boy's. Her voice is a high alto, her mannerisms childish. The whole package is impossible to take as a whole *or* to analyze. Almost the first thing she/he does in the nursery is to take a bar of soap and rub it all over her/his butt, trying to stick on the shadow. Or trying, much more deeply, to wave said butt in the audience's face, to appropriate a gesture only proper for a small boy to make in public and thus to assert her/his own boyishness, her own aggressive grasp of the character. She/he bends way over and looks back through her/his spread legs to see if the shadow has taken hold. It hasn't, of course; only Wendy's demure needle can attach it. But in bending over, Peter places himself, Mary Martin places herself, as firmly as possible in contrast to Wendy. She is a boy.

But she's not; once the shadow is sewn on and Peter starts to crow, he (she? the pronouns refuse to stay stuck, any more than a shadow stays on with soap)—he lies on his back with his legs spread in the air and plays shadow games on the shutters. The hem of his tunic falls and for a long second the costume tights are pulled taut over Peter's crotch, vividly outlining a female cleft even as he crows like a cock. Viewing the scene is like looking into the heart of all taboo. Yet it is not only shown to children, but given the best possible wholesome family rating. What the hell is going on here?

Van Leer reads Martin's *Peter Pan* postures, through the lens of Gwen Verdon's later body language as Lola in *Damn Yankees*, as "anything but inviting" (162). She is not sexually seductive, as a female. She is a female playing male in order to exude power. What a different sort of cross-dressing this is than the eighties or nineties cross-dressing of Dustin Hoffman in *Tootsie* (directed by Sydney Pollack) or Robin Williams in *Mrs. Doubtfire* (directed by Chris Columbus), in which a man plays at being a woman to tap into the (somewhat hysterically conceived) power that females possess, at least in some fin-de-siécle cultural codes.

Martin seizes male power at a terrible cost. Dressing as a boy, she makes a performative act. What does that act mean, when sized up against Judith Butler's characterization of the performative in *Gender Trouble?* "Acts, gestures, and desire produce the effect of an internal core or substance, but produce this *on the surface* of the body, through the play of signifying absences that suggest, but never reveal, the organizing principle of identity as a cause. Such acts, gestures, enactments, generally construed, are *performative* in the sense that the essence or identity that they otherwise purport to express are *fabrications* manufactured and sustained through corporeal signs and other discursive means" (136). On one level, this is certainly true of Peter Pan. The original "Betwixt-and-Between" (Barrie, *The Little White Bird* 129), Peter is literally neither flesh nor fowl, and on stage as a woman/boy, she/he is neither male nor female. The direction of such performative gestures, though, is not always to reveal their own fabrication. Particularly, in the case of Peter Pan, context and direction are everything. While Peter's centerless performativity may energize an audience of the nineties to new senses of essencelessness, Peter as manifest in the fifties and sixties was profoundly subversive of his own subversiveness. What Mary Martin performed for children—what she taught *me*—was that being a woman was the same as being a big child. Her performance does not cover a lack of identity. It nervously evades acknowledgment of the female essence of her character—and of the link between being female and being immature.

This is partly to say that Barrie's basic script plays differently in different eras, as one might expect. More specifically, *Peter Pan* met a cultural need for fifties America, that society that was always strapped for new justifications to keep women like my mother at home listening to Ethel Merman in place of more active cultural work. Mary Martin as Peter Pan is a distinctly American performance, her hard *R*'s and her back-slapping bonhomie suggesting a housewife in drag at a bachelor party (something that Lucille Ball and Vivian Vance used to act out literally on "I Love Lucy"). Martin's Peter warns Wendy early on in the play not ever to touch him, but where Barrie clinches this warning with the stage direction "He is never touched by anyone in the play" (*Peter Pan* 29), Martin's character soon forgets the warning and goes in for group hugs throughout. He is less an ethereal half-bird than the personification of hail-fellow-well-met.

Martin's Peter is male. As an evidently female male, he comes across as impotent and attention-deficient. His only real triumph is to defeat the fey Captain Hook, and even then he needs the help of the providential crocodile. His greatest failures are personal. When Wendy asks him, "What are your exact feelings for me, Peter?" and he answers, "Those of a devoted son, Wendy," the lines that Barrie wrote for an imaginary perpetual child take on what one might call the remorse of gender. Speaking the lines, Mary Martin seems less like the Peter called for in Barrie's stage direction ("determined to get at facts, the only things that puzzle him" 103), than like a lesbian impostor in a straight world. She/he cannot marry Wendy and really father the boys that are "yours and mine" as Wendy calls them, but not because she/he is a child—it is rather because she/he is a woman. When Wendy tests her/his affection, she/he is found out—the opposite of what she/he should be, and not inadequate because she/he is diminished, but inadequate because she/he is opposite.

One must understand that my reading of Martin's *Peter Pan* remains personal. "Why is Peter Pan played by a woman? Because a woman will never grow up to be a man," Marjorie Garber observes (168). When I recognize the force of Garber's insight, I also see what I internalized about men and women as I watched *Peter Pan* annually through the sixties. I learned that a woman is a man who isn't grown up enough or (more sinister) who *won't* grow up. And, conversely, a boy is a woman. The fulcrum on which my own powerlessness as a boy was balanced was the sense that somehow I too was a woman. The play was telling me, a young male, that I was an adult female. To grow up, in the play's terms, is to wear a tie and go to work. My mom didn't do that. The casting of a woman as Peter Pan is not a mere function of stagecraft, using the superficially boyish voice of the star actress to mimic the sound of a boy.[1] This is how I learned about power and gender. To rewrite the T-shirt: I'll be grown up tomorrow, but you'll be a woman your whole life.

"Take off your veil, and let me see your face," calls Captain Hook to the mysterious lady, who is a boy, who is a woman. Read as performative, she is all veil and no face beneath. Read as a statement, as an element of discourse instead of a character, she is pure ideology. A heterosexually seductive woman is really, when you get down to it, a boy, and she is a boy because she is a woman; women are boys. Straight and gay men alike, then, have a single sexuality. Paterfamilias Mr. Darling by day and cruisy Captain Hook by night (the parts in the Martin version are doubled, as usual, by the same actor, Cyril Ritchard), they seek the ideal woman/boy of their erotic economies.

When I watched *Peter Pan* as a preschooler, I didn't get the sexuality that the play exudes. I was blissfully innocent about the images that shock me today: the connections among eating, sickening, giving birth, child care, castration, penetration. Wendy in her nightgown, falling to earth pierced between the breasts with a gigantic rubber-tipped arrow, was to me an unfortunate accident rather than some parody of a Freudian nightmare. Peter's cutting off Captain Hook's hand was an act of bravery, not of symbolic sexual violence. It made perfect sense that Peter was at once Wendy's husband and Wendy's son. Even though I must have crossed the thetic divide several years earlier and was technically post-Oedipal, my sense of interpersonal boundary maintenance was still blissfully flexible. And when Mary/Peter lured pirate after pirate into a small dark room and stabbed them to death with her dagger, I swear that at the age of five the phrase *vagina dentata* never crossed my mind.

But for all that, the play imposed connections and distinctions on me, constructing gender for all it was worth. I reconstruct these connections now in memory, and see them as a work done, in fantasy, by adults and for adults. Yet I know that *Peter Pan* impressed me as I was growing up—or, rather, as I was trying not to. When I was four years old, my father tried to walk me to nursery school, and I sat down at the corner on the sidewalk and would not move. I always wanted to be a boy and to have fun, you see. To have fun somehow meant growing up not as a man but as a woman—didn't Peter Pan seem to do that? I inflated my preschooler rib cage and wished I had breasts, made doll furniture that my mother threw away in a rage. As Beaver Cleaver envied June, I envied mothers, grown women who had no pressure to work, for whom all was (so apparently) provided. The ideal, I suppose, would be to take the ultimate step and become Lassie—adult, female, and dog, in a permanent state of pampered bliss, with occasional time out for melodramatic heroics.

If this were a different kind of narrative, it would turn into a coming-out story now. I would move on to explain how only Mary Martin (or Judy Garland or Julie Andrews) could possibly understand me, and how I thwarted my mother's efforts to make me straight. Or I might wonder whether all those stacks of show tune albums kept me assured that she really accepted my gay dreams. However, I am coming to believe, in later life, that sexuality really is a matter of genetics. All the pressures of sixties high camp converging at once couldn't keep me from growing up straight. I am heterosexual to a fault, a forty-one-year-old straight man who just happens to be able to do a dead-accurate Carol Channing impression. Such are the strange things that happen when cultural construction meets the givens of the body.

I wanted to be (or stay) a woman, when I was a boy, not because I desired men, not because I wished I were a girl, but because I was comfortable as a boy and preferred not to change. The lesson I'd learned from Broadway and TV was that a boy could stay boyish as a woman. At least in Never Land. When I watch *Peter Pan* today, suspense and confusion alike give way to an overpowering sense of transience. The tragedy, and simultaneously the wonder, of growing old is that you both are and cannot be the child you once were. James Barrie described aging in his dedication to the 1928 first edition of *Peter Pan* in terms paraphrased by Lynn Fontanne when she introduced the 1960 video production of the play: "Some say that we are different people at different periods of our lives, changing not through effort of will, which is a brave affair, but in the easy course of nature every ten years or so. . . . I think one remains the same person throughout, merely passing, as it were, in these lapses of time from one room to another, but all in the same house. If we unlock the rooms of the far past we can peer in and see ourselves, busily occupied in beginning to become you and me" (xiii). Barrie gives the sense that he is the same person in a different "room," that the Llewellyn Davies boys he addresses are the same people, once children, now grown. His static image of the house full of rooms belies the secret that he always expresses but never makes overt: that we can move in only one direction, that we can look back but never *go* back.

The various contemporary films that I will discuss in chapter 6 are late twentieth-century attempts to go back, aided sometimes by computer graphics. Both the appeal and the inadequacy of these films are related to the direction of time in Barrie's house, the impossibility of retracing these steps, the pull of memory and fantasy toward the imagination of a step backward. So too is the appeal of much twentieth-century literature of self-exploration, from Proust to Larry Kramer's *The Destiny of Me*. In Kramer's play the protagonist spends much of the action in dialogue with an actor playing his younger self. The search for what we were, or for what room we left ourselves in, is part of a whole modern and postmodern genre that might be termed the autoerotics of nostalgia. "It is queer that the stories you like best should be the ones about yourself," as Wendy says (Barrie, *Peter Pan* 159). But who can understand us better than ourselves?

Perhaps Mary Martin could. Peter Pan is easy; he is the boy who would not grow up. Mary Martin is hard; she is the woman who is and isn't grown up, the boy who wants to stay a woman so she won't have to be a father. "No one's gonna catch me and make me a man!" Martin's Peter says to Wendy, a line not written by Barrie. One wants to remark that there's little danger of that, but the moment is too serious. It's the point when Peter decides not to accompany the Lost Boys back to London, not to be adopted by the Darlings. It follows a scene of wrenching realizations, a scene in which Martin's Peter suspects a sexual destiny that profoundly unsettles her/him. "There's something she wants to be to me, but she says it's not my mother," says Peter about Tinker Bell—Barrie's line, now. That something must remain unspoken. If we are honestly to "remain the same person throughout," we must never speak it. Only our relation to motherhood is safe. Here, we stay where Mary Lennox stays—always on the verge of discovering our sexual origin.

Things are safer in Martin's version than in Barrie's. The TV production excises Peter's harrowing lines about his own mother barring him when he tries to return home. (So does Disney's version. The barring-out scene was not realized in American film until Steven Spielberg's *Hook*.) For purposes of the American screen and stage, mothers are an idyllic breed. They are therefore never to be desired. Our culture never used to let us imagine a mother who could be less than perfect, who could, herself, desire. Why else did so many of those sixties sitcoms have absent or dead mothers: "My Three Sons," "Family Affair," "The Andy Griffith Show?" It was far easier to remove the mother than to represent her.

Martin's Peter forgets his "mother," Wendy. Then he returns years later for her but takes her daughter in his place. He's a serial fairy-dust sprinkler, locked in his own cycle of addiction. Barrie's Peter returns just once, a year later, making the whole story not cyclical but ending at the point when the cycle is broken. Barrie's version is harsher and less saccharine. Martin's Peter is the ultimate tease, always hovering at the edge of desire, pulling girls on the brink of womanhood into his Never Land and pulling back when they want him to commit. Such is precisely the "Peter Pan Syndrome" of contemporary pop psychology, of course. For Mary Martin's Peter Pan, none of the pop psychology applies, since she is never going to be a man—"No Sir!" And so her relation to others in the play is a level even deeper than the sexual, deeper than the level of the performances of gender.

One must remember that Peter Pan is not the seducer but the seduced. He comes to the Darlings' nursery for two reasons: to get his shadow back and to hear the end of "Cinderella." Once he has both, he is practically out the window when Wendy seduces him: "I know lots of stories!" He turns. Barrie's stage direction is savage: "How he would like to rip those stories out of her; he is dangerous now" (37). But Martin's reaction to Wendy's ploy has no danger in it. It is an exquisite take, a total melting of resolve. Little in it is directed toward Wendy, either in menace or desire. It is more the realization of an equation that doesn't quite balance. To get the stories, he must have a mother. By implication, the stories are about *him,* of course, the stories that only a mother can tell, of "once upon a time and long ago," stories that answer every child's longing question, "What was I like when I was a baby?" But to get the mother he must grow up, and if he grows up the stories will cease to matter. "Children know such a lot these days; soon they don't believe." He is poised on that windowsill for a long second, and it is very hard to know which way he will fall.

This seduction is nothing bodily. It is the seduction of narrative. Questions of sexuality and gender vanish in the face of its more complex performances, more complex because they are linguistic and not physical. That's not really such a high-faluting way of putting it, either. More than sex, more than touch, more then being held, we want to be told stories, preferably those long ritual storytellings during which we turn out to be the hero. *"Noi leggiavamo un giorno per diletto,"* says Dante's Francesca, "We were reading one day to pass the time." She and Paolo would have had no quality time at all if they hadn't been drawn together by a story. Whether it is desire for the story that William Gass prescribes, the tale that should be powerful enough "to charm a toothache," or the desire of the aliens in "Star Trek" episodes who barter whatever they have for fictions, narrative itself is desire, is the desire that drives Peter Pan.

I don't want to be a little boy again, even with the promise of having fun. Nor do I want to be a woman. My desire is simpler, and it may be triter: I want to turn on the VCR and hear the story of Peter Pan. And I already know, that while I am watching it, I will be the hero.

NOTE

1. An example of a purely functional use of a woman's voice as a boy's might be Nancy Cartwright's voicing of Bart Simpson in "The Simpsons." Since the character is animated, the fact that the boy's role is played by an adult actress is masked. It never comes into the viewer's consciousness except on those rare occasions when Cartwright voices a woman character in the same episode.

6

PANIC ATTACKS: CHILDREN AS ADULTS, ADULTS AS CHILDREN IN THE MOVIES

Homosexual panic is a unique phenomenon. It serves to control men and to enforce the patriarchal exchange of women, goods, and cultural capital. It takes its peculiar features from the nature of a society in which the institution of the closet prevails. The closet enables gay men to deny their sexuality to themselves and straight society to pretend that no one is actually gay, while suspecting that anyone might be. In such circumstances of multiple and mutual denial, no man can be sure of his own identity or even of the stability of his own performance of an identity.

Closets are rare in American culture, a culture that prefers to control people by means of ostensible indelible markings: gender, skin color, the accent of the immigrant. Homosexual panic, therefore, presents only fleeting and suggestive analogies to other dynamics of closeting and passing: the situation of light-skinned African Americans passing as white, the situation of Jews with Anglicized names passing for gentile. In each of these situations, the closeted individual is subject to panic, a panic that helps to reinforce social boundaries.

No adult is overtly panicked that he or she may be a child passing for an adult. It goes the other way around. It's the most charming of compliments to be taken for someone half your age, to be "carded" at the age of thirty in a liquor store by an unbelieving clerk. America seems to be a society that idolizes youth and is obsessed with staying young.

Why should anyone panic because other people are mentally taking years off his or her age while they interact with him or her socially?

Yet all adults were children once, and every adult has had the experience of being belittled and denied things by adults, an experience more or less unavoidable in child rearing. Central to such experiences is a feeling of inadequacy. This may be plain physical inadequacy (you aren't strong enough to pour the milk, aren't tall enough to reach something on the shelf). It may be also be the experience of inexperience, the feeling of not knowing an idiom, a practice, a routine that one's elders seem to fit into so naturally. Recalling such moments (Auden's "sighs for folly said and done," perhaps) is therefore part of the texture of adult life. As adults we now and then relive the embarrassment of being an inadequate child.

It is little wonder, then, that fantasies of returning to childhood figure so prominently in popular culture. Six American films from the decade 1986–96 feature this fantasy: Francis Coppola's *Peggy Sue Got Married* (1986), Penny Marshall's *Big* (1988), Brian Gilbert's *Vice Versa* (1988), Steven Spielberg's *Hook* (1992), Joe Johnston's *Jumanji* (1995), and Coppola's *Jack* (1996). In each, an adult actor portrays an adult transformed into a child or a child who inhabits an adult body. In half of these films, that actor is Robin Williams, who has marked the small genre as his own.

It's not quite clear how these films connect to their historical context. It may be too soon to decide what relation such fantasies have to the politics and culture of the late twentieth century. This chapter is only a first step toward exploring that problem. These pictures feature baby-boom-age actors in the personae of children. They address the generation born between 1945 and 1960 and play on that generation's sense of its collective past: its toys, music, and playground culture. In so doing, they construct childhood. They also construct a relation of the adult body to childhood, doing so via sense memory and sympathy. They also construct the return to childhood as a panic attack.

The first thing to notice about these six films is a gender imbalance. Five of the six have male protagonists. Only the earliest, *Peggy Sue Got Married,* has a female star, Kathleen Turner as Peggy Sue. Such imbalance could be an accident, of course, or could boil down to the fact that Robin Williams is a man. But *Peggy Sue* is the odd woman out in several other ways. In each of the male-centered films, the central role is taken by an adult actor who plays a preteen boy (in *Hook,* Williams plays Peter Pan—albeit a grown-up version of him—who it's safe to assume is a preteen boy.) Turner's Peggy Sue is a forty-three-year-old woman from 1985 magically transported back to 1960 when she was eighteen. She becomes a younger grown woman, not a true child. She has the choices that have brought her to the age of forty-three erased and re-presented to her as new options.

In each of the five "male" films, the plot complications and much of the physical and verbal comedy are provided by watching the obviously adult actor—Tom Hanks, Judge Reinhold, or Williams—do things that a child would do. No matter what the nominal direction of the transformation, whether boy-becomes-man (*Big*) or man-becomes-boy (*Hook*), the result is that we see a grown man behaving childishly.

In *Peggy Sue Got Married,* on the other hand, we see a grown woman acting *older* than she is, an eighteen year old with the mannerisms and habits of someone who is forty-three. Turner was just over thirty when she played the role, splitting the difference between the ages she portrays. Finding herself miraculously back in her parents' house just as it was twenty-five years before, Turner's Peggy Sue is a bit stressed, goes to the liquor shelf, and pours herself a drink. She laughs at her father's outrage and at his attempts to "ground" her. Later, she can barely suppress a laugh when her mother warns her to stay away from "penises"— because by 1985 she has been married longer than her mother had been in 1960.

Alongside the preternaturally mature Peggy Sue, the various men she meets back in the magically restored 1960 are both callow and *shallow.* They are engrossed in their own pretenses, boasting about their cars, their coolness, and their plans to become famous. She is variously attracted to a geeky science enthusiast, a rebellious poet, and the man she did marry, the electronics salesman Charlie (Nicolas Cage). All the men seem equally insubstantial in terms of her plans for her own life, which is now summed up in retrospect by the movie's title: "Peggy Sue got married. Case closed." She can do better, this time, without any of them.

By contrast, the women in the film, even the ones who are "really" eighteen, are far more mature than the eighteen-year-old men. They have their sights set on realistic goals: homes and cars, barbecues every weekend. The contrast between the film's men and women is underscored by the casting. Turner and the supporting actresses (including Joan Allen) are mostly about thirty in real life, but the male roles are taken by actors in their early twenties, including Cage and Jim Carrey. (All the actors play both 1960 and 1985 versions of their characters.) Against these really mature women, the men seem puerile.

Lest one think that *Peggy Sue* is therefore a film about women's empowerment, I will give away the ending: transported back to 1985, where it turns out that her return to 1960 may (or may not?) have been a hallucination, Peggy Sue meets her estranged husband, Charlie, the man she has repeatedly brushed off in the virtual 1960 she's been visiting. Back in "real time," Peggy Sue invites him to dinner, with the promise of reconciliation in the air. Her sojourn in a magical place seems to have taught her that there's no place like home, even if home features a burnt-out, weak-willed, lying, forty-three-year-old electronics salesman as its principal attraction.

In the male films, the experience of a man becoming a boy is seen as spiritually rejuvenating. Peggy Sue is not made younger by stepping backwards, though. If anything, she is reantiquated. She begins the film in 1985, in a retro-sixties prom dress that makes her look younger than ever, and several characters comment on how young she looks then, just separated from Charlie. She ends the film looking older, more hopeless, and more immured in her failed marriage than ever.

Back in 1960, Peggy Sue seems to learn that women have no childhood. They cannot become young again because they never were young, emotionally or spiritually. On finding herself young again, her first impulse is to play, but that impulse is thwarted. She sits her younger sister down and tries to get her to play Monopoly or Parcheesi, but her sister thinks she has just gone silly. As serious at twelve as the film's other women are at eighteen or at forty, the sister interprets Peggy Sue's sudden childishness as folly, not as frolic. Play, so integral to the men's films that we will look at later, is denied to women in *Peggy Sue*. The closest they come to letting their hair down is to swoon over the musical act performed by Charlie and his group, a reaction they play up for the benefit of the men's egos.

It is not accidental that the world Peggy Sue revisits is that of 1960. Mary Martin's *Peter Pan* does not figure in the movie, but it is contemporaneous with Peggy Sue's last year in high school and exemplifies the constraints of gender that channel her later life. Like Wendy Darling transported to Never Land, Peggy Sue escapes from the process of growing old only to find that she was never young. People want her to be various things—wife, mother, muse—but they never want her to be a playmate and certainly not always to be a little girl and have fun. On the evidence of the film, little girls aren't having much fun.

Peggy Sue is also, therefore, exempt from panic. She can't panic over growing young if she can never really *be* young. Instead she throws the male characters in the film into panic through her own self-possession. The male young-again film presents the man-becomes-boy experience as fraught with anxiety, but Peggy Sue is at ease and centered in her younger body, because her identity hasn't changed. The prohibition on retracing one's steps through the rooms of Barrie's house is not in force for women, here. They can move through time as through space and are always the same people. Always little, always subordinate, always the Other, a woman, in the dynamic of child and adult, is constructed at once as changeless Mother and changeless infant, Mary Martin and Peter Pan.

But men can change, and men are anxious about it. The male films use various pretexts to get into the situation of a man behaving boyishly. In *Big*, a boy makes a wish: "I want to be big." It is granted. He wakes up the next morning still himself, but in a thirty-year-old body. A father and a son, in *Vice Versa*, wish that they could trade places, and their wish is granted by an ancient magical object that has the power to switch souls from body to body. In *Hook*, Peter Banning, a man who may once have been Peter Pan, is transported to Never Land, where he undergoes training that strips away his growing up and turns him into a Lost Boy again. In *Jumanji*, an accursed board game traps a twelve-year-old boy in a fantasy world for decades. He ages there normally, but since he has been cut off from social contact at the age of twelve, he is a preteen in a man's body. The conceit in *Jack* is that the title character's body is growing at a rate four times faster than that of any normal child. Therefore, when he is chronologically and emotionally ten, he is physically forty.

From these different plot devices comes an identical effect: in each case a grown man does things only a child would do. The opposite is only once true in these films, though it is just as possible: a boy actor playing an adult role. It somehow lacks the same cultural impact to show a boy playing an man. Brian Gilbert's *Vice Versa* is a rare film that shows a boy instantly becoming a man. Divorced, harried corporate VP dad Marshall Seymour (Judge Reinhold) and his son Charlie (Fred Savage) have been "transmogrified"—Marshall is now in an eleven year old's body and Charlie now has the body of his thirty-five-year-old dad.

The premise is played mostly for screwball comedy. A pair of villains stalks the transmuted father and son, hoping to retrieve the magical object. Charlie (in his dad's body) strews his office desk with toys and keeps a frog in his executive washroom sink. Marshall (as a kid) has much less to do in the story. He sorts out a few bullies at school, using adult presence of mind rather than physical force, and he passes his math tests easily, but his presence as an adult in a child's body is mainly signaled by having him drink martinis and say things like "Holy shit!"

Vice Versa is a star vehicle for Reinhold, not for Savage. Playing Charlie, in an adult body, Reinhold undergoes transformations like those in other films in the man-to-boy genre. He loses inhibitions and preoccupations. He becomes nicer to his secretary, fairer to his business's customers, and more spontaneous and attractive to his girlfriend, Sam (Corinne Bohrer). In a climactic board room scene, Charlie, in his father's body, talks to the assembled brain trust of his company with childlike directness—and ends up winning control of a major project.

Vice Versa aligns well with *Big* and with the various Robin Williams films. Power is a central factor. Just after they trade bodies, Marshall and Charlie spar for the leadership role in their new relationship. "Try and remember I'm still your father," Marshall (Savage) warns. Charlie (Reinhold) simply picks Marshall up off the floor and says, "Try and remember I'm bigger than you now." To work together, the two develop an interdependence, of course. Neither can make his way without the other. But there at the start is a glimpse of the root of the dynamic. Bigger, not more mature, makes the rules—in companies, societies, and families.

The adult-bodied Charlie and the child-bodied Marshall also vie sexually. One interesting direction is summed up in a throwaway line, when Savage as Marshall realizes that he will have to go back and live with Robyn (Jane Kaczmarek), Marshall's ex-wife and Charlie's mother. "This is the woman I couldn't live with as a husband—and now I'm going to be her son. It's a Freudian nightmare." Perhaps, but the situation is taken nowhere in the film.

More developed is the pair's manipulation of Marshall's girlfriend, Sam. She is about to break off their relationship, realizing that Marshall's workaholic ambitions don't make for commitment to a significant other. But she is drawn back after Marshall and Charlie trade places. As an eleven year old, Marshall (Savage) can tell Sam that he loves her—or rather that Marshall loves her, since she believes him to be Charlie. The prospect of a mature and devoted stepson begins to appeal to her. In a thirty-five-year-old body, Charlie regains Sam's affections by taking her to rock concerts, behaving impulsively, shedding the cares of the office.

In the film's last scene, father and son go back to their proper selves. Charlie (now played again by Savage) says, "It sure feels good to be eleven again. . . . And it must feel good to be . . . How old are you, Dad?" "Younger than I used to be, kid," answers Reinhold as Marshall. At that point Marshall does not yet know that Charlie's last act in his body has been to propose marriage to Sam, and that she has accepted. All their problems—sexual, professional, familial, even academic—have been solved by this trading of places. But as in all films of the genre, the trade cannot be permanent. The father and son can learn from each walking in the other's shoes, but they do not stay in each other's identities.[1]

The relation of child to adult is not transitive. As a result, Savage's fine performance as Charlie/Marshall is the exception in movies. It is rare to see even a talented child actor seriously take on an adult role. Another exception, the eighties TV series "Doogie Howser, M.D.," proves the rule by throwing a child improbably into adult situations and responsibilities. The gimmick is that a boy is so brilliant that he graduates from medical school and begins practice while still a teenager. The gimmick, further, is that he *is* still a teenager and is forced nonetheless to cope with an adult role. He does not become an adult, even fantastically, except insofar as the whole scenario is fantasy, and a rather lame one at that.

The fantasies of the man-to-boy film are anything but lame. *Big* was a notable critical success, but none of the three Robin Williams films fully succeeded, critically or financially. The Williams films are full of interesting failure, of projections of a cultural fantasy that are perhaps too dark to look at. Their failure resides in their inability to span two genres—the kids' film and the adult film—and in the ways in which they make that generic divide problematic.

The man-to-boy film strongly implies an adult male viewer. Feminist film theory would say that the Hollywood movie always implies such a viewer. Laura Mulvey asserts that

> as the spectator identifies with the main male protagonist, he projects his look on to that of his like, his screen surrogate, so that the power of the male protagonist as he controls events coincides with the active power of the erotic look, both giving a satisfying sense of omnipotence. A male movie star's glamorous characteristics are thus not those of the erotic object of the gaze, but those of the more perfect, more complete, more powerful ideal ego conceived in the original moment of recognition in front of the mirror. (751)

Well, sometimes. It is fascinating to watch the opening scenes of *Big* with Mulvey's analysis in mind, because the film—made, of course, well after Mulvey's ideas had become commonplace in cinema theory—seems determined to unsettle the male viewer posed by Mulvey's feminism.

When we first see Josh Baskin, protagonist of *Big,* he is twelve years old. He is losing at a computer game. His interests include playing baseball—pretending, as most children do, to be a big leaguer—and trading baseball cards with his best friend, Billy. When the coolest girl in junior high, Cynthia, casually says hello to Josh, Billy convinces him that Cynthia wants to go out with him. We next see Josh at a carnival, weakly trying to ring the bell with a hammer stroke (a feat done easily by the grown man who follows him). Josh also isn't sure he wants to go on a particularly scary roller coaster—until he sees Cynthia waiting in the line. He goes up and begins to talk to her, only to find that she's at the carnival with a much older boyfriend. "He drives," she explains to Josh. As it turns out, Josh is not tall enough, by carnival rules, to go on the roller coaster. "It's a stupid rule," Cynthia tries to comfort him by saying, but he has been mortified. It's then that he sees the sideshow novelty that grants wishes, feeds it a coin, and receives a card saying, "Your wish has been granted."

Even before the appearance of Tom Hanks—Josh as a twelve year old is played by child actor David Moscow—the film engages an adult male viewer through the exact dynamics described by Mulvey, and attributed by her to the classic Hollywood film, with its male star and female love object. But the axes of power have been reversed. Instead of controlling the situation, Josh is at its mercy, down to being compelled by his mother to take out the garbage. He possesses an erotic gaze, but its object gazes *back*, is bigger than he is, prefers another male, and ultimately pities him. Most uncomfortable, for a grown man watching the film, is the sense that there is nowhere else to turn, no other point of view to choose in the visual dynamic that presents Josh, and his repeated humiliations, as the only point of identification for the male viewer.

Instead of a "satisfying sense of omnipotence," the film delivers images of impotence that make the reader sympathetic to Josh's desire to be "big." Ironically, in light of Mulvey's comparison of the male viewer's gaze on the male protagonist as being like the gaze directed at the self in the mirror, our first sight of the "big" Josh is when he catches sight of himself in the mirror the morning after his wish. His proprioception has given him no clues to his new size. Only when he sees himself in the door of the medicine chest does he suspect that he has changed.[2] But even the terms of the gaze in the mirror have been altered by his transformation. Instead of being an exchange of identification, a compact of power between gazer and image, Josh's look in the mirror is a look of misrecognition. He doesn't know who he is. Those may be the reasonably glamorous characteristics of Tom Hanks staring back at him, but the gazer is a twelve-year-old boy.

The feminist promise of those opening minutes is vitiated by the rest of *Big*, but these scenes provide insight into the power dynamics of this genre. These are guy movies, not really kid movies. Despite their marketing to children and their elaborate special effects and action scenes, neither *Hook* nor *Jumanji* was a major success on the kid picture circuit. *Vice Versa* quickly disappeared onto video, suffering from being released in the same year as *Big*. *Jack* is even less of a children's movie. Made by Francis Coppola, who directed *Peggy Sue Got Married*, it is every bit as melancholy as that film. But its promoters had no idea how to market it, falling back on the assumption that a movie in which Robin Williams plays a kid must be a gentle wacky romp. The picture got many negative reviews and failed to become a hit.

None of the movies in which Robin Williams plays a kid is a wacky romp, though each has its funny moments. Although Williams spends time in all three pictures playing the screwball moments of childhood, the films are more midlife crisis movies than children's adventures. *Hook* has all the elements of the midlife crisis fantasy. Under pressure in his high-powered job as a corporate lawyer, Peter Banning chafes at watching his daughter's school play and misses his son's big baseball game. He can't move without his cellular phone and throws fits when he's interrupted in the middle of business calls. As Jacqueline Rose notes, in *Hook* "Peter Pan appears as that part of human-ness which fathers must retrieve if families are to survive the material onslaught of the modern age (nostalgia about childhood as corporate capitalism's last saving grace)" (xiv). Here is a man in serious need of Spielberg magic to transform him into the practitioner of quality time that Hollywood norms require. Lacking a nearby dog to mediate the transformation, he must resort to more drastic means.

In *Jumanji* two children, Judy and Peter, begin to play an old board game that they've found in their house. In so doing, they violate the boundaries between real life and the mysterious dimension where Alan Parrish (Williams) has been trapped for twenty-six years. His ordeal in that wilderness has resembled the morass of a middle-aged man's journey through therapy: beasts, pursuers, elemental forces, and the destroying Father in the person of a hunter with an enormous gun all conspire to torment him there. The children, having freed him partially from the vortex, are his only hope for escape. Judy and Peter need a father. Their parents are dead. Their distracted aunt is herself having a midlife crisis and leaves them too much on their own. Alan forms a provisional nuclear family out of the children and his own old girlfriend Sarah (Bonnie Hunt, latterly the mom in the *Beethoven* pictures). With their support he slays his various demons and is restored to his twelve-year-old self again.

In both *Hook* and *Jumanji* the world is righted when the middle-aged hero confronts his wounds and reconstitutes a family. In *Hook* Never Land is cleansed (once more) of Captain Hook (Dustin Hoffman) and his evils. In *Jumanji* a decayed factory town is given a second chance at survival by the restoration of Alan to his rightful place in the universe. Both films have as their ultimate model *It's a Wonderful Life,* Frank Capra's 1946 Ur-midlife-crisis-story. In this archetype, a man fears that he is losing the love of his family and his stature in the community, something magical happens to him, and family and community are reconstructed around a reaffirmation of the enduring worth of a fortyish white guy.

Jack operates differently. It has fewer implications for the larger community, though it ends with a tableau of a high school graduating class, suggesting that the hero's coming to terms with himself is essential to the harmony of his peers. Jack's problems are internal and familial. While they are presented as the problems that a ten year old must face when his body is terribly out of scale with his mind and feelings, the movie is really a magical-realist version of the midlife crisis story. Jack is really ten, but he is also really forty. He has not just grown up too fast. His life has been magically compressed so that he's unlikely to live much past twenty by the calendar. The events of the film—going to school, making friends, having romantic misadventures, and having the first attacks of the angina that may someday kill him—are parallel to elements of the midlife crisis novel. Jack suffers through a new occupation, new friends, a midlife affair, the first heart attack. He is a Saul Bellow hero writ small.

Big and the three Williams films address an adult male viewer, a man who identifies with the hero both in anxiety and in triumph. All four films end with a measure of triumph. The hero reclaims his identity. The world comes back into balance. Josh Baskin is thirteen again, and Alan is once more twelve, his world restored. Peter throws his cell phone out of the window and vows to spend more time with his family. Jack graduates from high school, making a stirring valedictory address. But he doesn't forget to go out to the parties afterwards and have fun with the guys, either. The experience of panic leads in each case to a reintegration of personality and the promotion of community happiness.

The governing motif of each film is panic, a word that itself recalls the etymology of Peter Pan. The magical transformation that afflicts the central character is bad. The resolution is happy because it is a recovery. In *Hook* Peter simply disappears, in search of his children, who have been kidnapped by Captain Hook. Disoriented by that loss, he is further disoriented in Never Land, where he has trouble breaking out of his adult ways to become Peter Pan again. The characters in *Jumanji* are always in mortal danger. Each roll of the dice brings on a new catastrophe that threatens their lives. Jack's entering school has traumatic consequences, for him as he tries to fit in and for his mother as she tries to let go of him.

These problems are experienced both as external threats and as interior identity crises—for the protagonists and for viewers who identify with their plight. To get grown men to identify with their heroes, these movies represent the experience of inexperience, the embarrassment at not being able to do something competently that is at the core of so many lived childhoods. Jack doesn't go to school before the calendar age of ten because his parents have feared that he would be ostracized. When he does go, their fears come partly true. All the things that come naturally to other ten year olds, especially playground sports, are at first a mystery to him. As he stands awkwardly under the hoop watching a basketball game swirl around him, the male viewer has a sense of being transported into the worst playground nightmares of inadequacy. This anxiety is redoubled by a sense of loss of something that one has painstakingly gained. The film shows us a forty-year-old man. In fact, it shows us Robin Williams, whom we know as a screen performer capable of great athleticism. We expect him to dominate the game. (One measure of his prowess in *Hook* is an impromptu basketball demonstration, just after he regains the power to fly.) Then the film shows us this man as a hapless ten year old. His character has never had the skills we expect from him. As an adult male, he seems more ominously to have lost them. Of course, he gains (or regains) those skills and does end up dominating the basketball game. But the illusion, once broken, is destroyed. We can never be confident in the prowess of our hero in *Jack*. We have to relearn everything along with him.

In *Hook*, Peter has lost his skills, since the skills that he needs in Never Land are play skills, unsuited to adult competition. He can't fly, he can't fence, he can't crow, and he can't run and play all day, as he needs to do in order to outfight Captain Hook for the possession of his children. Most telling of all in the film's logic, Peter has lost his imagination. When the Lost Boys sit down to a pretend dinner—an element of Barrie's play excluded from other film versions—Peter is at a loss to know what to do. He's hungry, and he cannot enjoy the imaginary meal that the other boys are "eating." Only when he uses his lawyer's skills in the service of play—to win an insult contest started by the Lost Boys' current captain—does he break through the barriers of inhibition. Then, he is able to start a pretend food fight. As always in *Peter Pan,* once you believe in the fantastic, whether it's fairies or food fights, it turns real.

A key factor in *Big* is the inability of the film's adults to believe in magic. The film is magical realist rather than merely fantastic because it maintains a level of plausibility. One can imagine the situation of a suddenly "big" child played for laughs, as in *Vice Versa. Big* denies that possibility. On the morning when he first sees himself as Tom Hanks in the mirror, Josh evades his mother for a little while, doing slapstick routines as he escapes from the house without running into her. We retain the potential for a comic plot, one in which Josh and his family would work around his new status in awkward but endearing fashion. The film quickly demolishes this potential.

When Josh returns to the house in his adult body, his mother (Mercedes Ruehl) does not recognize him and despite his protests believes him to be an intruder bent on attacking her. She defends herself with a kitchen knife while asking Josh where Josh is. He cannot tell her, of course; he scarcely knows where he is himself. The violence of the scene underscores the realist end of the magical plot. *Big* is a world where a sudden confusion of child and adult is not the stuff of whimsical gags, but a descent into terror.

Panic is developed as a theme throughout the following scenes. The only person from his world who accepts Josh as himself is his friend Billy (Jared Rushton). Slightly older than Josh and decidedly the younger boy's mentor, Billy figures that the way to restore Josh to the correct body is to track down the carnival attraction that granted his wish. Since the search will take weeks, Billy finds Josh a room in a Manhattan flophouse. The place is seedy, inhabited by abusive men, prostitutes, and drug addicts. Gunfire is the ground bass of its life. The sight of a grown man and a preteen boy asking for a room doesn't even raise eyebrows there. What comes across as odd is Billy's aplomb in the situation. As the older friend, *he* manages the accommodation. He will steer the search for the carnival, help get Josh his first job, and find him a better apartment when he succeeds in that job.

On that first night in the city, when Billy has to leave Josh in the flophouse, Billy steers him around the place like a seasoned street person. Billy's manner is the bravado of someone almost-thirteen wanting to seem worldly in the eyes of someone still-twelve. Yet the assumption of such bravado by the character played by a child stands in contrast to the nervousness of Josh, the character played by an adult. When Billy strides out into the night and the city, Josh, terrified, pushes a heavy dresser against the door of his room. He lies down on the mattress to cry. One wonders how many thirtysomething business travelers do the same thing, every night, all over America.

Big shifts from pathos into corporate comedy. Josh's mother all but disappears from the picture. Instead of family dynamics, the film focuses on Josh's rise up the corporate ladder. In so doing, *Big* strays into different generic territory, a territory it helped define. It becomes a child-at-heart-executive-transforms-soulless-corporation movie. Within a few years it had been joined by Joel Coen's *The Hudsucker Proxy* (1994), starring Tim Robbins as the child-at-heart executive, and by Barry Levinson's *Toys* (1992), starring, naturally, Robin Williams.

The cultural work of the child-at-heart-executive movie is easier to define than that of the man-becomes-boy picture. Child-at-heart movies take their cue from the ideology of Charles Dickens. They critique corporations as impersonal and profit-driven, but the critique is never an anticapitalist one. Such films suggest that an entire corporation can be redeemed by an executive's rededication to a spirit of community, as Scrooge or Boffin is reformed in Dickens. So, in *The Hudsucker Proxy*, Tim Robbins's infantile faith in the power of circles—the Hula Hoop, the Frisbee—rescues the Hudsucker toy company from cynical mismanagement by Paul Newman. In *Toys*, Robin Williams, a connoisseur of virtual-reality thrill helmets and fake vomit novelties, wrests the Zevo toy company from the mismanagement of his militaristic uncle.

In *Big*, Josh Baskin gets a job with a toy company, that curiously persistent model for American business in late twentieth-century film.[3] Josh rises to power within the firm by being himself, a kid who loves toys. He bonds with the company's crusty founder, MacMillan (Robert Loggia), who is also a child at heart. Josh's actions are consistently childish—he's still twelve—but they register differently in different contexts. He becomes a master of the toy development business, able to predict whether kids will like playing with MacMillan's products or not. At the same time, as the same person, he is tactless socially, embarrassing himself in the famous scene in which he nibbles the kernels off an ear of baby corn and can't bring himself to swallow a caviar canapé. Josh's route to corporate success, like that of Chance the gardener in *Being There* (1979, directed by Hal Ashby) depends on others' fortuitous misinterpretations of his words and actions.

Running through all these scenes of Josh in corporate life is an undercurrent of terror—will people find out that he is a twelve year old? That current is mixed with the sense that he cannot be found out even if he wants to be. In an adult body, Josh is condemned to adulthood—he can act as childishly as he likes but he can never truly be suspected of what Peter Hollindale calls "childness," the condition of being a child, by the adults around him. They misinterpret him, reading him as an innocent adult. As the impostor who cannot be exposed, Josh cannot back out of playing a role for which he realizes he is inadequate. The film offers this experience to the viewer as more than a fantasy. That a viewer can identify with Josh's dilemma underscores the film's cultural argument. *Big* seems to say that men are all really boys and spend time worrying about exposures of their boyishness—exposures that can never really shake the core identity of adulthood. Whoever dies with the most toys wins, says another T-shirt—and it's quite serious.

Panic, in *Big* and in the other films discussed here, is represented in order to be redeemed. These films suggest a conflicted attitude toward the situation of a man fearing to be unmasked as a child. They point to a range of cultural attitudes that are given play but never fully worked out in the logic of their scripts. It is good, for instance, for an adult to behave like a child. Josh helps redeem the toy company and improves the lives of those around him because he is a child at heart. Jack, after years of being taught by a private tutor (Bill Cosby), finds human connections when he is accepted as part of the local treehouse boys' club. Peter rescues his children when he drops the role of corporate pirate and recovers his original refusal to grow up. Individuals, families, and businesses profit from the childishness displayed by apparently grown men.

Childishness is evoked in these films to be put away. At the end of each, the compartments are resealed. Children must never aspire to become adults too quickly. Hollindale notes that "whether by social ritual or life's accidental shocks, some people move from child to adult in one fell swoop. Most do not. There is for most people an intermediate time . . . which used to be called 'youth'" (30–31). The man-to-boy pictures have as a central value the maintenance of the transitional period of youth (American adolescence). They never become growing-up-too-fast movies.

Josh wishes to be a kid again, and is. Alan returns to his own childhood, shedding his adult self. Peter is reintegrated into his adult self, choosing for the second time to grow up and leave Never Land. Jack accepts the maturity of graduation (in his now over-seventy-year-old body). The asymmetric logic of these endings seems to work this way: for a man to recover the disinhibitions of boyhood is good; for a boy suddenly to take on the mantle of manhood is bad. Men get to be better men by rediscovering what it is to be kids. Kids must revert to being kids if they succeed too well at being men. There are no twist endings in these films. Children do not stay on as infiltrators in the adult world, as Chance stays in power at the end of *Being There*. Order is reasserted in the child-to-adult movie.

The boys who become men suddenly in *Jumanji, Jack,* and *Big* all succeed at being men, after initial humiliation. Their core success is sexual, just as Charlie and Marshall work out their success sexually in

Vice Versa. In each of these three films, a just-pubescent boy in an adult male body is first embarrassed and then ultimately successful sexually. *Jack* presents the initial humiliation most clearly. Jack develops a crush on his teacher (Jennifer Lopez) and asks her to a school dance. She refuses, citing the relationship between teacher and student as her primary reason. That justification helps shade the refusal into something quite different. She does not say that she is not attracted to him. Perhaps she shouldn't; who knows? Student teaching probably doesn't cover situations where one's ten-year-old students have forty-year-old bodies. Her affection for him, and the body language she uses in his presence, suggest otherwise. She *is* attracted to him, and only the circumstance of the teacher-student relation keeps her from going out with him.[4]

Jack is irresistible to all the grown women he meets. His best friend's mother (Fran Drescher), tricked into believing that Jack is the school principal, is attracted to him from the moment she meets him. She even bails him out of jail after he's been in a bar fight over her. More disturbingly, Jack is deeply attractive to his own mother (Diane Lane). It's a comic moment early in the film when Jack, ten but forty, leaps into bed between his parents when he's scared one night. It's a bizarre moment later on, when Jack's newfound school friends come to the door of his home. They find his mother playing a sort of laser tag game with him, clearly sexually aroused as she and her "grown" son chase each other around the house. When Jack is depressed, he finds solace by climbing into an old cardboard shipping carton. His mother, when depressed, tends to crawl into the same carton. In a later scene Jack's father crawls in after her and they begin to make love in the shelter she's shared with her son.

Jack gets to have it both ways. It openly presents elements of desire for children that are typically unshown. It shows a teacher's erotic delight in the energy of her young charges, a young mother's excitement in banter with her son's friends, and the desire of a mother for her son. All of these situations of desire are made possible by presenting the boy in the body of a man. At the same time, each situation is made culturally "safe" by use of taboos involving incest and professional relationships. With the Drescher character, for instance, Jack is for almost the whole film ostensibly her son's school principal. They flirt, but they never become involved sexually. Similarly, we can't really imagine that the film will ever show us Jack sexually involved with his mother or his teacher. The picture is a tease.

Because older women desire him, Jack transcends the initial embarrassments of bad judgment that lead to rejection. He's in the wrong place at the wrong time, but his core identity is strongly attractive to women. The film is not articulate about this desirability, however. *Big* much more fully explores the nature of sexual desire within the dynamics of adult-child relationships. As Josh Baskin climbs the corporation in the business comedy subplot, he is pursued sexually by his co-worker Susan (Elizabeth Perkins).

The romantic subplot in *Big* is more fully realized than the one in *Jack*. *Big* avoids *Jack*'s tendency to play the sexually themed scenes for laughs (with Drescher) or for Oedipal fantasy (with Lane). Like *Jack*, *Big* starts its romantic plot with an embarrassment. After the party at which Josh cannot eat the canapés, he goes for a drive with Susan. They return to his apartment. She says she wants to stay the night, and Josh delivers the line that became the film's trademark: "You mean sleep over? OK—but I get to be on top!" . . . of the bunk bed, of course. Hanks's reading of the line is so chipper that it epitomizes every awkward thing that anyone has ever said on a date.

That famous line also signals a shift in the movie's dynamics. "I get to be on top" is distressingly gauche. It's childish even for an innocent twelve year old. It is his home, but he is claiming the better sleeping place rather than offer it to his guest. Yet the brazenness of the remark carries with it a shift in power between Josh and Susan. She has been the sexual pursuer, senior to him in the company, attracted initially by his meteoric rise in the business hierarchy. When he tells her he wants to be "on top," it is, for perhaps the first time in the film, *her* embarrassment and not his that the viewer feels. Susan of course understands the comment as a sexual gambit. She hears Josh expressing desire not just for a sexual position but for control of the budding relationship. She understands him, moreover, as offering a rejoinder to her own sexual forwardness, as if she were the kind of woman who would manage to get "on top" in all senses if she weren't warned off.

Of course, the evening at Josh's apartment is not one of sex, but of play. It's a romp around the furnishings—basketball hoop, trampoline—with which Josh and Billy have decorated the huge studio, as they express their twelve-year-old tastes on a corporate VP's budget. Now Susan is embarrassed. She's unable at first, in her office party clothes, to make much headway on the trampoline. At the end of the night, when they go to bed, the meaning of Josh's initial comment becomes clear, as he comes from the bathroom toward the bed where Susan sits invitingly on the lower bunk—and vaults cleanly into the upper.

She lies there bemused but charmed beyond words. The gaze shifts toward *Susan.* Josh settles in "on top," out of sight. The viewer sees her desire and her lack of balance, her loss of control of the situation. The episode, to a male viewer, is one of the most richly satisfying love scenes in Hollywood cinema. What more could the male viewer want than the desire of a disarmed heroine, tucked into the lower bunk with a glow-in-the-dark compass ring "so she won't get lost"? Rhett Butler never got half so abandoned a look from Scarlett O'Hara.

After that pivotal scene, *Big* segues into conventional romantic comedy. The attraction between Josh and Susan is threatened by pressures at work and by the blocking character Paul (John Heard), the ex-boyfriend who's been displaced by Josh professionally and romantically. The misprisions that have been a source of embarrassment to the adult viewer who identifies with the clueless Josh now start to work to Josh's advantage.

When Josh says to Susan, "You're one of the nicest people I've met," she replies, "How do you do it?" He's stuck for an answer because he has no idea what she means. She means, "How can you be so unassuming, so direct," but there's only one answer to that: he's immature. He stares at her in earnest silence. His wordless gaze seems yet another proof of his maturity. Susan next breaks up with Paul, who asks her, "What is so special about Baskin?" She replies, "He's a grown-up." It's a laugh line that, like so many lines in the film, is resonant far beyond its one-liner status. Susan's remark becomes one of the guiding paradoxes in *Big.*

Josh is a grown-up because he has access to his "inner child." He *is* a child. Susan asks him, during their climactic date, "What were you like when you were younger?" He answers, "Oh, I wasn't much different." "I believe that about you," she says. The dynamic of power that started to tip in Josh's direction during the scene in his apartment shifts back for a moment. Josh is about to confess to Susan that he is really thirteen years old—a near-impossible confession to bring off—but her desire, now palpable, throws him off his aim, and he ends up kissing her.

They make love, tentatively but passionately, and the love scene marks the film as indisputably for adults, not children. It is not so much that the sex is explicit; it is not. Josh touches Susan's breast once, but her breast is never uncovered, and that is as far as the simulated sex goes. But he is *thirteen*. In fact it is his thirteenth birthday. (At this point in watching the picture, my then seven-year-old son, who had seen his share of choreographed love scenes on TV, said, "Yuck! What is he *doing?*" Josh continued to be a *kid* for him all along, and kids don't do that in movies.) The move into a sexual relationship unsettles Josh, though he and Susan are briefly happy. It is at this point that his nostalgia for his (recent) childhood becomes overwhelming.

In giving in to Susan's sexual desire, Josh is not merely "growing up too quickly," however. He—remember that "he" exists in the viewer's identification with him, not independently—is upset by the implications of that desire. To Susan, Josh is a "grown-up." She can also believe that he is like a child. She still wants to go to bed with him. His panic intensifies in the face of a desire so fluid that it refuses to demand chronological rites of passage. Doesn't she recognize any boundaries?

At the same time, of course, the film is twisting toward an emphasis on Josh's power. It becomes less feminist as it goes and more the standard fantasy of sexual power that Mulvey critiques. *Big* too gets to have it both ways. It can assure us men that even as emotional twelve year olds we are irresistible to the gorgeous Elisabeth Perkins. At the same time, it can be deeply sympathetic with our terror about women's lack of emotional boundaries.

This terror comes to a head in a pair of scenes that bracket Billy's discovery of the location of the carnival (and therefore Josh's ticket back to his childhood). As they sit discussing development of a new toy idea, Susan suddenly asks Josh, "What is it we're doing?" Josh doesn't understand her. They're developing a comic book. She tries to ask, obliquely, if they're just having an affair or whether he might be serious about marrying her—an outcome she would clearly prefer. Again, Josh cannot answer. He adopts his typical mode of staring blankly at her and then starts hitting her with a comic book. They wrestle into an embrace on the floor.

Josh's reticence can be read in two ways. To the viewer who knows his real age, he doesn't know what to say because her message is too subtle for him. He can't read the intricacies of adult relationships. To Susan, who assumes that he's thirtysomething, he reads her all too well. If he accepts her gambit, he's caught in adult commitments.

Whatever she's saying, it means he can't be thirteen any more if he stays. Susan accepts and even admires Josh for his childishness. That prevents her from really understanding that he is a child. When he confesses the truth in the second of the two scenes that close their relationship, she continues to take his statements the wrong way. "I'm a child, Susan, and I'm not ready for all of this!" he exclaims; "I'm thirteen years old." She answers in stride: "Oh, and who isn't. You think there isn't a frightened kid inside of me too?" Everything that he tells her about his status as a child is preinterpreted as a statement that any man might make about his own diffidence. Being a child is always an available metaphor for being unable to cope.

Something more significant is at stake here than Josh's desire to reclaim his appropriate role as an early teenager. At stake is an entire culture's investment in constructing boundaries between adults' and children's identities. Josh (and the viewer through him) is momentarily exhilarated to know that a grown-up woman desires him even though he's only thirteen. After that exhilaration comes the terror of thinking that no woman may ever desire him for anything except the exuberance he shows at thirteen. Susan (in all innocence, herself) runs together identities. She accepts Josh as a whole person. But he can't accept himself that way. Some rite of passage, some self-division is necessary for him to claim the role of an adult male. It is unthinkable to him that he can come of age without ever coming of age.

Susan finally lets Josh go. In fact she has no choice. He makes his wish before she can dissuade him. She won't go back to being thirteen herself—she's been through all that growing and doesn't want to try it again.

(Or, maybe, like Peggy Sue, she has always been grown up and has never placed great value on stepping across the threshold of age.) She'll possibly wait for him. It won't be that long before he's twenty-one. But they must part, he to turn small and she to go back to the world of the big. The distinction is maintained.

The distinction between adult and child in *Big* is absolute, a distinction repeated in the other films of the genre. Growth is not an insensible progress along a continuum, but a sudden crossing of a threshold. The terms of the crossing are not just magical, as with Josh Baskin: "I went to bed one night and I was a kid, and when I woke up the next morning I was a grown-up." There is also a sense in which being an adult is a total putting away of childish things—or boyish things, since these transformations are so often male.

The child-adult dichotomy is highlighted by the indeterminate playing of Josh's age in *Big*. One wonders at times whether he's supposed to be thirteen or three. Hanks plays the energy and the moodiness of a new teenager well, whether Josh is thinking about his computer games or his new girlfriend. In some scenes, as when he plays with his food at a lunch counter, he seems to be thirteen, but acting in a deliberately childish way. But Josh does other things that would cause a real thirteen year old to cringe with embarrassment, even if he were safely in the body of someone much older: playing with noisy toy trucks on his office table or keeping huge play balls—the kind that toddlers play with—on his apartment trampoline.

The screenwriters present Hanks with assorted eclectic elements of childhood. Though his performance is resourceful, even he can't blend them into a coherent child. Josh Baskin is Anychild, Everychild, and stands for the tastes and impulses of all children. As embodied by an adult actor, this representative quality is highly suggestive. All the stages of Josh's life, from toddler to adult, meet in the combined experiences and sense memory of the adult actor's body. But as a consistent depiction of the personality of a thirteen year old (granted that no thirteen year old has ever found himself in Josh's situation), the performance fails.

The performance fails suggestively, in the service of maintaining a dichotomy. It is a truism to say that adults are still children, that they still feel like children in their adult bodies. This truism is, like many, often true. One purpose of the social construction of male adulthood is to deny that truth. Psychology of various sorts, clinical and popular, hunts out a man's inner child in order to expel it. We acknowledge the Peter Pan syndrome in order to grow up more effectively. Our self-knowledge may be a continuum, but culture forces us to draw divisions. Children of all ages, back beyond the pale of adulthood, are simply children. Accused of being childish, no adult ever retorts, "Do you mean childish like four? Or childish like twelve? There's a difference, you know."

These films resolve the panic situation, the anomaly of not being sure of one's own age and identity, into a reaffirmation of boundaries between adult and child experience. The child is the necessary complementary term for the adult, the mechanism whereby every adult body can be assured of a status in the social order. That status is defined by laws and privileges. The work of maintaining it is reinforced by the stories and images of popular culture.

Peter Pan remains the keynote of this cultural work. *Hook* is an entry not just in the "Robin Williams" genre, the man-plays-boy movie, but in the collaborative myth of *Peter Pan*. *Hook* intervenes in the Peter Pan myth in order to straighten it out and reclaim it for the corporate nineties. The first straightening that the film does is to recast Peter Pan as a male. It does so even before we know that Robin Williams's character is the "real" Peter Pan. Preoccupied with business cares, Banning watches a school production of *Peter Pan* in which his daughter plays Wendy. Opposite her is a boy playing Peter. It's a small but telling choice of detail. In this film, whatever form Peter Pan assumes, it will not be the form of a woman.

Sexual maturity, as so often in these pictures, is the threshold between childish and adult experience in *Hook*. Peter Banning is Peter Pan, grown up. Far from remembering his former status as the eternal child, Peter has become a "pirate," as Wendy (Maggie Smith) reminds him. He's a cutthroat corporate attorney specializing in hostile takeovers. Peter can't even remember how he turned from Peter Pan into Peter Banning. When he finally does remember, it becomes clear that sexual desire is once again the threshold between staying a child and growing up. On one of his erratic spring-cleaning visits, it seems, Peter Pan had seen a girl in bed at Wendy's house: Wendy's granddaughter, Moira. At that moment he gave up staying a boy and having fun and decided to return to the world, grow normally, and marry Moira. Wendy abetted this plan by pretending that Peter was an everyday orphan and raising him as her ward.

Peter tells this story to Tinker Bell (Julia Roberts) during his own sojourn back in Never Land. He's in crisis. He has failed to regain his skills and win back his children. He originally rolled away in his pram as an infant, he tells Tinker Bell, because he did not want to die. Everyone who grows up must die. The sight of Moira stirred in him a desire specifically sexual, but not specifically directed at Moira except as its conduit: he wanted to become a *father*. Thinking of the joys of being a father, Peter finds his "happy thought" and relearns how to fly.

The logic of this sequence is complicated and in fact circular. To save his children, Peter must become a boy again and learn to fly. He can't fly because he's too old, too inhibited, and can't think lovely thoughts anymore. So he meditates on his own abandonment of childhood, thinks on the sequence of events that made him a parent, and finds the thought that makes him a child again, so that he can become a parent again. It's a bit of a mixed message, even for a Betwixt-and-Between.

The message gets mixed more after Peter starts flying and regains the confidence of the Lost Boys. When he is again able to fly and fight and crow, Peter reassumes the role of Peter Pan. He's Peter Pan as you've never seen him before: fortysomething, virile, six feet tall. Emotionally, he has reverted to the Peter he was before he grew up. He now cannot remember why he's returned to Never Land. He flies off to play with Tinker Bell and asks her excitedly, "Don't we have the greatest adventures?" He now wants to be a little boy again and have fun. His meditations on fatherhood and maturity have vanished. Tinker Bell tries to keep him on task. But it's no use. Able at last to meet the challenges of Never Land, Peter lacks purpose. He cannot integrate the child and the adult in himself. Their needs are incommensurable.

Tinker Bell resorts to a drastic course of action. She transforms herself into a grown woman. (As the fairy, Roberts has played the whole picture to that point in process-shot, shrunk to about six inches high.) Finally standing on the same set as Williams, she looks, as Peter tells

Tinker Bell, "humongous." She explains: "This is the only wish I ever wished for myself. Oh, Peter, this is the biggest feeling I've ever, ever felt . . . this is the biggest feeling I've ever had, and this is the first time I've been big enough to have it." She kisses Peter, passionately. For once, she expresses the desire that Mary Martin's Peter could never understand, that wanting to be something to Peter that isn't his mother. (Or, in effect, she expresses a version of the crush that the Disney cartoon Tinker Bell has on the animated Peter Pan, a crush that that Peter brushes off with preadolescent insouciance.)

The aim of Tink's kiss is hard to define, however. It clearly expresses a real desire, the desire Tinker Bell always implicitly has for Peter Pan but can never enact because the timing has always been wrong: either she's small or he's big or he's a boy or he's a woman or she's a fairy or she's a spotlight or she's a cartoon. Now at last she is Julia Roberts, pretty woman, America's sweetheart. Strategically, the kiss shocks Peter into action. Tactically, it is Tinker Bell's expression of a sexuality that can now be put into play. Peter now has a man's body, and he doesn't want to leave Never Land. He's back on her level of fantasy (or alternative reality). For once, they are both the same size and are both well past puberty.

After the kiss, Peter says simply, "More," but the word leads him to associate: "More . . . Moira. I love Moira . . . And Jack and Maggie." Once kissed, Peter experiences, for an instant, a mirror image of the panic that Josh Baskin feels at greater length, when desired by Susan, the panic that Alan Parrish feels in *Jumanji* when Sarah is about to kiss him. Peter snaps back to adulthood. The boundaries are redrawn. Tinker Bell realizes that she's lost the point, but may have won a different game. Saying wistfully, "When it's all over you'll never come back," she blows fairy dust on Peter and sends him off to rescue his children.

As in *Big*, as in *Vice Versa*, as in all these films, the message returns: you must mesh boy and man to find yourself, and you must immediately separate them again. Mixing boy and man has the potential for power, eroticism, and subversion. The films show us this mixture for a moment and whisk it away. In terms of implied affect—of how they are supposed to appeal to the sentiments of the audience—we are expected to revel for a moment in nostalgia and then to accept the reinforcement of the divide between adult and child.

The sobriety induced by the endings of these films is a powerful cultural statement. It is a reassertion of patriarchy against the sea of confusions of the post-Reagan era. Troubled by all sorts of imaginary cultural attacks that threaten to blend him with the Other and to take away his special status, a white adult man is blended for a moment with that ultimate Other, himself as a boy. He uses the fantastic space provided by this blending to augment his power and emerges a better man than ever. Or a better boy, who will grow into a doubly stronger man. Patriarchy is displayed as the power that adult men have not just over adult women but over children, and especially over boys, those continual threats to replace them in positions of power.

This representation of patriarchy gets a colonial twist in *Jumanji*, as if to load all the nightmares of laying down the white man's burden into one set of images. When he rolls the dice that transport him into the weird areas of the board game Jumanji, Alan Parrish is sucked into "the jungle." This jungle is a patchwork of bits of jungles from all corners of the Western imagination. Not a specific geographical location, the jungle is simply "out there," threatening to break into the peace of a New England village. The jungle is chock-a-block with quicksand, poisonous vines, and Great White Hunters.

The film *Jumanji* follows the Goosebumps formula—two prepubescent children, brother and sister, orphans who are semineglected by their busy guardian, are drawn into the mysterious world of the board game. When they free Alan from his own kind of Never Land, the jungle grabs them too, putting them all in grave danger. An even graver danger, culturally, is posed by the mixing of generations in the world of children's horror. Suddenly, in the territory usually populated by resourceful twelve year olds (as in Goosebumps), there is a grown man, himself a twelve year old, but in a thirty-eight-year-old body.

Alan's expertise, the fruit of his twenty-six years in the jungle, helps Judy and Peter to cope with the irruptions of the Jumanji universe into their lives. But the three of them cannot free themselves from the game without the help of Sarah, the girl with whom Alan had started to play the game twenty-six years before. Sarah (Bonnie Hunt) is now grown, a semirecluse herself since Alan's disappearance back in 1969. She and Alan recommence their relationship where it left off that quarter-century before. In a strange way, Alan and Sarah, adults who are still twelve year olds with respect to each other, supplant the real children in the adventure plot.

Joe Johnston's film of *Jumanji*, then, is a sort of colonization of a children's book. The formula of the preteen heroes left to their own resources is invaded by grown-ups. The original book *Jumanji* by Chris Van Allsburg, which features the two children left completely to their own devices, is taken over by the film's need to place its adults at the heart of the childish adventure. Somehow, *Jumanji* on the big screen would be unthinkable without Robin Williams swinging from vines and wrestling crocodiles.

Neither the rambunctious monkeys nor the stampeding rhinoceroses of the children's book are big enough obstacles for the film's heroic couple. To balance the grown-up heroes of the film, as if to underscore that patriarchy is the real name of this game after all, Johnston provides a blocking character who appears only tangentially in Van Allsburg's book, the hunter Van Pelt. Van Pelt is Alan's nemesis. He carries a huge gun and keeps trying to shoot Alan. Since the rules of Jumanji require the players to finish the game before the jungle horrors disappear, they have to keep rolling the dice. Van Pelt, though he does not directly threaten Sarah, Judy, or Peter, indirectly threatens to strand them in the jungle. Not only will they be stuck there if Alan gets shot, but at one point Van Pelt takes the game box away from them, threatening to take control of this alternate universe from within and seal off all hope of escape. It's a plot twist taken not from Van Allsburg but from assorted holodeck episodes of "Star Trek."

When Van Pelt enters the story, it becomes a "guy" movie. Sarah and Judy are still there, in various states of distress. But the emotional dynamic of the picture wheels around to center on the three males: Van Pelt, Alan, and Peter. Like Captain Hook pursuing Peter Pan, Van Pelt chases Alan across the never land of Jumanji. He's very like Captain Hook, in fact. As in most stage productions of *Peter Pan*, the father and the villain are played by the same actor (Jonathan Hyde). Hyde plays both Van Pelt and Sam Parrish, Alan's father. Back in the film's 1969,

146

Sam was the domineering owner of the town's shoe factory, bent on training his son along the same aristocratic lines he was trained in, hectoring Alan never to back down from a fight. Transformed into the homicidal Van Pelt, Hyde stalks the grown Alan, making him feel, as the board game announces in sinister tones, "just like a child."

In turn, Alan begins to domineer over Peter. *Jumanji* constitutes a nuclear family out of the people who come together during the game. The outcast group of four become parents and children in this provisional family unit (not unlike the embattled scientists and children in Steven Spielberg's *Jurassic Park*). What matters most in this new family is the father-son dynamic. Alan begins to dress down Peter for various failings and is unable to congratulate him for his triumphs. Alan realizes ruefully, "Twenty-six years buried in the deepest darkest jungle, and still I became my father."

Not permanently, of course. Hollywood could hardly turn Robin Williams into an uptight patriarch. As the film resolves itself, he turns into a jolly Dickensian dad, another avatar of George Bailey. (The picture actually ends at Christmas, with Williams in a Santa suit.) At the crucial moment of the game, when Van Pelt has him cornered at gunpoint, Alan faces up to his Oedipal terror and drops the dice, ending the game. Then, he becomes twelve again. The entire "future" (seen from 1969) and "past" (seen from 1995) are wiped clean. Sarah and Alan are back in Sam Parrish's house, the game has set them free, Alan can give Sam a hug, and Sarah can give Alan a kiss, something she had tried to do in the fantastic 1995 that has now become their secret shared "past." She failed then. Alan, still twelve though played by Robin Williams, shied away. Back to twelve again in body, but with a lifetime of experiences "behind" him, he returns her kiss.

They are kids again. In the film's final tableau, they are adults again, in an ameliorated 1995 in which the shoe factory has not been abandoned, in which Alan can distribute largess as the happy patriarch of the town, and in which he and Sarah, long since married, can keep an eye on a new Judy and Peter, whose parents they hire to work in the company in order to save the children from being orphaned.

Of the films I have discussed here, *Jumanji* is in literary terms the most revealing, because it is not an original story. I've said that it "colonizes" a children's story, the picture book *Jumanji* by Chris Van Allsburg. It colonizes a particular genre of children's book that is the latest territory of children's culture to be invaded by Hollywood: the picture book. In this colonization, the film *Jumanji* loads an entire structure of meanings onto the bare space created by Van Allsburg out of gray-scale drawings and a cryptic story. What the film adds to the book—almost everything—reveals by contrast what the book fails to provide—also, almost everything. I will turn next to those great spaces of silences, picture books, in an attempt to read what they pointedly leave out.

Notes

1. *Vice Versa* is not an original idea. The 1988 film is a remake of a 1948 film by Peter Ustinov. The 1977 Disney version of *Freaky Friday* (directed by Gary Nelson) is another precursor. Important, however, here is the cultural need to make *so many* of these films in the late eighties and early nineties.

2. *Big* differs from *Vice Versa*, which has a similar mirror scene, in a telling detail. In both films, the boy in a man's body looks into his shorts to see if he has pubic hair. In *Vice Versa*, Charlie (in Marshall's body) gives a look of satisfaction and begins to swagger. In *Big*, Josh panics and snaps the waistband shut. The moment in *Big* rings truer, if there can be a "true" representation of something so fantastic. Altering the body of the hero has scary consequences in *Big*; it's not just a joy ride.

3. The summer of 1998, for instance, featured another struggle for the soul of toy companies and toy shops in Joe Dante's *Small Soldiers*.

4. The power of this particular fantasy—the attraction between a teacher and her grade school students—is awkwardly represented in Tamra Davis's film *Billy Madison* (1995). A grown man who goes back to grade school on a bet, Billy Madison (Adam Sandler) hits on his third-grade teacher, Veronica Vaughan (Bridgette Wilson), who at first rejects him. Later she begins a sexual relationship with him, for no apparent reason except to fulfill the fantasy of a boy making it with his third-grade teacher. Somehow it is crucial for grown men, fantasizing that they are boys again, to carry into that fantasy a corresponding fantasy of sexual potency and attractiveness.

7

AMBIGUITIES:
PICTURE BOOKS FOR THE VERY YOUNG

Turning from Joe Johnston's film of *Jumanji* to Chris Van Allsburg's 1981 book, one is struck by how little is on the pages. Almost none of the plot and character framework of the film is found in Van Allsburg's book. In the book, Judy and Peter have parents. The parents go out to the opera one night. Judy and Peter find the board game and begin to play. Strange things happen. A lion, some monkeys, and some rhinoceroses appear. But there is no plot similar to the Alan/Van Pelt plot in the movie. There is no Alan, no Sarah, and only a brief suggestion of Van Pelt.

The book takes up just fourteen pages of large-print text, each one facing a full-page plate in black and white. The film's screenplay is an interpretation in every sense. In this interpretation, *Jumanji* undergoes a transformation. Its key elements are given histories and motivations. We still don't know *how* the game accomplishes its magic, but we learn the interpersonal dramas surrounding Judy, Peter, their aunt, their house. We know Alan's family romance. We see the career trajectory of the shoe-designer-turned-cop who tries to cope with the crisis in the town. We know that there *is* a town, a community absent from Van Allsburg's book, where it is suggested merely by the presence of a park, the mention of an opera, and the appearance at the end of a Mrs. Budwing and her two sons (who become the next players of the game). In Johnston's film, everything is explained for us.

There's something backwards here. On the one hand, the transformation of *Jumanji* is easily accounted for. The book is a picture book for primary-grade children; it's short, literally sketchy. The film tries to appeal to older children, adolescents, and adults. The need to flesh out a scanty plot to feature-film length accounts for the new elements in its adaptation to the screen.

On the other hand, why should the filmmakers need to add so many explanatory devices to a children's book? It makes sense that the children's story can allow rhetorical elaboration. We can always expand, qualify, and spin out elements of a children's story, introduce new characters, and whip up new subplots. It makes less sense, though, to see a children's story as something needing a clearer *explanation* to an adult audience. Shouldn't a book for little kids be easy to understand? We think of adult themes as needing explanation to children, not the other way around. At work here is an imperative of interpretation that also accounts for elements in the film adaptations of *Black Beauty, The Secret Garden,* and *Shiloh.*

The book *Jumanji* makes several refusals to explain itself. We don't know where the game comes from. We don't know the characters' histories. We don't know the relation of the disastrous events within the game to the history that the characters are living. The game may be hallucinatory, real, magical, or deliberately imagined. The nature of the game in the film is the subject of lots of conflicted talk. The impact of the game on Judy and Peter in Van Allsburg's book is impenetrable. The book is ambiguous.

Yet it is a children's book. What else could it be? A large-format (25 by 28 centimeters) illustrated book, *Jumanji* is found in the children's section, is described on its dust cover as the author's "second book for children," and is the winner of a major prize for children's book illustration, the Caldecott Medal. Yet the mysteriousness of the book marks it as an exception to the canons of children's literature as prescribed by some theorists.

Nicholas Tucker, in his study of how children read literature, *The Child and the Book,* says that ambiguity and the younger reader don't mix. Books for the very young, says Tucker, must be clear-cut:

The next stage, when it is possible to hold two contradictory, abstract ideas together in one concept, such as the notion of a good-bad character, or an act that may be positive and negative in its implications, will generally have to wait until most children are at least around the age of eleven.

It follows, therefore, that younger children will not on the whole welcome ambiguity into their literature. (9)

Tucker's observation is drawn from solid premises in developmental psychology. Its inspiration is Piagetian, though the great Swiss developmental psychologist Jean Piaget had little to say about children's literature. Tucker's contention is that children's appreciation of books develops in Piagetian stages, from the ability to comprehend clear moral lessons and distinct narrative situations to a greater ability to deal with moral subtlety, narrative complexity, and situational uncertainty.

Whether children welcome ambiguity into their literature or not, a text like *Jumanji* suggests that ambiguity is already there. Granted that the ambiguity of *Jumanji* is less moral than situational, more a matter of a surreal confusion of boundaries than a moral graying of issues, the book is still unclear, even morally. Is it a good thing for Judy and Peter to leave the game for the Budwing children to play, without warning? Maybe, maybe not.

The classic picture books of the twentieth century in the United States are masterpieces of ambiguity and terseness. In their unwillingness to communicate unequivocally, many picture books are sites for the exploration of power and desire. The books that I discuss here are by several canonical children's writers: Dr. Seuss, Arnold Lobel, Maurice Sendak, and Margaret Wise Brown. I assemble these picture books not to make any grand generalization about the nature of the picture book. Picture books have generated their own body of theory, as in the work of Perry Nodelman. The books I treat here have had a cumulative effect on me as I've read them to children over the years and have shown me how complex the treatment of desire is in children's culture.

I read these books because the classic children's book is just as much addressed to adults as to children. Books like *Goodnight Moon* and *Green Eggs and Ham* are rarely read by children alone as "first readers." These texts *seem* elementary, but they are not really reading primers. By the time a child can read *Goodnight Moon*—barely over 120 words, only about 60 different words in all, but some of them difficult—he or she will have already reached a more sophisticated verbal level than the one represented by the simple concepts and phrases of that text. A child will likely read alone texts that are more complex than *Goodnight Moon* first, return to it, but find it too easy.

These books are therefore rarely experienced first by children who actually "read it all by themselves," as the Beginner Books motto proclaims. Seuss's Beginner Books are initially experienced, as Lynn Atkinson points out to me, by an adult and child reading together as a unit. This realization parallels Ellen Handler Spitz's concept of "conversational reading": "the interactive participation of adults in children's cultural experience" (xiv). The implied address is multiple and brings together different levels of reader. It is not that either adult or child is addressed at the expense of the other or that one is taking in different things than the other can understand or that the natures of these two addresses, as in Barbara Wall's formulation, are necessarily somehow opposed. The whole reading experience, which governs the rhetorical form of the text, is collaborative.

Picture books, because they include adult readers, often appeal to adults long after the context of reading them as, or to, children has disappeared. Adults frequently tell me that they cry while reading *Goodnight Moon*. I doubt that nostalgia lies behind this kind of affective response. These books affect adults powerfully because they are powerful texts. I put this tautologically in order to blur the distinction between a text that might affect an adult only via memory or kitsch sentimentality and a simply powerful poem like *Goodnight Moon* that has the potential to affect adults and children differently, but with comparable intensity.

My concern in this chapter will be with the texts of picture books, and only tangentially with their illustrations. While text and picture undeniably function as an artistic whole, my primary experience of these books was as an oral interpreter of language. My enduring interest is in the text of these books as a type of modern poetry. My approach is partial, but it is that of a parent who reads aloud—a crucial interpreter of these books. I spent much of my early thirties as an oral interpreter, for example, of verse by Dr. Seuss.

Dr. Seuss is a touchstone in my classes on poetry and literary theory. He's good for a laugh, to deflate pretensions, to serve as a contrast to esoteric texts and approaches. He marks a stoutly defended barricade of the literary, a barricade constructed voluntarily by students struggling to gain cultural prestige. Seuss is silly. Everyone knows that Seuss is silly. He is a byword for the frivolously childish. When my students compare a modernist poet to Seuss, they are saying that the poet is puerile. Conversely, and from quite the other direction, to suggest that a critical approach should be applied to Seuss is to suggest the sterility of that approach. Seuss thus becomes the bastion of common sense against the navel-gazing of literary theory. He is the malleable common ground we all share, at least in American culture. Dr. Seuss is the artist everyone can understand, the writer who is easy, the artist that truly difficult art must transcend, the artist whose transparency mocks the hermeneutics of the literary interpreter. He is also the good guy writer beyond whose simplicity all else is really pretension.

Seuss, in commentary on his work, is simply zany. Clifton Fadiman claims that Seuss "aims to create nothing more than what meets the eye or ear" and that Seuss supplies "oddity instead of wholesome instruction, wild humour instead of mere pleasantness" ("Professionals" 320, 322). Introducing the collection *Six by Seuss*, Fadiman characterizes Seuss's language as "jingly-jangly," sees him as a master of "the wild, the grotesque, even the mildly lunatic," and pictures him figuratively "whacking with the slapstick of comic fantasy the backside of whatever is stuffy or overinstructive or mannered or self-consciously whimsical" ("Introduction" 6, 8). Or, to quote a more portentous commentator, Jonathan Cott: "Imagination and play are at the basis of all our hope" (37). In reading Dr. Seuss we find imagination and play at their purest. Such poetry exists, as W. H. Auden put it, "in the valley of its own making / Where executives would never want to tamper."

Executives, indeed, tampered with Dr. Seuss at their own risk. As Judith Morgan and Neil Morgan show in *Dr. Seuss and Mr. Geisel*, Seuss, during his lifetime, was a law unto himself at Random House, especially after the founding of the Beginner Books imprint. In becoming an independent creative force, Seuss became an executive, too. Toward the end of his career, Alison Lurie argues, Seuss equated happiness, in books like *Oh, the Places You'll Go* (1990) "with wealth, fame, and getting ahead of others" ("Cabinet" 79).

Implicit in the way that Lurie deplores Dr. Seuss's Reagan-era celebration of entrepreneurship is her recognition that Seuss's earlier work was liberal, even occasionally leftist in its sympathies. Lurie explicitly points to the progressive nature of the earlier Seuss: the anti-authoritarianism of "Yertle the Turtle," the integrationist message of "The Sneetches." Seuss, it appears, has a political impact, but that impact is simplistic and easily suppressed when it is more convenient to think of his work as politically *degagé*. As one of the more overtly political of the classic children's writer-illustrators, Seuss helps mark one boundary of the extent to which picture books are usually politicized. However, even at this extreme, in trying to fix the political reference of a Seuss book, one keeps finding that the book itself comes to operate as a great empty signifier, shedding meanings as quickly as one can attach them.

What, for instance, is the oobleck in Seuss's *Bartholomew and the Oobleck* (1949)? This question really asks what the book means, because the book is all about attitudes toward oobleck. Sick of the same four things always falling out of the sky—rain, sunshine, fog, and snow— King Derwin of Didd demands that his magicians create a new kind of weather for him. Bartholomew Cubbins, who first encountered the king in *The Five Hundred Hats of Bartholomew Cubbins* (1938), is horrified: "Your *magicians*, Your Majesty? . . . Oh, no, Your Majesty! Don't call *them!*" (7) but the king persists. He asks the magicians for a new kind of weather, to "make something fall from my skies that no other kingdom has ever had before" (8). The magicians promise to make "oobleck"—but they cannot explain exactly what "oobleck" might be.

The magicians retreat to the Mystic Mountain Neeka-Tave, where they mutter spells all night. (Presumably they are the same magicians who were incompetent to remove Bartholomew's hat in *The Five Hundred Hats*, but this failure has been forgotten by everyone but Bartholomew.) The next morning, oobleck begins to fall. It is a green sticky substance. Oobleck is like no kind of weather ever seen, and King

Derwin is delighted. Yet as the oobleck falls thicker and faster, it clogs things up: the royal trumpeter's instrument, the hoes and plows of farmers, the royal cook's kitchen gear. It even sticks the king to his throne, until Bartholomew shames him into admitting that he has made a mistake, and the king says, "I'm sorry" (44). At that moment, the oobleck melts away.

Given the date of the book, 1949, it makes strong historicist sense to identify the oobleck as radioactive fallout. A king (the American government) becomes dissatisfied with the weather (conventional warfare) and appoints a team of magicians (the Manhattan project) to create something new (the atomic bomb). The magicians retreat to a mountain fastness (Los Alamos) and produce oobleck (the bomb) but the results (radioactive contamination) threaten to destroy society. Since this is a children's fantasy, the whole episode is wished away by the person responsible (the president?).

Or is the oobleck something else? Sperm, milk, food, flesh, snot, Silly Putty? Is it (as Maggie Dwyer suggests to me) that stuff inside of lava lamps? Seuss attributed oobleck to a remark he overheard in France in 1944: an American serviceman complaining, "Rain, always rain! . . . Why can't we have something different for a change?" (Morgan and Morgan 122). The genealogy of oobleck starts in an absurd remark, the wisecrack of a soldier trying to imagine a new kind of weather. Oobleck is so far beyond the ordinary that it fails to fit into any structure of mimetic signs. Seuss emphasized this uncanny nature of the oobleck in his design scheme, eschewing pink and purple tones as too much like flesh or blood. He finally decided to make the oobleck a dusty green color—the only color that appears in an otherwise black-and-white book (Morgan and Morgan 123). Oobleck looks like nothing on earth.

Therefore, oobleck looks like anything one might want it to be. In the dynamics of the story, it is the object of Lacanian desire, as Slavoj Zizek might define it. The oobleck stands, for King Derwin, as the *objet petit a,* "the void of that unattainable surplus that sets our desire in motion. . . . Desire is by definition caught in a certain dialectic, it can always turn into its opposite or slide from one object to another, it never aims at what appears to be its object, but always 'wants something else'" (134). The king cannot define his desire. His desire comes to light only as a pure signifier, the meaningless word *oobleck*. Once his desire is attained, he doesn't want the oobleck anymore. Once he renounces this object of his desire, it disappears. It's the obscure object indeed, this oobleck.

King Derwin demands a nameless desire. Perhaps the magicians, obeying his demand, "carry out the operation of changing this precious gift into a gift of shit" (129), as Zizek puts it, paraphrasing Lacan. For, as Lurie notes, in requital of his desire for a new kind of weather, the king "gets a sticky, smelly substance which, though it appears as green, is clearly excrement ('you're sitting in oobleck up to your chin')" ("Cabinet" 74). The oobleck appears as a "disgusting, meaningless fragment of the real" (Zizek 129).

Ted Geisel himself was amused by the readings of literary critics. "Dr. Seuss as icon yielded theses, dissertations, and book chapters, some so pretentious that Ted was appalled" (Morgan and Morgan 214). In the work of Dr. Seuss, the children's nonsense book becomes a deflector of meaning. Any meaning ascribed to the text can be dismissed as pretentious. The armor is doubly layered. Within the text are images impervious to the imposition of meaning. The text is further shielded by its generic assignment to the category of nonsense. The oobleck is everything, nothing, *objet petit a;* but when we come to define it as *objet petit a,* we find that it can't even be that. To define the oobleck as the obscure object of desire is too pretentious. So the green stuff and the text that surrounds it become insulated from even the vaguest attempts to tie them down to signification. The children's book, finally, escapes the hermeneutic circle and oozes away, as free (and as sticky) as oobleck.

Seuss books like *The Lorax* (1971) and *The Butter Battle Book* (1984), with their obvious indictments of polluters and arms race hawks, drew fire from critics for their explicit and undisguised polemics (Morgan and Morgan 211, 254–55). The more obscure earlier books that point toward political engagement, like *Horton Hears a Who* (1954), were more readily suffered, because they are less referentially fixed. *Horton Hears a Who* is dedicated to a Japanese friend of Geisel and is obliquely an attack on dehumanizing prejudices toward the Japanese. But it might also be a statement against prejudices about black people, the working class, immigrants, women, even children themselves. It becomes a generalized liberal-humanist message. "Reading" its political statement becomes synonymous with "reading too much into it," a practice that can be disavowed when necessary. When one ceases to "read too much," the text can return to the realm of inactivated fantasy.

The meaning of Dr. Seuss is ostensibly transparent. Or it is nonexistent. The text is something to play with, not to be fixed. Or the text is an enclosed modernist object. As in Archibald MacLeish's "Ars Poetica," it "should not mean / But be." Or Seuss is Umberto Eco's "open text," the aesthetic object that stays ambiguous, inviting a suspension of judgment. Therefore not just the "meaning" of Seuss, in E. D. Hirsch's sense of authorial intention, but also its "significance," in Hirsch's sense of cultural importance, is at issue. The text may not have a Hirschean meaning, particularly if its author, like Dr. Seuss, ascribes the intention behind the work purely to whimsy. With meaning absent, significance also becomes problematic, because the text lacks both internal and external authorities on which critics can ground significances.

In the rest of this chapter, I choose books that trace my own reading experiences of picture books I met and became involved with as an adult. I work backward toward the most minimal possible use of text and finally to the almost abjuring of text. I see in the books I've chosen here a desire for an open affective situation, for the maximum resonance of the minimal text.

Leonard S. Marcus quotes Margaret Wise Brown, writing to a friend for guidance in word choice: "I wallow in uncertainty about punctuation, wording, and form. Whether I should use *If you become I will become*, or *If you are I will be* or mix them both up so that the rythm [sic] gets broken from page to page and isn't too soporific, or what is consistancy [sic] and what makes the best poetry. . . . Which is stronger the sense of a line or the meaning" (150). The book whose problems incited this letter is *The Runaway Bunny* with pictures by Clement Hurd. *The Runaway Bunny* would not appear to have made Flaubertian demands on the perfectionism of the writer. But the crafting of this book cost Brown tremendous effort because of the stakes involved. She wanted to convey the maximum affective impact through the minimum means.

In the works of Brown, Seuss, Sendak, and Lobel, I see a desire to achieve direct contact with a child too young to respond articulately, perhaps too young to respond in language. Language, in *Goodnight Moon* or *Green Eggs and Ham,* is purged away. Language is reduced to its elements by impulses partly pedagogical and partly aestheticist. I think that Brown and Seuss, in particular, work to increase the aesthetic rationale at the expense of pedagogy, despite the fact that both were active in early-learning programs. When we see Brown struggling with the cadences of *The Runaway Bunny,* she does not ask herself how best to present a vocabulary set or convey a mathematical concept but, "what makes the best poetry"?

One Fish Two Fish Red Fish Blue Fish (1960) is perhaps the clearest example of the aestheticist impulse in Seuss's Beginner Books. The Beginner Books started with *The Cat in the Hat* (1957), an attempt to create a basal reader that would be more interesting than the Dick and Jane series. The key element of Beginner Books was a curtailed vocabulary—250 words in the case of *The Cat in the Hat,* an astonishing 50 words in *Green Eggs and Ham* (1960). An even simpler version of Beginner Books, the Bright and Early series, had its inspiration in *Hop on Pop* ("the simplest Seuss for youngest use"), a phonics-based collection of simple phrases and sentences from 1963.

One Fish stands somewhere in the middle of this group. A collection of poems rather than a unity, a menagerie rather than a narrative, a sequence of one-liners built around nonsense words for nonsense animals, *One Fish* is neither reader nor phonics text. Neither is it a trickster fable like *The Cat in the Hat* or *Green Eggs and Ham.* It lacks the narrative conventions that would produce coherent meaning. The keynote to the book is that " funny things are everywhere" (2). The governing principle here, as in Seuss's "big books" *If I Ran the Zoo* (1950) and *On beyond Zebra* (1955), is that of carnival.

One Fish starts with fish, as the title proposes. There are a lot of fish. They come in all shapes and sizes and do extraordinary anthropomorphic things, like the fish in *McElligott's Pool* (1947). Then on page 9 the fish motif is suddenly dropped. The refrain sounds for the first time. The book's guiding characters appear, a boy and a girl. They are drawn in nearly identical manner. Only the girl's ponytail, held in place by a ribbon, distinguishes her gender from that of the short-haired boy.

"Fish" cede to "things." The boy and girl watch many things go by. The things are people, perhaps. Perhaps they are animals. Most likely these creatures are Betwixt-and-Betweens. Some can do stuff, others are useless. All are fabulous, and the little boy and girl seem to have an intimate relation to them, one of knowledge and of power. No human adult is pictured, only a collection of Nooks and Goxes and Gacks.

These child protagonists are so spare, so generic. Compare them to the heroine of Ludwig Bemelmans's *Madeline* (1939) and note how little we know about them. Madeline is a wealthy convent school girl in Paris with real-life tastes and a definite size (she is "the smallest one"). She has a named adult teacher and doctor. The Seuss children, however, are unnamed, stripped of detail. Increasingly throughout Seuss's career, his protagonists are drained of socially identifying features and become approximations to the pure liberal subject. They are like Goose-bumps characters in their tendency toward the default-value, but Seuss's protagonists are even more stripped of identity. In their half-fusion with animals, some Seuss heroes, as in *Green Eggs,* become perfect neutral vessels for representing your average American. They are like Beethoven or other movie dogs, perfectly absorbent identities.

Anybody can read themselves into these kids. When Lurie says that "the typical Seuss hero is a small boy or a male animal" ("Cabinet" 75), her point is, selectively, true enough. From Marco to Bartholomew to Gerald McGrew, the "I" of the Seuss books is a boy. But he is an I increasingly drained of markings of gender distinction or privilege. By the point reached in *The Cat in the Hat,* though the I is still a boy, he narrates in the first person plural, speaking for his sister too. "Sally and I" becomes the plural narrator of *The Cat* books, equal partners in the illustrations. (I do recognize, however, the frequent silence adopted by Sally on major issues and her pronounced lack of leadership on the spot-removal problem.)

Gender does not disappear from *One Fish.* The protagonists reflect gender stereotypes. The boy boxes the Gox; the girl brushes and combs the hair of her blue-haired pet. In most things, though, they are partners or interchangeable. They share unisex dress and equal mastery of the technologies of fun. The boy and girl of *One Fish* are part of the same dynamic that constructs Sam-I-Am, the androgynous central character of *Green Eggs and Ham.* Tim Wolf describes this unisex dynamic in Seuss's later work: "Although I believe females could read beyond the specifically male characters in Seuss's first three books [*And to Think That I Saw It on Mulberry Street* (1937), *The Five Hundred Hats of Bartholomew Cubbins* (1938), and *The King's Stilts* (1939)] to make an androgynous identification . . . the readers of *Green Eggs and Ham* are even more free to view Sam as male or female or both" (154). Or neither. These books speak for an ideology that is both compelling and at the same time oddly detached from necessity. They seem to say that the younger we are, the less constrained we are, the more plastic and malleable. Here is a classical liberal dynamic. Dr. Seuss tries to become the first person to put chalk to the collective American tabula rasa. The unformed child is the perfect audience for his art.

The generic child in the Seuss canon, far from erasing social dynamics, encodes them again with more at stake. As Seuss characters shed ethnicity, class, gender, color, and even humanity (*and* animality) to become just "things," they appeal to a swath of hyphenated and assimilated Americans. They are a neutral middle ground into which we can read any American identity. The American subject is unmarked in Seuss's texts, and therefore capable of anything, especially having fun. All it takes is your own determination to do so, no matter who you are.

The dominant theme of *One Fish* is "fun," a fun that the boy and girl rehearse over and over. They move through a milieu in which the "things" that parade through the book's pages are harnessed as domestic animals, toys, or entertainments. When the book opens, the things that go by are "funny." The children are spectators. As *One Fish* progresses, the things become servants that feed the kids' appetite for "fun," now coded as an activity rather than a quality. (To see the distinction between the activity and the quality of fun, think of the Cat in the Hat's phrase "lots of good fun that is funny.") And so, the thing Mike sits on the back of a three-seater bike and pushes the pair uphill when it gets steep (22–23). The enormous hoofed Zans allows its horns to be used as can openers (36–37). The Ying provides harmony for singing in the shower (40–41). The Gack sits patiently as the children play ring-toss with its antlers as targets (58–59).

Entwined with these images of pressing "things" into the service of "fun" are other images and texts that stress exclusive knowledge. Although early on Mr. Gump allows many different children to bump on the humps of his Wump (18–19), later in the text the curiousness of these creatures works more to the exclusive advantage of the protagonists. The boy and girl encourage the reader to identify with their privilege and their expertise. They deride a Nook, who tries to use a cookbook but fails because he cannot read (31). They approve of quiet things and expel noisy ones (34–35). They assert control over their domestic spaces, taming the carnival. They prescribe things for every home—every home should have a Zans, a blue-haired combing pet (46), a Yink who drinks pink ink (42–43). They use a language that comes to resemble, perhaps to parody, the rhetoric of advertising. Every home needs one. If you get one first, you will "have the only / Gack in town" (58).

The insistence of the pair on access to fun becomes more strident as the book goes on, leading to a climax (50–51). The boy and girl ask if "you," the reader, have ever done some outlandish things: flying a kite while in bed, walking with ten cats on a board balanced on your head, milking a grotesque Seussian cow. They conclude that one should do such things because "fun is good" (51). The children confront the reader, their noses in the air, their eyes closed, slightly dowdy in the unisex attire that takes on preppie-weekend-wear overtones as the book goes along. They are the picture of smugness and self-satisfaction. "Fun" has shifted from the register of a carnivalesque assemblage of crazy animal types, wildly following their individual drives, to the patience of the animals who are processed into consumer fetishes.

Fun may be good, the reader wants to protest, but can I afford "this kind of cow?" Let alone a Zans for cans. The children's management of the world of play has its foundation in an access to the stability of an economic order, an order defensible because (and perhaps *only* because) of the amusement it lavishes on its children. One can become uneasy, then, in the presence of the "Clark" episode cited by Alison Lurie as one of the best examples of Seuss's advocacy of "the free-ranging imagination." The children find a grotesque Seussian monster called "Clark" and take him home. Clark is a gigantic sea mammal, impossibly pressed into an glass ampule full of water, scarcely bigger than himself. It must weigh tons, but the boy and girl effortlessly trot home with it against the dark of the night sky, preparing to climb what looks like a huge flight of steps, presumably into their house. They cannot be repressed. The only possible damper on their enjoyment might be a parsimonious mother unwilling to cede house room to their new pet.

Yet as Clark bubbles up out of the crepuscular imagination of the children, he brings questions of power and knowledge with him from the deep. We imagine this mother, off the margin of the page, as oppressive. But like all such mothers in Seuss, she is oppressive only in theory. She never appears to enforce her oppressions. Meanwhile, though she may balk at Clark, she has underwritten the furnishing of the house with a Zans, a Gack, a boxing Gox, and a cycling Mike. These kids have everything. Their mother rubs the children's noses in their own imaginations, challenging them to produce fantasies she'd be unwilling to fulfill. Like the mother in *The Cat in the Hat* and *The Cat in the Hat Comes Back,* she abandons the field to her kids, letting them wreak the utmost in ludic havoc on the place, with only one condition: that her indulgence be suspected of having strict limits.

Fun, in *One Fish Two Fish Red Fish Blue Fish,* is an uneasy proposition. It is manic and prodigal on the one hand. The world of the imagination is staffed by the likes of Ish, who will wish for fish and make them suddenly appear on a dish (56–57). On the other hand, play centers on a fulfillment of consumer fantasies that is not only acceded to, but promoted by, detached and distant parents. (Such parents are the precursors of the equally detached Goosebumps parents.) The fun of carnival seems to slide into the kind of mandatory fun endorsed by the organizers of corporate picnics. You "should" have this kind of fun; "fun is good."

One Fish is nonsense. Its affect is open, its animals and "things" fantastic, its signifiers impossible to fix. Yet as a whole, as aesthetic object, it serves as a kind of talisman that an adult gives to a child in order to sanction a certain exercise of the child's imagination as proper. This book may be seen as an intervention into the imagination of early childhood—an imagination that the Beginner Books generally *create* as much as they *address,* of course.

Is Dr. Seuss liberating for children? Is he an anarchist of the nursery? In many senses, he is. Rupert the Bear would never have brought home Clark, if he had found him in the dark. It is difficult to imagine the well-mannered denizens of Richard Scarry books doing things half as wild as the Seuss children manage to do. Far from training children with decorous iambic lessons, Dr. Seuss injects an anapestic kitschiness into their earliest literary tastes. While it's silly to "blame" Dr. Seuss for the sexual revolution and the drug culture of the 1960s, one senses that the head shop T-shirts that show the Grinch holding a margarita or smoking a joint are not far from his own intentional biases. On the overtly political level, his progressive statements outweigh his reactionary ones—or at least balance them. The misogyny of *Horton Hatches the Egg* (1940) is countered by the human rights stand of *Horton Hears a Who*. Ted Geisel was a liberal hero of the twentieth century who got a little conservative in the 1980s—well, didn't we all. There is nothing necessarily oppressive about his work.

Yet there is also the status of Beginner Books themselves as commodities, the relentless marketing of them book club style, the sample copies in pediatricians' waiting rooms, the direct mail ads. These initiatives were part of Random House strategy while Geisel himself still controlled the imprint of Beginner Books. Since his death, the culture industry devoted to Seuss has intensified and proliferated, with a TV show ("The Wubbulous World of Dr. Seuss"), many new marketing and franchising agreements, and Seuss characters showing up as everything from soft toys to jam jars. This is liberation, but liberation under corporate control. Like Mick Jagger in the telecommunications ad wailing, "You can't always get what you want" and being answered by the chirpy company motto "Yes you can," the anarchism of Dr. Seuss ceased to be fantasy as soon as it left his drawing board and entered into a complicated exchange of power and money.

The work of writer-illustrator Arnold Lobel is less commodified. He established his position during his lifetime without becoming the source of much of a spin-off industry—so far, at any rate. Like Seuss, Lobel produced some of his work for a reader series, HarperCollins's I Can Read books. Like Seuss's, Lobel's beginner fables are nondidactic and ambiguous. Regret, nostalgia, and desire stretch thinly but tenaciously over Lobel's tales of slapstick and animal follies. In these books, we see the expression of things uneasily put into words, a sense that fun must be balanced by thoughts of temporality and the constraints that the body places on desire.

Heady themes, you are thinking, for preschool readers. Yet Lobel's Frog and Toad series offers an analogue, for the youngest readers, to the situation that Kenneth Grahame's *Wind in the Willows* (1908) presents to young adults. *The Wind in the Willows* is a children's book about the voicing of desire. Grahame, like Lobel, treats the devoted friendship that two anthropomorphic—and amphibious—animals bear each other. George Shannon documents the influence of Grahame's work on Lobel and demonstrates many parallels between their works (101–4). Lobel's achievement, like that of Grahame, assumes that child readers can grasp, and be affected by, subtle and understated themes. Or perhaps one should say that Lobel exploits the complex situation of the children's book in order to approach the themes that matter strongly to both kids and adults.

Lobel's early readers are story collections. Frog and Toad, the friends of four books in the I Can Read series, have several adventures in each of their sixty-page-long books. *Grasshopper on the Road* (1978) has a journeying hero, *Owl at Home* (1975) one that stays at home, but each has a series of adventures. I will focus here on two collections of stories about mice, *Mouse Tales* (1972) and *Mouse Soup* (1977). These collections combine the two impulses in Lobel's other work—a desire for adventure and a return to stasis.

Lobel's work is suffused with fables. George Shannon stresses Lobel's connections to Aesop and other sources of classic fables, and indeed Lobel's major work is the Caldecott Medal book *Fables* (1980). But fables can have many directions, from moralism to satire to surrealism. Shannon looks at the two mouse volumes as pure escapism: "*Mouse Tales* and *Mouse Soup* are the epitome of Lobel's perception of nonsense humor as the primary song of Arcadia. As he tells his tales of absurdity, Lobel echoes the burlesque and comic songs of Victorian England in laughing for laughter's sake rather than as social critique" (122). In particular, Shannon cites "The Journey" and "The Bath," from *Mouse Tales*, as "examples of reductio ad absurdum" (118). Pure fantasy in each case, these tales seem to be throwaways even within a fanciful collection of stories. But the tone of the book is at its darkest just when Shannon announces that it is meaningless.

"The Journey" is, indeed, a bit of a shaggy-dog (or shaggy-mouse?) story. A mouse is desperate to visit his mother. He will use any means necessary to get to her house. He drives his car until it breaks down, wears out pairs of roller skates, boots, and sneakers, and finally wears out his own feet. Whereupon he buys a new pair of feet and walks the rest of the way to his mother's. She says: "Hello, my son. You are looking fine—and what nice new feet you have!" (*Mouse Tales* 47).

Does this mother keep receding as one draws closer to her, or has the hero of the story seriously miscalculated the length of his journey? Unlike the pursuing mother in Brown's *Runaway Bunny*, who matches every transformation her child proposes, this mother outwaits—or outwits—a variety of shape-shiftings on her son's part. The story is presented with tiny illustrations within the lines of text, so that we see graphically the course of the transformations. Only the final illustration, a small circle encompassing mother and son, breaks out of the lines of the text. The mother waits at the end of the tale in a circular home that the hero cannot penetrate without mutilating himself. For that is what he does. The punchline of the story is a throwaway. Very young children can appreciate the absurdity of the hero's putting on a new pair of feet at the end of a sequence of replacing the replaceable parts of himself. But any child, and perhaps still more the collaboratively reading adult, may be taken aback for a moment by the hero's desire to cut off his own feet to see his mother and by his mother's relative indifference to the sacrifice. Like Roald Dahl's mother unemotionally contemplating the removal of his adenoids, this mouse mother is an affective mystery.

The mother in "The Journey" is a type of Edward Lear's Aunt Jobiska, the cheerful relative who celebrates the Pobble's pointless crossing of the Bristol Channel by announcing, "It's a fact the whole world knows, / That Pobbles are happier without their toes" (244). Yet the Pobble in "The Pobble Who Has No Toes" starts with a concern about missing extremities and keeps fretting over them and compensating for their loss. The mouse in "The Journey" just suddenly amputates them. The mouse's mother in "The Journey" hugs and kisses him, but she is a cold parent compared to Aunt Jobiska, who cooks the Pobble eggs and buttercups and fusses over him. Just beneath the surface of "The Journey" is the sense that one must make great sacrifices even for a routine hug and kiss.

Danger is also present in "The Bath." Added is a sense of moral anomie. A mouse who is dirty takes a bath. He is so dirty that he keeps washing and washing, letting the water run and run, until the whole town is flooded and the other mice are clinging to the rooftops of their homes. "By then the town was all wet. But the mouse did not care. He rubbed himself with a big towel until he was very dry. And then he went right to sleep" (*Mouse Tales* 61).

"The Bath" is another piece of (literally) free-floating imagination. It is set in a community without mutual responsibilities. The bather plays the role, there, of moral infant. He sees only his own needs. He is oblivious to the harm he does to the other mice in town. One suspects that he expresses his desires in an overmotivated way. He bathes because he is dirty. That assertion resurfaces like a refrain: "But the mouse was still dirty," repeated four times in four pages (56–59). He is dirty enough to fill his bathtub, to flood his room, his house, and the whole town. He nullifies the desires of the other mice with the force of his own. (In one illustration [57], a mouse couple are sitting down to a romantic drink in their home, while the floods of the bathwater rise ominously outside.)

The bather cannot be as dirty as he protests or as he leads himself to believe. Or if he is, his dirt is not just physical. He bathes in order to cleanse himself spiritually. Or he wants to soak in a hot tub, to return to the womb, to remake the world as womb—and what better excuse than to code himself as dirty, to try to persuade himself and others that his contamination is so great that only the general flood can wipe it out? He is the last word in passive-aggression. That passive-aggressive side of him can be satiated once the world is flooded on his terms, once it has come, through catastrophe, to recognize the depth of his need. At that point, as in many Lobel stories, he falls comfortably asleep in his own bed.

Bedtime is the frame of *Mouse Tales*. The father of a family of seven mouse children promises to tell them one story apiece if they will all fall asleep at the end of the series. They fall asleep just as the bather— and the child being read to—falls asleep. "The Bath" is the last story in the book. Bedtime is a recurrent setting in Lobel's I Can Read series. The owl in *Owl at Home* spends much of his time in bed. The Frog and Toad stories frequently find their resolutions at bedtime (or, as in "Tomorrow" from *Days with Frog and Toad* [1979], the story begins with Toad's resolution not to get *out* of bed). In the final tableau of both mouse books (and of *Frog and Toad All Year* [1976]), the resolution comes at the moral equivalent of bedtime: an easy chair safe by a roaring fire at night.

"The Crickets" from *Mouse Soup* ends just as "The Bath" does, with a mouse comfortably under the covers. Its governing mode is similar to that of "The Bath": an insistent force presses against someone's resisting will. In "The Crickets," a mouse is trying to sleep when a cricket starts to make noise outside her window. She tries to ask it to be quiet, but each of her successive pleas is comically misunderstood. The cricket makes more noise, brings more crickets, and all the crickets together make *much* more noise, until the mouse finally impresses on them that she wants them to leave. (In a deft crossing of a boundary, Lobel has the mouse utter her finally effective "GO AWAY" not in the text of the story, but in an illustration [40].) Here a desire is continually denied and yet resurges, until a catastrophe, the mouse's visible shout, explodes the tension and leads to a resolution.

"The Crickets" is a funny story for children because of the insistence of the crickets on making noise, because of their willful misprision of the desires of the mouse. It is absurd. But the absurd can take many forms. In Dr. Seuss's catalogs of the absurd, like *On beyond Zebra* and *If I Ran the Zoo*, the absurd is seen as *menagerie*. Seuss gives a sense that the elements of the absurd are tamed and placed on view. The absurd in Arnold Lobel's work is a force that overwhelms his characters: the Dark Frog (in *Days with Frog and Toad*), a runaway sled or uncontrollably melting ice cream (*Frog and Toad All Year*), a fluffy cloud that turns into a threatening cat ("Clouds" from *Mouse Tales*). Frequently, the force of the absurd, as desire or perhaps as drive (the drive "circulates around its object, fixed upon the point around which it pulsates," Zizek 134), wells up from within the characters themselves.

"Two Large Stones" from *Mouse Soup* is both typical and atypical of Lobel's stories. It is atypical because the protagonists of this story are not animals but stones. It is typical because though the characters are static, their drives are tremendous. They live on the side of a hill, immobile. They are vaguely personified, with indentations on their sides suggesting noses, the beginnings of a face. They wonder what's on the other side of their hill but know that they will never travel to see it. They ask a bird to tell them what's there; the bird answers, "I can see towns and castles. I can see mountains and valleys. It is a wonderful sight" (25). The stones despair because the rest of the world contains wonders they will never see. A hundred years later, a mouse comes by, and they ask the mouse what's on the other side of the hill. "Earth and stones . . . grass and flowers," he replies (29). The stones are happy again, because the bird, it seems, had lied. They are not missing anything.

The bird, of course, is long since dead, a point easy to miss in the story. The stones' capacity for longing is proportional to their capacity for endurance. Feeling "sad for one hundred years" (26) is a brief depression for them. The story contrasts perception with reality (Shannon 121) and becomes a reworking of the blind-men-and-elephant theme. The truth is as we are capable of conceiving it. Yet the truth in "Two Large Stones" is the truth of time and its longings. It is not a tale that seems attractive for children since it depends on stasis instead of action and on a trick of perception (one might call it situated knowledge) that is unillustrated: the bird can see farther than the mouse, who in turn sees farther than the stones. In Lobel's drawings, we see just the stones. We do not stir from their perspective. In this respect, "Two Large Stones" works more subtly and indirectly than Seuss's "Yertle the Turtle" (1950) and "The Big Brag" (1950), which depend on showing amplified perceptions of the world.

"Two Large Stones" works not by amusing a child with slapstick (something Lobel also does well) or by telling a joke, but by portraying the constraints of a located body—a stone. By asking readers to identify with stones, the story suggests that we are all stony in some way, that we all desperately want to see the other side of our hill. Despite the power of story to tease or to satisfy us, we never really will see it.

"Two Large Stones" is odd because the usual pattern in children's stories is to insist that imagination can transcend physical limitations. Imagining one's way beyond obstacles is a frequent motif in Dr. Seuss, from the make-believe parade of *And to Think That I Saw It on Mulberry Street* to the inventive urgings of *On beyond Zebra* and *Oh, the Thinks You Can Think!* Characters in Lobel's work are frequently immured in their own limited worlds, however. In one of his most beautiful stories, "The Letter" (from *Frog and Toad Are Friends*), Frog finds Toad depressed because no one ever writes to him. Rather than invent an imaginary recompense, Frog writes Toad a real letter—one that takes four days to arrive. They wait for it together. Frog has already told Toad its contents; but "Toad was very pleased to have it" (64), all the same. Discouragement about quotidian things is cured by redoubled attention to the delights of the quotidian. We transcend our limits by becoming more ourselves.

In contrast, when Max is sent to bed without his supper in Maurice Sendak's *Where the Wild Things Are* (1963), imagination helps him overcome his disappointment. A forest grows in Max's room. The forest is presented as literal, but it is a forest of the imagination, perhaps a forest of dream. This imaginary transgression of imprisonment is in line with other classic transcendences. It is marked by ambiguities and by an uncertain take on the power dynamics of exile, imprisonment, and nurturing. *Wild Things* is ambiguous, enmeshed in power relations between child and adult.

It is not a new observation to say that *Wild Things* is ambiguous. That is at once the scandal of the book and its identifying feature. John Cech maintains that the book "broke a taboo against the expression of the powerful emotions of childhood" and asserts that "the arrival of *Where the Wild Things Are* was the aesthetic equivalent for the picture book that the famous 1913 premier of Igor Stravinsky's *The Rite of Spring* was for modern music" (110). Cech cites the anxiety of parents and educators over the book and also Bruno Bettelheim's about-face in moving from a condemnation of *Wild Things* to the position that the book helps children to manage the expression of fear therapeutically (111–12).

Cech's reading of *Wild Things* focuses on its mythic elements and its challenge to the larger mythic web of American culture. My reading here is much more circumscribed. I have been struck by how the text and pictures circumscribe a power struggle. Cech argues that the book "reassures the child reader that the monsters are tameable through the imagination" (123). Amy Sonheim stresses a circumscribed reading of the book ever more firmly: "As a result of clear-cut directions in and out of the fantasy, Sendak creates a controllable place for Max to work out his confusion and, consequently, a non-threatening place where readers can explore their own encounters with wild things" (86). Critical attention to *Where the Wild Things Are* reads at times like an effort to reassure adults that everything, even a wild rumpus, is really under control.

There is something dangerous about *Wild Things*, something more dangerous than the clumsy monsters who are easily cowed by Max. The danger in the book comes from a relation not illustrated in the book's pictures and obliquely indicated by its text. Max has his imaginary adventure because he has offended his mother. (The mother is not pictured.) As punishment, she denies him food. The punishment is ephemeral, in fact momentary. Even after the adventure that occupies most of the pages of the book, Max's dinner is waiting for him *and it is still hot!* His mother relents almost at once.

Here is one of the keys to the scandal and to the management of *Where the Wild Things Are* in criticism. Max puts on his wolf suit and makes mischief. By exerting his imagination, a tendency usually encouraged in children's books, he gets in trouble and is punished. So he exerts his imagination on a grander scale, conjuring up the forest, the private boat, and the land of the Wild Things. The upshot is that he is not only not punished further but actually rewarded right away. His mother gets his dinner ready within pages of denying it to him. The book has it one way, and then turns around and has it another.

Where the Wild Things Are represents an elemental power struggle between a parent and a child. If the child misbehaves, he is starved. (I exaggerate, but anyone who has ever suggested "no dinner" to someone Max's age will know the child's sense that inanition is just around the corner.) The duration and consistency of punishment are crucial in the rhetoric of discipline. Advocates of punishment recommend that the punishment should last long enough to extract all willfulness from the child. As Philip Greven, critiquing such rhetoric, asks, "How long is long enough? When will the child's will be broken? What sounds indicate to a parent 'not tears of anger but tears of a broken will'?" (68). In Sendak's book, none, apparently. The punishment is no sooner inflicted than withdrawn, in the strict temporal sequence that the temperature of the dinner would indicate.

The context of the events, in the text, suggests one explanation. Max is making his mischief when "his mother called him 'WILD THING!' / and Max said 'I'LL EAT YOU UP!' / so he was sent to bed without eating anything" (5). Max's mother does not enforce traditional discipline. She does not at first punish him so much as she lashes out, almost playfully. Only when Max retorts in kind does she punish him. The punishment is inflicted, in the passive voice, by an unseen arbiter or force. The parent is never again named in the book. Her presence is only implied by the still-hot dinner that waits for Max at the end.

A possible scenario is that the mother reflects for a moment, realizes that Max's cheekiness has only been a response to her own cheekiness, and rushes to provide food for him. Yet the mechanism of punishment and repentance is shown as impersonal. The book does not name the process in which an adult repents of a decreed punishment, but it represents that process by implication.

The critical need to make the story of *Wild Things* into a simple allaying of a child's fears may mask a larger and more important ideological need. Critics may need to turn the childishness of the mother in the story into something as fantastic as the monsters of Max's private world. Is the mother weak in inflicting an unjust punishment—unjust, among other things, because it doesn't match the "crimes" but overreacts, invoking a withdrawal of nurturing altogether? Do readers need to mask her weakness? Is Max a reliable witness? Does he perhaps skew the whole situation in his own direction, imagining the punishment scenario as well as the land of the Wild Things? There's much more at stake here than the problems of scariness and the imagination.

Where the Wild Things Are is a book about falling asleep that can serve as a bedtime book that encourages a sleep purged of monsters, as Bettelheim finally argued, by the invocation of those monsters themselves (and, of course, by teaching "the magic trick of staring into all their yellow eyes"). Margaret Wise Brown's *Goodnight Moon* (1947) is the classic text of this falling-asleep genre.

The book apparently had its origins in waking up. Brown "had written the text one morning upon waking" (Marcus 184). The impact of the book is hard to account for. It is no more than a handful of noun phrases followed by the repetition of those same noun phrases prefaced by the word *goodnight*. The illustrations by Clement Hurd are spare and stylized, but also restrained. As night falls and the bright colors of "the great green room" fade toward the gray that is the book's final chord, the cumulative force of Hurd's drawings complements Brown's words and underscores their impact.

Written in the simplest of phrases, *Goodnight Moon* is an overwhelmingly nominative book. It deals in nouns. As Leonard Marcus observes, the reader "takes possession of that world by naming its particulars" (187). Marcus sees parallels to Twain and Hemingway, arguing that Brown's sense of precision in detail is worthy of those American masters. While appreciating the need to connect Brown's work to the pillars of the male canon, I think that we should turn to the work of Gertrude Stein as the major analogue to Brown's work in English.

This move does not so much elevate Brown by connecting her to Stein as it explicates Stein by referring her to the more popular master, Brown. Margaret Brown admired Gertrude Stein and helped to acquire Stein's children's book *The World Is Round* for the publishing firm Harper in the late thirties (Marcus 99–101). Despite this, Brown was not able to become Stein's disciple. Their correspondence was never intimate and faded quickly. Nevertheless, Brown stands as an important popularizer of Stein's technique.

Goodnight Moon is a redoubled book. It names things and then names them again as it tells them goodnight. Between the first iteration and the next, one might almost say, with Stein, "Everything is the same except composition and as the composition is different and always going to be different everything is not the same. Everything is not the same as the time when of the composition and the time in the composition is different. The composition is different, that is certain" ("Composition as Explanation," 516). Hurd's drawings so clearly reinforce the sense of the passage of time in *Goodnight Moon* that one comes to think of them as prior to the words. Since the composition of the text was in fact prior, one can see suggested there the quality of time indicated by the mere fact of iteration. The objects and words are the same, but objects and words are changed through the sheer happening of night.

This reiteration is not mechanical. Clocks and socks show up to be said goodnight to, but they don't appear in the first round of phrases. The telephone doesn't get wished goodnight, but a "nameless, imponderable 'nobody'" does appear and is wished goodnight, between the brush and the mush (Marcus 187). Everything is the same, except everything is not the same. On the scale of one room and a single bedtime, Stein's observation about the nature of composition is realized.

The great green room of the book is a place with no realized social context. The objects that fill it are suggested by the verbal resemblances of rhyme. The room is like one of the set-piece descriptions in Stein's *Tender Buttons*. While Stein saw her project in *Tender Buttons* as that of "ridding myself of nouns" (460), *Goodnight Moon* takes the opposite tack and rids itself of almost everything else. *Tender Buttons* is an interrogation of words, an unsettling of the notions that come packed into them:

> A table means does it not my dear it means a whole steadiness. Is it likely that a change.
> A table means more than a glass even a looking glass is tall. A table means necessary places and a revision a revision of a little thing it means it does mean that there has been a stand, a stand where it did shake. (474)

Goodnight Moon by contrast evokes delight in the persistence of naming, a persistence against which the transience of time and the altered state of sleep are measured.

This is a long way around explaining the feelings evoked by *Goodnight Moon*, one of the best American poems of the twentieth century. In the dress of a children's word book, the text offers the inexplicable lesson that things are different, that time passes, and that time has a direction—lessons perhaps too subtle for its very youngest readers to articulate. Even in *Where the Wild Things Are* time is subjective, subject to the constraints of the imagination and the will. In *Goodnight Moon* time is outside us and bigger than we are. It is bigger than any grown-up, which is why few grown-ups can come to the words "Goodnight stars / Goodnight air / Goodnight noises everywhere" without what Emily Dickinson, like Brown a great poet of the temporal, once called "a tighter breathing."

I know the work of Brown, Lobel, Seuss, and Sendak well because I read it continuously with my son just a few years ago, when he was in kindergarten or younger. Once he was in the third grade, as I've said, I read to him much less often. He established his own reading tastes and has gone into fields where it's difficult or unadvisable for me to follow. He knows the mythology of the Scholastic SF series Animorphs almost religiously and quotes to me frequently chapter and verse about Hork-Bajirs, Yeerks, and Andalites as they struggle for the souls of earthlings. I think I will leave these books to him, at least for now. In fact, I think it's important that he develop independent preferences, even independent obsessions, about reading. It's a rite of passage into adult literacy.

Still, we do, sometimes, read together aloud. We nearly always choose poetry. Fran will take a book of Shel Silverstein, and I will get some by Edward Lear, Dr. Seuss, or Margaret Wise Brown, and we will take turns reading to each other. It's not for the story or for information, naturally; it's for the delight in voicing the words of poets. Their work, of almost vanishing simplicity on the verbal level, unites us in common appreciation of poetic language.

You're only young once, indeed, but you can in fact be immature your whole life, and that leads me around to the paradox of my title. You are young twice, three times or more in the sense of a kind of surrender to the childishness of poetry. Literature only rarely offers a haven from cultural contentions and power struggles. My personal tour through children's literature and film has left me more embedded in the professional and social struggles over the meaning of childhood and childishness than ever. Years of struggle over the canon have convinced me that "high" or "great" literature is never aloof from politics, either. But perhaps somewhere at the limit of language reached in the work of Margaret Wise Brown is that place where all of us adults can be young twice—a place where literature, after all, can become "universal."

Works Cited

Adorno, Theodor, and Max Horkheimer. "The Culture Industry: Enlighten-
ment as Mass Deception." Trans. John Cumming. *The Cultural Studies
Reader*. Ed. Simon During. London: Routledge, 1993. 30–43.

Ashby, Hal, dir. *Being There*. United Artists, 1979.

Barrie, J. M. *The Little White Bird*. London: Hodder and Stoughton, 1924.

———. *Peter Pan; or, The Boy Who Would Not Grow Up*. London: Hodder
and Stoughton, 1928.

Bemelmans, Ludwig. *Madeline*. 1939. New York: Puffin, 1977.

Benezra, Karen. "Scholastic's Cool Ghouls." *Brandweek* 3 June 1996: 46–48.

Bertolucci, Bernardo, dir. *The Sheltering Sky*. Warner Brothers, 1993.

Brown, Margaret Wise. *Goodnight Moon*. Illus. Clement Hurd. New York:
Harper, 1947.

———. *The Runaway Bunny*. Illus. Clement Hurd. New York: Harper, 1942.

Burnett, Frances Hodgson. *Little Lord Fauntleroy*. New York: Scribner, 1886.

———. *The Secret Garden*. 1911. Philadelphia: Lippincott, 1962.

———. *Surly Tim and Other Stories*. New York: Scribner, Armstrong, 1877.

Butler, Judith. *Gender Trouble: Feminism and the Subversion of Identity*. New
York: Routledge, 1990.

Capra, Frank, dir. *It's a Wonderful Life*. RKO, 1946.

Carlei, Carlo, dir. *Fluke*. MGM, 1995.

Cech, John. *Angels and Wild Things: The Archetypal Poetics of Maurice
Sendak*. University Park: Pennsylvania State University Press, 1995.

"Children's Bookbag." *Publishers Weekly* 2 Sept. 1996: 41.

Coen, Joel, dir. *The Hudsucker Proxy.* Warner Brothers, 1994.

Columbus, Chris, dir. *Mrs. Doubtfire.* Twentieth Century Fox, 1994.

Coppola, Francis, dir. *Jack.* Buena Vista, 1996.

———. *Peggy Sue Got Married.* TriStar Pictures, 1986.

Cott, Jonathan. *Pipers at the Gates of Dawn: The Wisdom of Children's Literature.* New York: Random House, 1983.

Cross, Gary. *Kids' Stuff: Toys and the Changing World of American Childhood.* Cambridge, Mass.: Harvard University Press, 1997.

Dahl, Roald. *The BFG.* New York: Farrar, 1982.

———. *Boy: Tales of Childhood.* Illus. Quentin Blake. New York: Farrar, 1984.

———. *Charlie and the Chocolate Factory.* 1963. Illus. Joseph Schindelman. New York: Puffin, 1988.

———. *James and the Giant Peach.* New York: Knopf, 1961.

———. *The Witches.* New York: Puffin, 1983.

Daniel, Rod, dir. *Beethoven's 2nd.* Universal, 1994.

Dante, Joe, dir. *Small Soldiers.* DreamWorks, 1998.

Davis, Tamra, dir. *Billy Madison.* Universal, 1995.

DeLillo, Don. *Great Jones Street.* Boston: Houghton Mifflin, 1973.

Disney's Pocahontas. N.p.: Mouse Works, 1995.

Dixon, Franklin W. *Hunting for Hidden Gold.* New York: Grosset and Dunlap, 1928. New York: Grosset and Dunlap, 1963.

———. *The Missing Chums.* New York: Grosset and Dunlap, 1962.

"Dixon, Tex W." "Ghost Story." *Texas Monthly* 23.9 (Sept. 1995): 60–64.

Donehue, Vincent J., dir. *Peter Pan.* Goodtimes Home Video, 1960.

Eckford-Prossor, Melanie. "Colonizing Children: Dramas of Transformation." Ms.

Fadiman, Clifton. Introduction. *Six by Seuss.* New York: Random House, 1991. 6–8.

———. "Professionals and Confessionals: Dr. Seuss and Kenneth Grahame." *Only Connect: Readings on Children's Literature.* Ed. Sheila Egoff, G. T. Stubbs, and L. F. Ashley. Toronto: Oxford University Press, 1969. 316–22.

Fitzhugh, Louise. *Harriet the Spy.* 1964. New York: HarperTrophy, 1990.

Friday, Nancy. *My Secret Garden: Women's Sexual Fantasies.* New York: Pocket Books, 1973.

Gadamer, Hans-Georg. *Truth and Method.* 2d rev. ed. Trans. W. Glen-Doepel, rev. Joel Weinsheimer and Donald G. Marshall. New York: Continuum, 1993.

Garber, Marjorie. *Vested Interests: Cross-Dressing and Cultural Anxiety*. New York: HarperPerennial, 1993.

Gilbert, Brian, dir. *Vice Versa*. Columbia, 1988.

Grahame, Kenneth. *The Wind in the Willows*. 1908. Illus. Ernest H. Shepard. New York: Scribner's, 1954.

Greven, Philip. *Spare the Child: The Religious Roots of Punishment and the Psychological Impact of Physical Abuse*. New York: Vintage, 1992.

Harris, Susan K. *Nineteenth-Century American Women's Novels: Interpretative Strategies*. Cambridge: Cambridge University Press, 1990.

Hines, Anna Grossnickle. *Daddy Makes the Best Spaghetti*. New York: Clarion Books, 1986.

Holland, Agnieszka, dir. *The Secret Garden*. Warner Brothers, 1993.

Hollindale, Peter. *Signs of Childness in Children's Books*. Stroud: Thimble Press, 1997.

Ingoglia, Gina. *Disney's Pocahontas*. New York: Disney Press, 1995.

Johnston, Joe, dir. *Jumanji*. Columbia, 1995.

Kipling, Rudyard. *Captains Courageous*. 1897. New York: Odyssey Press, 1965.

Knight, Eric. *Lassie Come-Home*. 1940. New York: Holt, 1978.

Leaf, Munro. *The Story of Ferdinand*. Illus. Robert Lawson. New York: Puffin, 1977.

Lear, Edward. *The Complete Nonsense of Edward Lear*. New York: Dover, 1951.

Levant, Brian, dir. *Beethoven*. Universal, 1992.

Levinson, Barry, dir. *Toys*. Twentieth Century Fox, 1992.

Litvag, Irving. *The Master of Sunnybank: A Biography of Albert Payson Terhune*. New York: Harper and Row, 1977.

Lobel, Arnold. *Days with Frog and Toad*. 1979. New York: HarperTrophy, 1984.

———. *Fables*. New York: Harper and Row, 1980.

———. *Frog and Toad All Year*. 1976. New York: HarperTrophy, 1984.

———. *Frog and Toad Are Friends*. 1970. New York: HarperTrophy, 1979.

———. *Grasshopper on the Road*. 1978. New York: HarperTrophy, 1986.

———. *Mouse Soup*. 1977. New York: HarperTrophy, 1983.

———. *Mouse Tales*. 1972. New York: HarperTrophy, 1978.

———. *Owl at Home*. 1975. New York: HarperTrophy, 1982.

Lodge, Sally. "Life after Goosebumps." *Publishers Weekly* 2 Dec. 1996: 24–27.

Lurie, Alison. "The Cabinet of Dr. Seuss." *Popular Culture: An Introductory Text.* Ed. John G. Nachbar and Kevin Lause. Bowling Green: Bowling Green State University Popular Press, 1992. 68–79.

———. *Don't Tell the Grown-Ups: Subversive Children's Literature.* Boston: Little, Brown, 1990.

Luske, Hamilton, Clyde Geronimi, and Wilfred Jackson, dir. *Peter Pan.* Walt Disney. 1953.

Marcus, Leonard S. *Margaret Wise Brown: Awakened by the Moon.* Boston: Beacon Press, 1992.

Marshall, Penny, dir. *Big.* Twentieth Century Fox, 1988.

Meek, Margaret. "What Counts as Evidence in Theories of Children's Literature?" *Children's Literature: The Development of Criticism.* Ed. Peter Hunt. London: Routledge, 1990. 166–82.

Miller, Alice. *For Your Own Good: Hidden Cruelty in Child-Rearing and the Roots of Violence.* Trans. Hildegarde Hannum and Hunter Hannum. New York: Noonday Press, 1990.

Miller, Troy, dir. *Jack Frost.* Warner Brothers, 1998.

Monette, Paul. *Becoming a Man: Half a Life Story.* New York: Harper, 1993.

Morgan, Judith, and Neil Morgan. *Dr. Seuss and Mr. Geisel: A Biography.* New York: Random House, 1995.

Morris, Timothy. *Making the Team: The Cultural Work of Baseball Fiction.* Urbana: University of Illinois Press, 1997.

———. "Returning to the Hardy Boys." *Raritan* 16.3 (Winter 1997): 123–42.

Mulvey, Laura. "Visual Pleasure and Narrative Cinema." *Film Theory and Criticism: Introductory Readings.* Ed. Gerald Mast, Marshall Cohen, and Leo Braudy. New York: Oxford University Press, 1992. 746–57.

Murray, Heather. "Frances Hodgson Burnett's *The Secret Garden:* The Organ(ic)ized World." *Touchstones: Reflections on the Best in Children's Literature,* vol. 1. Ed. Perry Nodelman. West Lafayette, Ind.: Children's Literature Association, 1985. 30–43.

Naylor, Phyllis Reynolds. *Shiloh.* New York: Dell, 1992.

Nelson, Gary, dir. *Freaky Friday.* Walt Disney Productions, 1977.

Nodelman, Perry. *Words about Pictures: The Narrative Art of Children's Picture Books.* Athens: University of Georgia Press, 1988.

Noonan, Chris, dir. *Babe.* Universal, 1995.

Paul, Lissa. "Enigma Variations: What Feminist Theory Knows about Children's Literature." *Children's Literature: The Development of Criticism.* Ed. Peter Hunt. London: Routledge, 1990. 148–64.

Petrie, Daniel, dir. *Lassie.* Paramount, 1994.

Piper, Watty. *The Little Engine That Could.* 1930. New York: Grosset and Dunlap, 1978.

Pollack, Sydney, dir. *Tootsie.* Columbia, 1982.

Prince, Gerald. *Narratology: The Form and Functioning of Narrative.* Berlin: Mouton, 1982.

Roback, Diane. "The Year of the Paperbacks." *Publishers Weekly* 4 Mar. 1996: S24–S31.

Rose, Jacqueline. *The Case of Peter Pan or the Impossibility of Children's Fiction.* Philadelphia: University of Pennsylvania Press, 1992.

Rosen, Judith. "Battle of the Book Fairs." *Publishers Weekly* 19 Feb. 1996: 134–37.

Rosenbloom, Dale, dir. *Shiloh.* Legacy Releasing Corporation, 1997.

Rud, Rita. "How about Asking a Child for a Change? An Interview with a Ten-Year-Old Goosebumps Fan." *Bookbird* 33.3–4 (Fall–Winter 1995–96): 22–24.

Sacks, Oliver. *Awakenings.* New York: HarperPerennial, 1990.

Scarry, Elaine. *The Body in Pain: The Making and Unmaking of the World.* New York: Oxford University Press, 1985.

Sendak, Maurice. *Where the Wild Things Are.* 1963. New York: HarperTrophy, 1988.

Seuss, Dr. [Theodor Seuss Geisel]. *And to Think That I Saw It on Mulberry Street.* New York: Random House, 1937.

———. *Bartholomew and the Oobleck.* New York: Random House, 1949.

———. "The Big Brag." *Yertle the Turtle.* 1950. *Six by Seuss.* New York: Random House, 1991.

———. *The Butter Battle Book.* New York: Random House, 1985.

———. *The Cat in the Hat.* New York: Random House, 1957.

———. *The Cat in the Hat Comes Back.* New York: Random House, 1958.

———. *The Five Hundred Hats of Bartholomew Cubbins.* 1938. *Six by Seuss.* New York: Random House, 1991.

———. *Green Eggs and Ham.* New York: Beginner Books, 1960.

———. *Hop on Pop.* New York: Beginner Books, 1963.

———. *Horton Hatches the Egg.* New York: Random House, 1940.

———. *Horton Hears a Who.* New York: Random House, 1954.

———. *If I Ran the Zoo.* New York: Random House, 1950.

———. *The King's Stilts.* New York: Random House, 1939.

———. *The Lorax.* New York: Random House, 1971.

———. *McElligott's Pool.* New York: Random House, 1947.

———. *Oh, the Places You'll Go.* New York: Random House, 1990.

———. *Oh, the Thinks You Can Think!* New York: Random House, 1975.

———. *On beyond Zebra.* New York: Random House, 1955.

———. *One Fish Two Fish Red Fish Blue Fish.* New York: Beginner Books, 1960.

———. "The Sneetches." *The Sneetches and Other Stories.* New York: Random House, 1961.

———. "Yertle the Turtle." *Yertle the Turtle.* 1950. *Six by Seuss.* New York: Random House, 1991.

Sewell, Anna. *Black Beauty.* 1877. Harmondsworth, England: Puffin, 1977.

———. *Black Beauty.* Adapted by Deidre S. Laiken. Illustrated Classic Edition. New York: Playmore, 1977.

Shannon, George. *Arnold Lobel.* Boston: Twayne, 1989.

Sonheim, Amy. *Maurice Sendak.* New York: Twayne, 1991.

Spielberg, Steven, dir. *Hook.* TriStar Pictures, 1992.

———. *Jurassic Park.* Universal, 1993.

Spitz, Ellen Handler. *Inside Picture Books.* New Haven: Yale University Press, 1999.

Spottiswoode, Roger, dir. *Turner and Hooch.* Touchstone, 1989.

Stanzel, F. K. *A Theory of Narrative.* Trans. Charlotte Goedsche. Cambridge: Cambridge University Press, 1984.

Stein, Gertrude. "Composition as Explanation." *Selected Writings of Gertrude Stein.* New York: Vintage, 1972. 513–23.

———. *Tender Buttons. Selected Writings of Gertrude Stein.* New York: Vintage, 1972. 461–509.

Stierle, Karlheinz. "The Reading of Fictional Texts." Trans. Inge Crosman and Thekla Zachrau. *The Reader in the Text: Essays on Audience and Interpretation.* Ed. Susan R. Suleiman and Inge Crosman. Princeton: Princeton University Press, 1980. 83–105.

Stine, R. L. *Attack of the Jack-o'-Lanterns.* Goosebumps 48. New York: Scholastic, 1996.

———. *The Barking Ghost.* Goosebumps 32. New York: Scholastic, 1995.

———. *Beware, the Snowman.* Goosebumps 51. New York: Scholastic, 1997.

———. *Bienvenidos a la casa de la muerte.* Escalofríos 1. New York: Scholastic, 1995.

———. *The Blob That Ate Everyone.* Goosebumps 55. New York: Scholastic, 1997.

———. *Chicken Chicken.* Goosebumps 53. New York: Scholastic, 1997.

———. *Cry of the Cat.* Goosebumps Series 2000, 1. New York: Scholastic, 1998.

———. *The Curse of Camp Cold Lake.* Goosebumps 56. New York: Scholastic, 1997.

———. *The Curse of the Mummy's Tomb.* Goosebumps 5. New York: Scholastic, 1993.

———. *Deep Trouble.* Goosebumps 19. New York: Scholastic, 1994.

———. *Fright Camp.* Goosebumps Series 2000, 8. New York: Scholastic, 1998.

———. *Ghost Camp.* Goosebumps 45. New York: Scholastic, 1996.

———. *The Haunted Mask 2.* Goosebumps 36. New York: Scholastic, 1995.

———. *The Haunted School.* Goosebumps 59. New York: Scholastic, 1997.

———. *The Horror at Camp Jellyjam.* Goosebumps 33. New York: Scholastic, 1995.

———. *How I Learned to Fly.* Goosebumps 52. New York: Scholastic, 1997.

———. *How to Kill a Monster.* Goosebumps 46. New York: Scholastic, 1996.

———. *Let's Get Invisible!* Goosebumps 6. New York: Scholastic, 1993.

———. *Monster Blood.* Goosebumps 3. New York: Scholastic, 1992.

———. *Monster Blood 2.* Goosebumps 18. New York: Scholastic, 1994.

———. *Monster Blood 3.* Goosebumps 29. New York: Scholastic, 1995.

———. *Monster Blood 4.* Goosebumps 62. New York: Scholastic, 1997.

———. *My Best Friend Is Invisible.* Goosebumps 57. New York: Scholastic, 1997.

———. *Phantom of the Auditorium.* Goosebumps 24. New York: Scholastic, 1994.

———. *Say Cheese and Die.* Goosebumps 4. New York: Scholastic, 1992.

———. *Say Cheese and Die—Again!* Goosebumps 44. New York: Scholastic, 1996.

———. *The Scarecrow Walks at Midnight.* Goosebumps 20. New York: Scholastic, 1994.

———. *Stay Out of the Basement.* Goosebumps 2. New York: Scholastic, 1992.

———. *Tales to Give You Goosebumps: Ten Spooky Stories.* New York: Scholastic, 1994.

———. *Vampire Breath.* Goosebumps 49. New York: Scholastic, 1996.

———. *Welcome to Camp Nightmare.* Goosbumps 9. New York: Scholastic, 1993.

———. *Welcome to Dead House.* Goosebumps 1. New York: Scholastic, 1992.

Stine, R. L., and Joe Arthur. *It Came from Ohio! My Life as a Writer.* New York: Scholastic, 1997.

Stuart, Mel, dir. *Willy Wonka and the Chocolate Factory.* Warner Brothers, 1971.

Terhune, Albert Payson. *Lad: A Dog.* New York: E. P. Dutton, 1919.

Thomas, Betty, dir. *Doctor Dolittle.* Twentieth Century Fox, 1998.

Thompson, Caroline, dir. *Black Beauty.* Warner Brothers, 1994.

Tompkins, Jane. *Sensational Designs: The Cultural Work of American Fiction, 1790–1860.* New York: Oxford University Press, 1985.

Tucker, Nicholas. *The Child and the Book: A Psychological and Literary Exploration.* Cambridge: Cambridge University Press, 1990.

Van Allsburg, Chris. *Jumanji.* Boston: Houghton Mifflin, 1981.

Van Leer, David. *The Queening of America: Gay Culture in Straight Society.* New York: Routledge, 1995.

Wall, Barbara. *The Narrator's Voice: The Dilemma of Children's Fiction.* New York: St. Martin's Press, 1991.

Warner, Susan. *The Wide, Wide World.* New York: Feminist Press, 1987.

White, E. B. *Charlotte's Web.* New York: Harper and Row, 1952.

Wilcox, Fred M., dir. *The Secret Garden.* MGM, 1949.

Wolf, Tim. "Imagination, Rejection, and Rescue: Recurrent Themes in Dr. Seuss." *Children's Literature* 23 (1995): 137–64.

Zizek, Slavoj. *Looking Awry: An Introduction to Jacques Lacan through Popular Culture.* Cambridge, Mass.: MIT Press, 1991.

INDEX

TIM MORRIS is the author of *Becoming Canonical in American Poetry* and *Making the Team: The Cultural Work of Baseball Fiction.* He directs the graduate programs in English at the University of Texas at Arlington.

Typeset in 11/14 New Caledonia
with Handle Oldstyle display
Designed by Dennis Roberts
Composed by Jim Proefrock
at the University of Illinois Press
Manufactured by Maple-Vail
Book Manufacturing Group

University of Illinois Press
1325 South Oak Street
Champaign, IL 61820-6903
www.press.uillinois.edu